Windows for Seniors

Windows 11 Edition

Kevin Wilson

www.elluminetpress.com

Windows for Seniors: Windows 11 Ed

iStock.com/golibo, PeopleImages, ymgerman. Photo 130859010 © Kaspars Grinvalds - Dreamstime.com. Photo 103557713 © Konstantin Kolosov - Dreamstime.com. Yuri Arcurs via Getty Images, Cover Image by Chris Bardgett / Alamy Stock Photo

Publisher: Elluminet Press
Director: Kevin Wilson
Lead Editor: Steven Ashmore
Technical Reviewer: Mike Taylor, Robert Ashcroft
Copy Editors: Joanne Taylor, James Marsh
Proof Reader: Mike Taylor
Indexer: James Marsh
Cover Designer: Kevin Wilson

eBook versions and licenses are also available for most titles. Any source code or other supplementary materials referenced by the author in this text is available to readers at www.elluminetpress.com/resources

For detailed information about how to locate your book's resources, go to www.elluminetpress.com/resources

Table of Contents

About the Author

With over 20 years' experience in the computer industry, Kevin Wilson has made a career out of technology and showing others how to use it. After earning a master's degree in computer science, software engineering, and multimedia systems, Kevin has held various positions in the IT industry including graphic & web design, programming, building & managing corporate networks, and IT support.

He serves as senior writer and director at Elluminet Press Ltd, he periodically teaches computer science at college, and works as an IT trainer in England while researching for his PhD. His books have become a valuable resource among the students in England, South Africa, Canada, and in the United States.

Kevin's motto is clear: "If you can't explain something simply, then you haven't understood it well enough." To that end, he has created the Exploring Tech Computing series, in which he breaks down complex technological subjects into smaller, easy-to-follow steps that students and ordinary computer users can put into practice.

Acknowledgements

Thanks to all the staff at Luminescent Media & Elluminet Press for their passion, dedication and hard work in the preparation and production of this book.

To all my friends and family for their continued support and encouragement in all my writing projects.

To all my colleagues, students and testers who took the time to test procedures and offer feedback on the book

Finally thanks to you the reader for choosing this book. I hope it helps you to use your computer with greater understanding.

Have fun!

Windows 11

Windows 11 is the next major release of Microsoft Windows, and is the successor to Windows 10.

Windows 11 was released on the 5th October 2021 as a free upgrade to compatible laptops, PCs, and larger tablets. However, Windows 11 is far more strict with hardware requirements than Windows 10, so some older machines won't be supported or be able to upgrade.

Windows 11 features a modern, simplified interface that is intended to inspire productivity and creativity with its more intuitive and visually pleasing design.

In this chapter we'll take a look at:

- What's New
- Common Features
- Windows Editions

To help you better understand this section, take a look at the video resources. Open your web browser and navigate to the following site:

`elluminetpress.com/win-11`

What's New?

Windows 11 includes a major overhaul of the user interface with translucent windows, new icons, fonts, and rounded corners.

A more noticeable change is the start menu and taskbar, which are now centred. Although for die hard Windows fans, you can still align the taskbar to the left if you prefer. It's worth noting that the centred approach is easier to use, as the start button and apps are more easily accessible with a mouse.

Widgets make a comeback to Windows 11, allowing you to add widgets for weather, photos, news, stocks and so on.

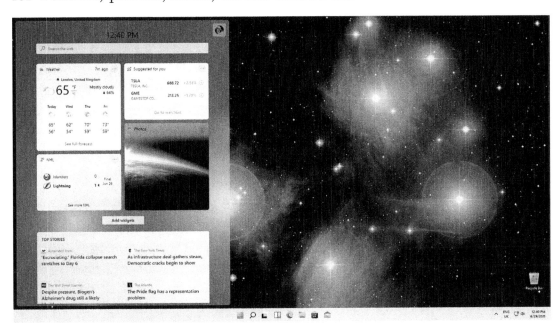

Chapter 1: Windows 11

A new combined calendar and notification centre.

Multiple or virtual desktops has a few new features, you can now access your desktops using a button on the taskbar.

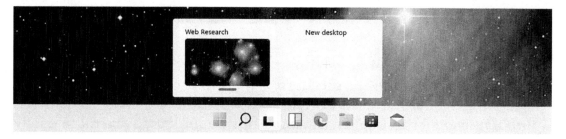

You can also have different wallpapers allowing you to easily distinguish between your desktops, and you can add names, as well as change the order of the desktops on the desktop bar at the bottom of the screen

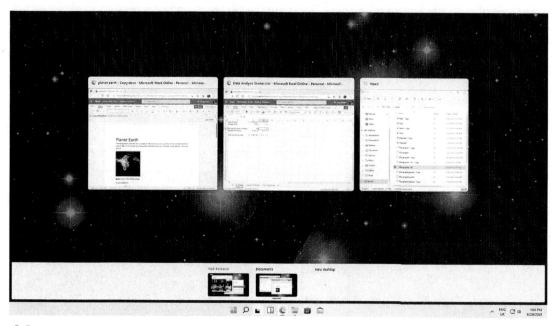

Windows Search has been reduced to a magnifying glass icon and allows you to search for apps, files and settings.

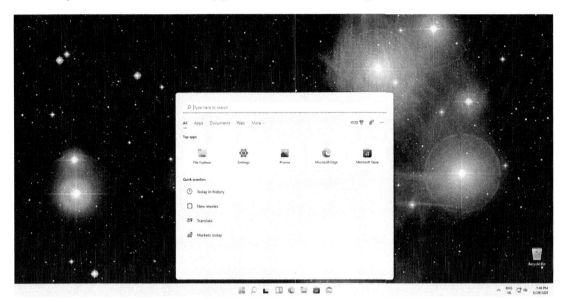

New snap layouts make multi tasking easier. This feature allows you to quickly arrange your windows on the screen using various pre-set templates.

Here, you can see Edge, OneNote and File Explorer snapped to a layout.

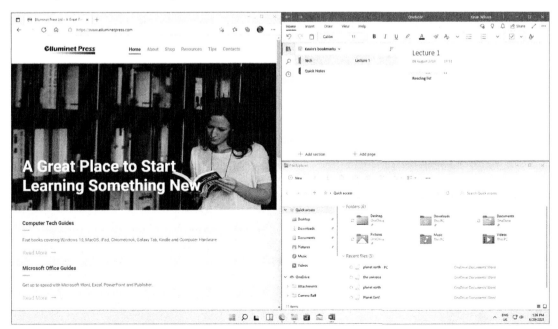

Chapter 1: Windows 11

File Explorer has been redesigned with a more modern looking interface. The ribbon along the top has been reduced to some commonly used tools. You'll also see some new icons for devices, files and folders.

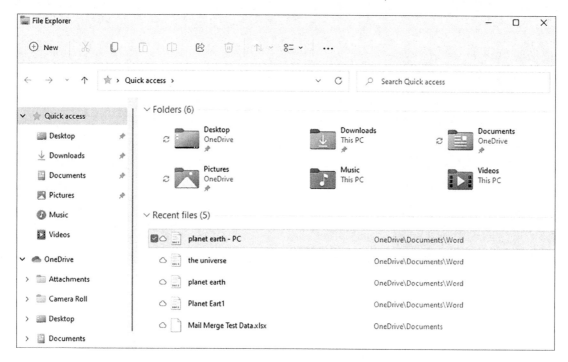

The Settings App has also been redesigned, giving a more intuitive and consistent look across the available settings. The main categories are now listed down the left hand side, with settings in the categories appearing in the right hand panel.

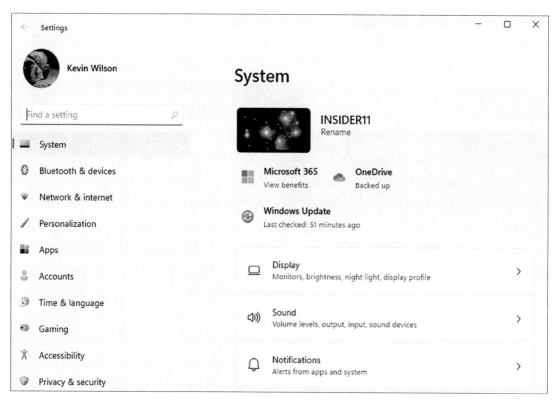

A new redesigned Microsoft Store store plus android apps.

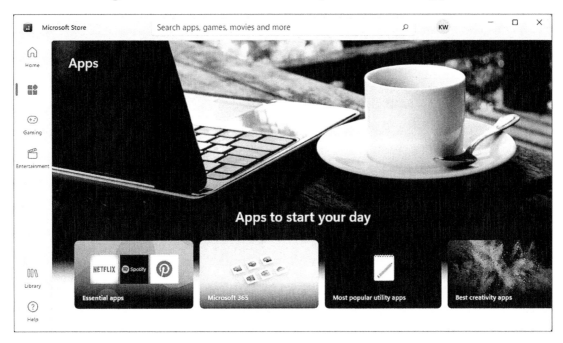

Microsoft Teams has been integrated into Windows 11 allowing better connectivity. You can chat right off the taskbar...

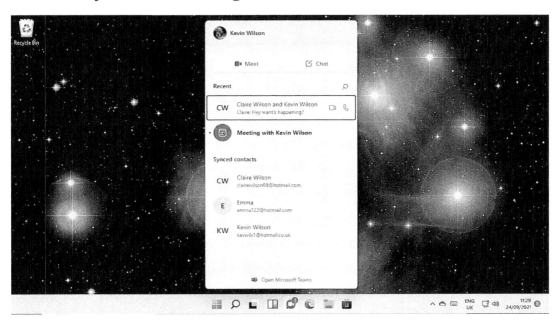

In Windows 11, there is no separate tablet mode for touch screen devices. Instead, when you detach a keyboard from a surface tablet or other hybrid device, icons on the taskbar move further apart, and window edges become more visible making them easier to select. There are also various touch gestures you can use to move between apps, as well as the usual tap, scroll and zoom gestures.

The Mail, Calendar, Paint and Photos apps have had a minor update

Windows Editions

There are two editions of Windows 11 available to consumers: Home and Pro.

Windows 11 Home is designed for use on PCs, laptops and tablets. This edition is intended for the every day home user. If you bought a laptop or tablet device from a computer store, then this is the version you're most likely to have. Below is a list of features included in this edition.

Feature	Windows 11 Home
Device encryption	✓
Find my device	✓
Firewall and network protection	✓
Internet protection	✓
Parental controls and protection	✓
Secure boot	✓
Windows Hello	✓
Windows Security	✓

Windows 11 Pro is the same as the home edition, except it has additional features that are oriented towards business environments and power users. Here in the list below, you can see a list of windows 11 pro features in the right hand column.

Feature	Windows 11 Home	Windows 11 Pro
Device encryption	✓	✓
Find my device	✓	✓
Firewall and network protection	✓	✓
Internet protection	✓	✓
Parental controls and protection	✓	✓
Secure boot	✓	✓
Windows Hello	✓	✓
Windows Security	✓	✓
Assigned Access		✓
Dynamic Provisioning		✓
Enterprise State Roaming with Azure		✓
Group Policy		✓
Kiosk mode setup		✓
Microsoft Store for Business		✓
Mobile device management		✓
Support for Active Directory		✓
Support for Azure Active Directory		✓
Windows Update for Business		✓
BitLocker device encryption		✓
Windows Information Protection (WIP)		✓

2

Setting up Windows 11

New PC laptops, tablets and computers will come with Windows 11 already installed, usually the home edition.

If you have an older machine purchased in 2017 or later, you may be able to upgrade to Windows 11. It is unlikely older machines will be able to run Windows 11.

In this chapter we'll take a look at:

- Upgrading to Windows 11
- System Requirements
- TPM
- Secure Boot
- Checking your PC
- Upgrading using Windows Update on Windows 10
- Upgrading using the Windows 11 Installation Assistant
- Running Windows 11 for the First Time

To help you better understand this section, take a look at the video resources. Open your web browser and navigate to the following site:

elluminetpress.com/using-win-11

Upgrading to Windows 11

If you have a fully licensed version of Windows 10 installed, then if your PC is compatible, you will receive the Windows 11 update for free.

Requirements

If you're upgrading, make sure your PC meets the following specification.

Processor:	1 gigahertz (GHz) or faster with 2 or more cores on a compatible 64-bit processor or System on a Chip (SoC)
RAM:	4 gigabyte (GB)
Hard Disk:	64 GB or larger storage device
System firmware:	UEFI, Secure Boot capable
TPM:	Trusted Platform Module (TPM) version 2.0
Graphics card:	Compatible with DirectX 12 or later with WDDM 2.0 driver
Display:	High definition (720p) display that is greater than 9" diagonally, 8 bits per colour channel

Two things to take note of. First, you'll need a device that has a trusted platform module v2.0 (TPM 2.0). TPM is a chip usually mounted on the motherboard that securely stores passwords, digital certificates, or encryption keys that are used to authenticate a PC or laptop, so that malware can't access or tamper with that data. If you purchased your PC after 2017, you most likely have this feature installed.

You can check this in device manager. Right click on the start button, select 'device manager' from the menu.

Scroll down the list, double click on 'security devices'. You should see 'trusted platform module 2.0'. If you see 'trusted platform module 1.2', or 'security devices' doesn't appear at all, you won't be able to install Windows 11.

Go to www.elluminetpress.com/enable-tpm for details on how to enable TPM on your machine.

Secondly, your device will also need secure boot enabled. Most modern devices include this feature. Secure Boot is a security feature that only allows approved operating systems to boot up, thereby preventing malware from taking control of your device at boot time.

Check your PC

To check if your PC is compatible, use the PC Health Check tool. To do this go to

    www.microsoft.com/en-us/software-download/windows11

Click 'PC Health Check' at the top of the web page.

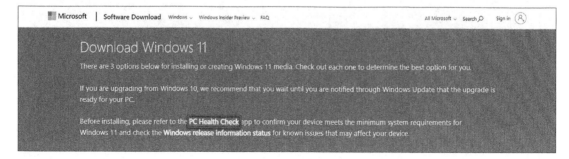

Click 'download pc health check app'

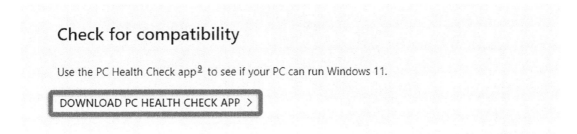

Click 'open' when prompted by your browser. Run through the installation wizard. Once the installation is complete, click 'check now' at the top of the screen.

If you see the message on the left, you're all set, otherwise you can't install Windows 11.

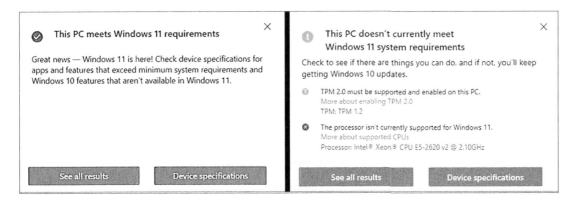

Upgrade using Windows Update on Windows 10

If you are running Windows 10 and your device meets the requirements, then you should automatically receive a notification in Windows Update. In Windows 10, open the Start Menu. Click the settings icon.

Chapter 2: Setting up Windows 11

Click 'update & security'.

Then select 'Windows Update' from the list on the list. Then click 'check for updates'.

Windows 10 will check for any available updates. When Windows 11 is available, you'll see a 'feature update' notification in windows update. Click 'download and install now'.

To complete the update, you'll need to restart your machine when it's finished. Go to Start > Power Icon > 'Update & Restart'.

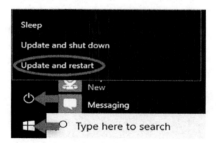

If you only see 'restart' on the menu, then the update hasn't finished downloading yet. Once the installation is complete see "Running Windows 11 the First Time" on page 31.

28

Windows 11 Installation Assistant

The Installation Assistant downloads and installs the latest version of Windows 11.

First, download the health check tool, then run it to confirm your PC is compatible. See page 26.

Next, you'll need to download installation assistant. To do this, open your web browser and navigate to the following website.

`www.microsoft.com/en-us/software-download/windows11`

Scroll down to 'Windows 11 installation assistant', then click 'download now'.

Click on the file in the downloads prompt, or click 'open' if prompted by your browser. If not, you'll find the file in your downloads folder.

Once the tool confirms the device hardware is compatible. You'll land on the 'install windows 11' screen. Click 'accept and install'

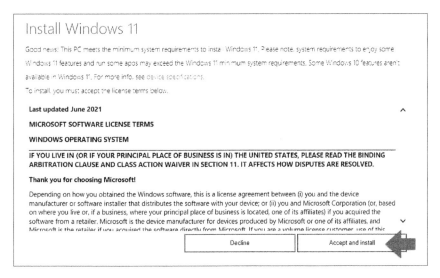

Select 'accept and install' on the license terms.

The install assistant will download and install Windows 11. This might take a while. Once this step is complete, your PC will restart.

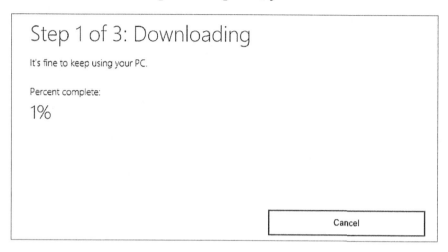

Click 'restart now'.

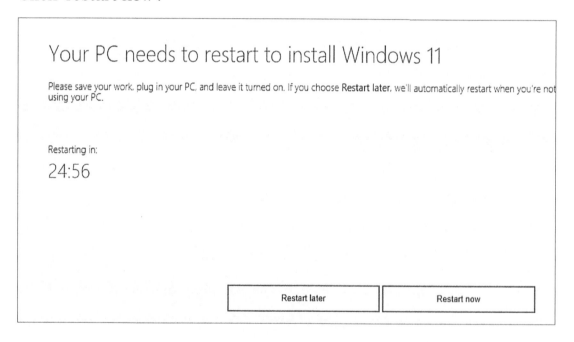

Once your PC reboots, the update will install. This will take a while.

Once the installation is complete see "Running Windows 11 the First Time" on page 31.

Running Windows 11 the First Time

If you've just bought a new computer with Windows 11, or installed a fresh copy, you'll need to run through the initial set up procedure. This will allow you to connect your computer to your WiFi/Internet, enter your Microsoft Account email address and password, and set a login method such as a PIN, fingerprint, or face ID.

Select your country or region from the list and click 'yes'.

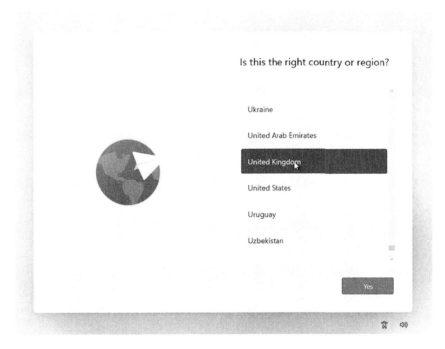

Select keyboard layout for your country, then click 'yes'.

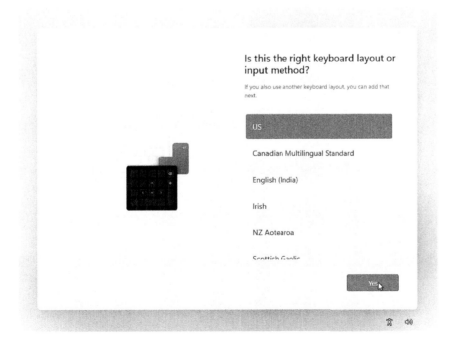

Skip secondary keyboard if you don't have one.

On the terms and agreements page click on 'Accept'.

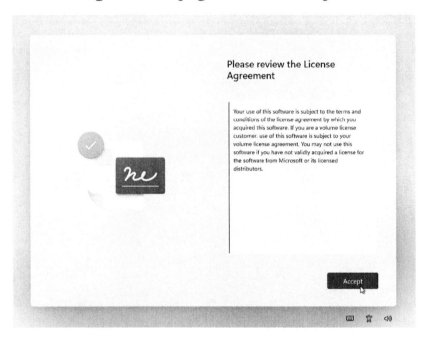

Select your WiFi network from the list of detected networks. This is usually printed on your router/modem or you can find out from your service provider. Click 'next'. Enter your WiFi password.

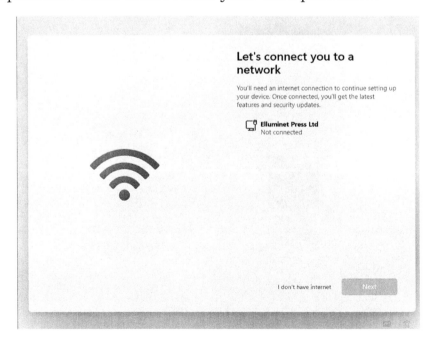

Give your device a meaningful name. You can name your device after the person who uses it, or what room it's in. For example: "Kevin's Laptop", or "Office-01". Click 'next'.

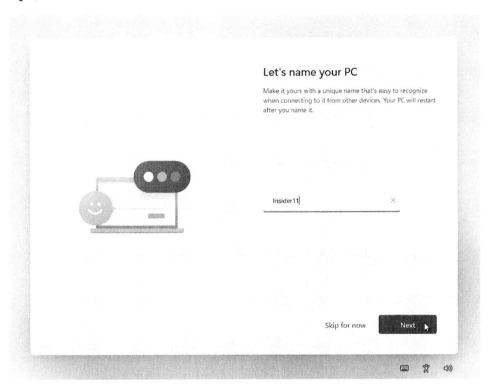

Select 'set up for personal use' if you're going to use your device at home. If you are setting up a device to use at school/college or a corporate network at work, select 'set up for work or school'. Click 'next'.

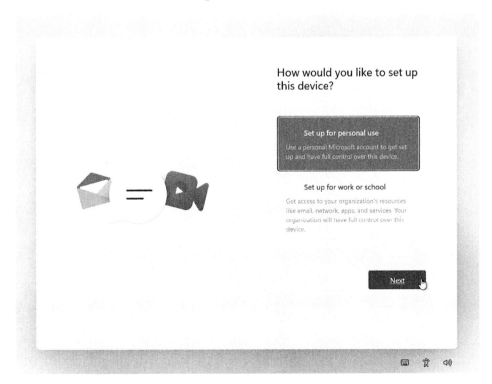

Chapter 2: Setting up Windows 11

Sign in with your Microsoft Account email address and password, then click 'next'. This allows you to make use of OneDrive, email, purchase apps from the App Store, buy music and films.

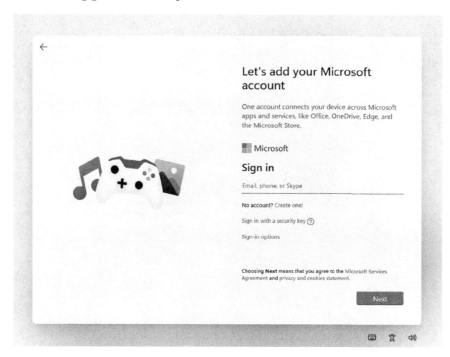

Set up your sign in method. You'll have certain options available depending on your device. If you have a finger print scanner on your device select that option. If no other options are available, select PIN.

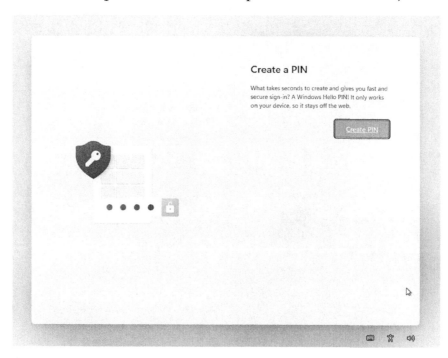

Click 'create pin', then enter a 4 digit pin code. This will is the code you'll use to sign into Windows on your device, so don't forget it.

If you have upgraded from another machine, you'll get the option to restore your device. This means you'll be able to pull over settings, apps and files you had on your other machine. If you want to restore from data from another machine, select it from the list, otherwise select 'set up as new device'. Click 'next'.

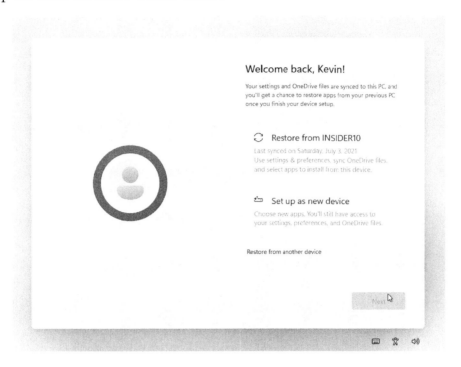

This allows windows to determine your physical location. This enables you to use location based apps such as weather, local interest, news as well as maps, and getting directions. To turn it on select 'yes'. If you don't plan on using any of these apps, then turn it off. Select 'accept'.

This is useful if you're setting up a tablet and allows windows to periodically report its location. This can help if you lose your device or it is stolen. You'll be able to see its location in your Microsoft Account settings. Select 'yes', then 'accept'.

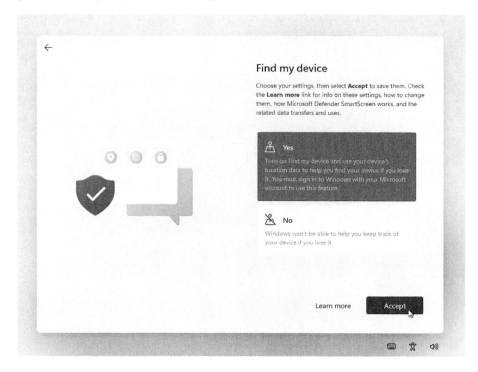

Diagnostic data is what Microsoft uses to troubleshoot problems and make improvements to its services. I'd suggest you select 'required only', so the only data that is sent to Microsoft is your device settings and its current state of operation, select 'accept'.

This is data collected when you use Windows Ink and allows Microsoft to use the data to improve its product. Leaving this feature on is usually ok, but you can also turn it off. Select 'no' then 'accept'.

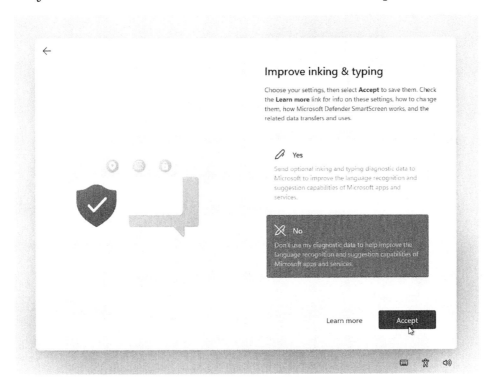

Allow Windows to tailor your computing experience to your personal tastes. This will give you tips and recommendations based on how you use Windows. To enable this, select 'yes', then 'accept'.

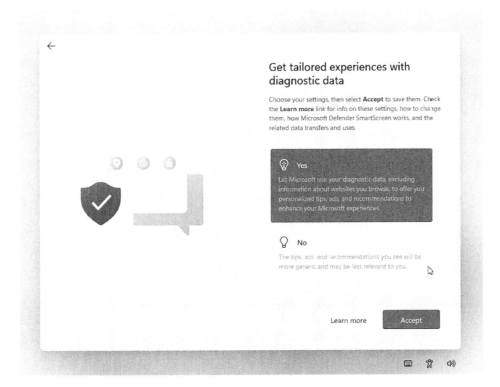

Chapter 2: Setting up Windows 11

Advertising ID, this means any ads that appear will be tailored to your personal computing habits. Select 'yes', then 'accept'.

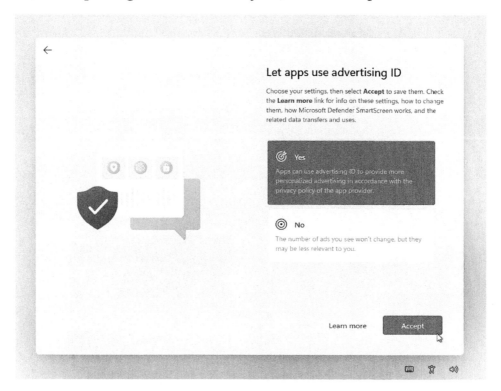

Here you can further customise Windows 11. If you're a gamer, click the 'gaming' box. If you're a creative, click 'creativity', and follow the steps. You can skip this section for now and customise Windows later. Click 'skip'.

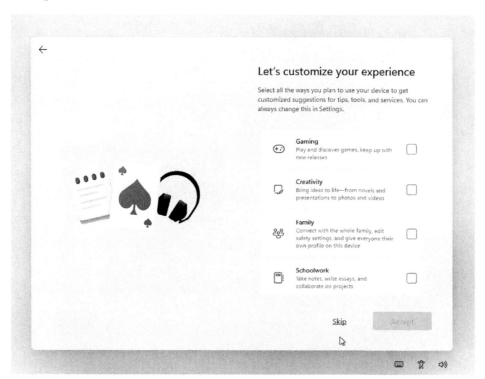

Enable OneDrive. Click 'automatically store my files in OneDrive', then click 'next'.

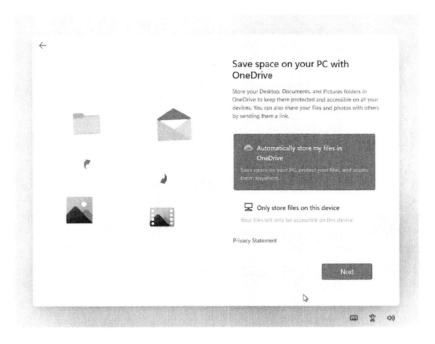

This section allows you to sign up for a Microsoft 365 account. This gives you more OneDrive space and access to Microsoft Office Apps such as Word, Excel, PowerPoint, and Outlook for a monthly or annual fee. Click 'no thanks' for now, you can always sign up later if you choose to.

Once Windows has all your preferences and details, it will configure your computer. Time for a coffee... this will take a while. Once the configuration is complete, you'll land on the Windows 11 desktop.

3

Settings and Personalise

You can personalise Windows according to your personal taste and how you intend to use your PC.

In this chapter, we'll take a look

- Adjusting System Settings
- General Settings
- Keyboards
- Mouse
- Internet & Networks
- Printers
- Bluetooth Devices
- Audio Settings
- Display Settings
- User Accounts
- Windows Hello & Sign In Options
- OneDrive
- Linking your Phone
- Dynamic Lock
- Focus Assist
- Notification Settings
- Storage Sense
- Search Settings
- Fonts
- Linux Subsystem
- Family Safety

To help you better understand this section, take a look at the video resources. Open your web browser and navigate to the following site:

elluminetpress.com/using-win-11

Adjusting System Settings

To adjust system settings, you'll need to use the settings app.

Settings App

To open the settings app, click the start button, then select the settings app icon.

On the top left, you'll see your Microsoft Account. You can click on this to edit your info, sign in options, email accounts and so on. Underneath that, you'll see a search field that is used to search for settings.

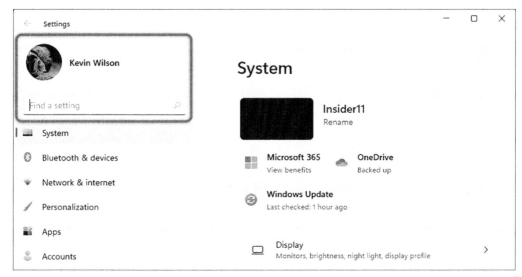

Chapter 3: Settings and Personalisation

Down the left hand side you'll see a list of categories. Settings for different features and options are grouped into these categories.

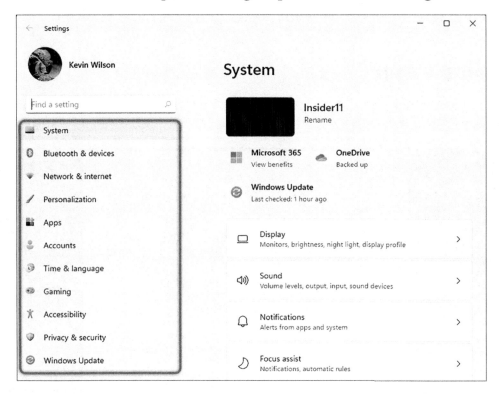

For example, all settings to do with devices such as printers, mice and keyboards can be found in the 'bluetooth & devices' category.

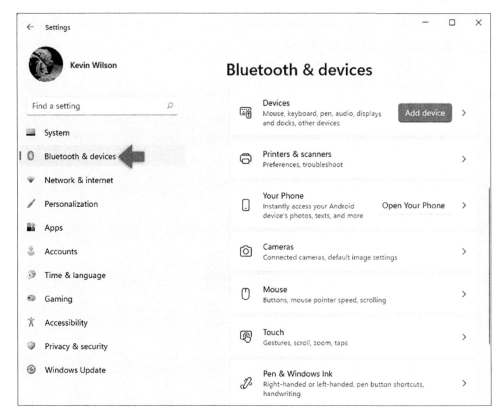

Searching for Settings

The quickest way to change a setting is to search for it using the search field on the settings app.

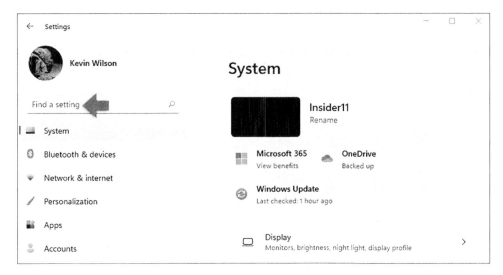

If I wanted to change the printer settings, I'd just type 'printer' into the search field.

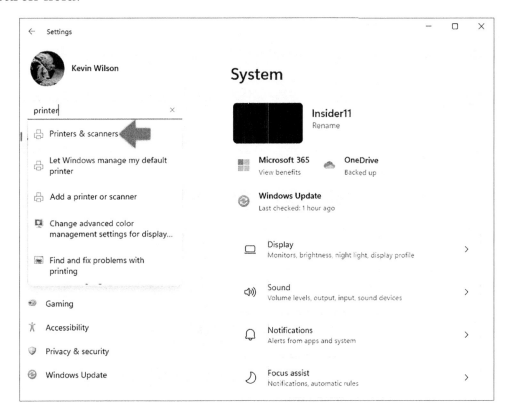

Click on 'Printers & Scanners' in the list of suggestions in the drop down box.

You can do this for any setting you need to change.

General Settings

General configuration settings worth noting are date and time, power saving options, regional settings and keyboard layouts.

Desktop Background

To change the wallpaper or background on your desktop, right click on your desktop, then from the popup menu, select 'personalise'.

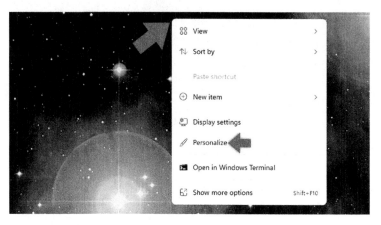

Scroll down the page, then click on 'background'.

Scroll down to the 'personalise your background' section. You can put a picture in the background, a colour, or create a slideshow.

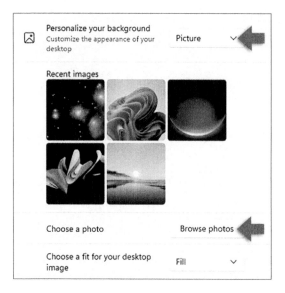

Colour

To set the background to a colour, change the dropdown box at the top from 'picture' to 'solid color', then select a colour from the palette.

Picture

To use a picture, select 'picture' from the first drop down box at the top. Select a picture from the recent images. If you want to add your own, click 'browse photos.

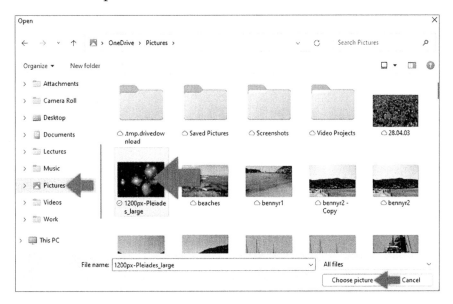

Select 'fill' from the drop down box that says 'choose a fit for your desktop image'. This will resize and crop your photo to fit your screen size.

Slideshow

To create a slideshow, select 'slideshow' from the drop down box at the top.

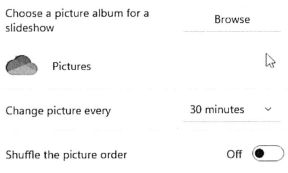

Click 'browse' to choose your photos. Navigate to your pictures folder, then click 'chose this folder'.

Set the amount of time to show each picture - eg 30 mins, or 1 hour...

Click the switch at the bottom to turn on 'shuffle the picture order'. This will select random photos from the pictures folder you selected above.

Start Menu Folder & Settings Icons

You can add your documents, downloads, music and the settings icon to the bottom right of your start menu next to the power button.

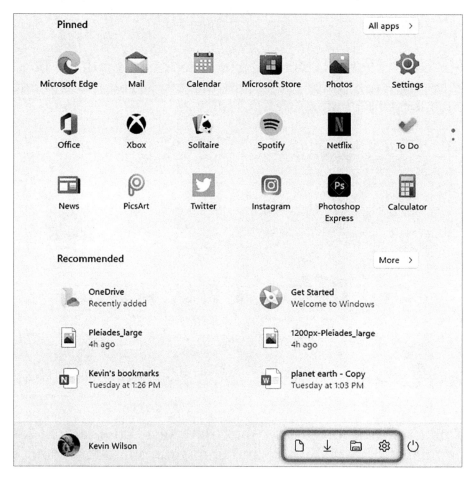

To do this, open your settings app, select 'personalisation' from the list on the left hand side. Scroll down the list on the right, select 'start'.

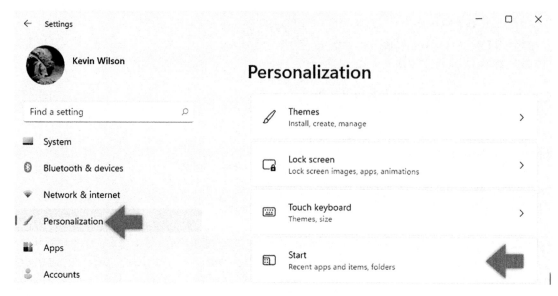

Here, you can show recently added apps, most used apps, as well as jump lists and recently opened documents in file explorer.

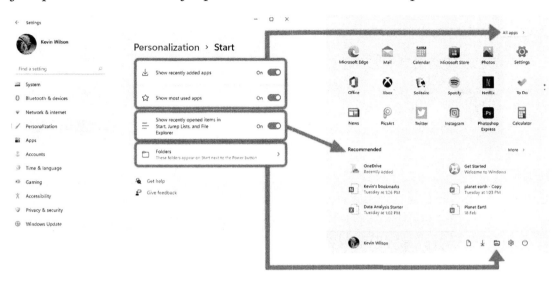

Underneath that, you can add your folder icons to the bottom right of the start menu. Click on 'folders'.

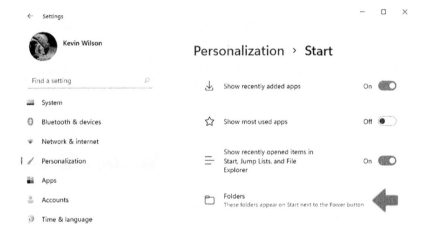

Choose the folders you want to appear on the bottom right of your start menu. It is useful to add your most used folders such as documents, downloads, or pictures, as well as the settings icon.

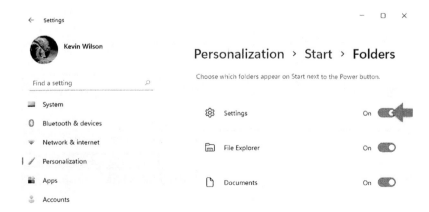

Taskbar Personalisation and Alignment

You can personalise the taskbar in Windows 11. To do this, right click on the taskbar, then select 'taskbar settings' from the popup menu.

Click on the small arrows on the right to open up the sections. In the 'taskbar items' section you can add or remove the buttons that appear next to the start button.

In the 'taskbar corner icons' select which icons you want to appear in the corner. In the 'taskbar corner overflow', select which icons you want to hide in the overflow section. Turn the switch 'on' to show the icon in the overflow, turn the switch 'off' to hide it in the overflow.

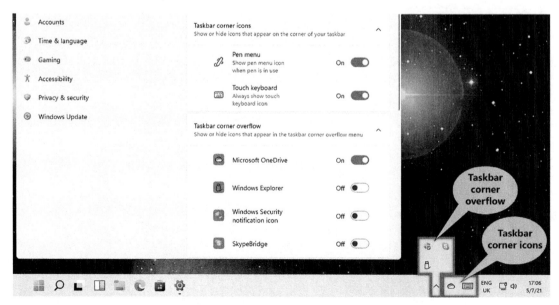

In the 'taskbar behaviours' section, the Windows 11 taskbar is by default aligned to the center.

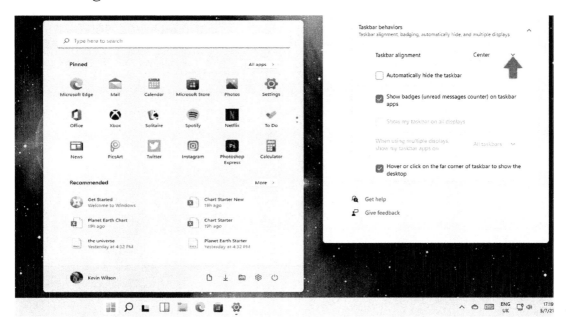

You can change this if you prefer the traditional left aligned taskbar as seen in previous versions of Windows. Select 'left' from the 'taskbar alignment' drop down box.

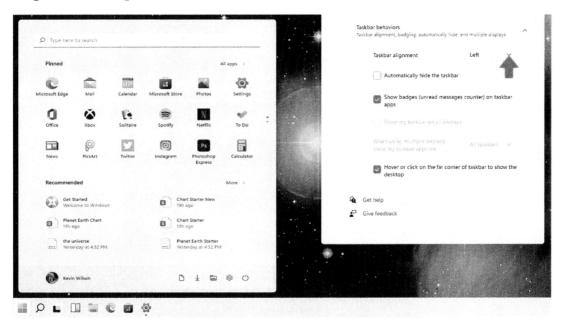

You can automatically hide the taskbar which means the taskbar disappears when you navigate away to something else, and reappears when you move your mouse pointer back to the bottom of the screen.

You can also show or hide the taskbar on other displays if you have more than one.

Colours & Effects

You can change on screen colours and effects in Windows 11. To do this, right click on your desktop then select 'personalise' from the popup menu.

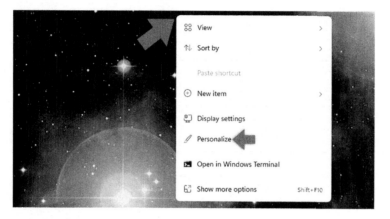

Scroll down the list on the right, select 'colours'.

Scroll down to 'transparency effects' and 'accent colours'.

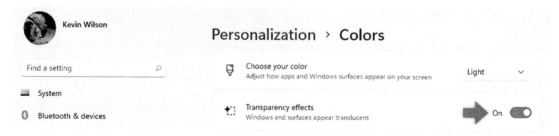

Transparency effects create panels that look like frosted sheets of glass such as the widgets panel, or the semi translucent start menus and windows. Use the switch to turn the effect on or off.

Accent colours are the colours of switches, scrollbars, progress bars, sliders, highlighted text, hyperlinks, and buttons.

Using the drop down box next to 'accent colour', set this to 'automatic' to allow Windows to select a colour based on your desktop background, or set it to 'manual' and select a colour from the pallet below.

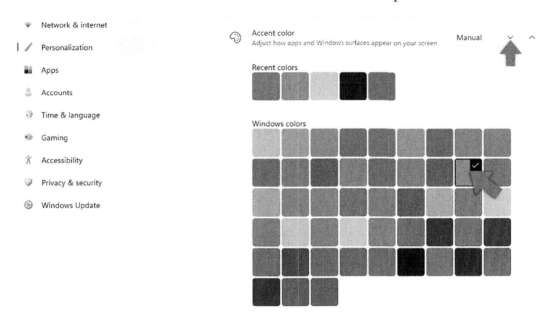

Light Mode & Dark Mode

Dark mode makes looking at your screen a bit easier on the eyes. It replaces the bright white backgrounds in Windows Apps with a dark acrylic background. This only works with Windows Apps such as explorer, photos, news, groove music, mail, or calendar, and not with applications such as Word, Chrome, or Photoshop. Below you can see light mode vs dark mode.

Chapter 3: Settings and Personalisation

Right click on your desktop then select 'personalise' from the popup menu.

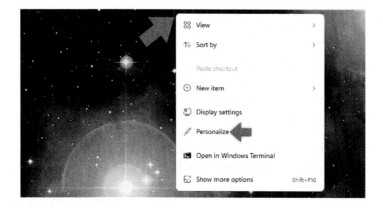

Scroll down the list on the right, select 'colours'.

Scroll down until you see 'choose your color'. Select 'light' for light mode, and 'dark' for dark mode.

You can also customise the colour. To do this select 'custom' from the drop down.

Now you can choose between dark and light mode. 'Windows Mode' sets the colour mode for the start menu, taskbar, search, and system tray. 'App Mode' sets the colour mode for all windows apps including, mail, calendar, file explorer, news, weather, app store, and so on.

Here, you can see windows is dark, and the app (eg settings) is light.

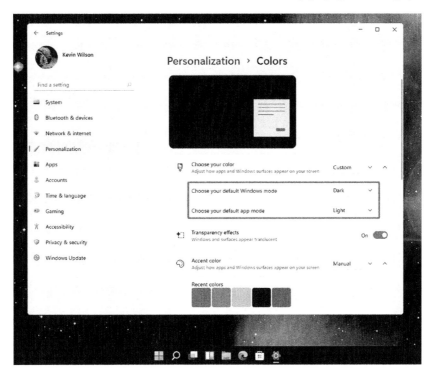

If I wanted the apps dark, and windows light...

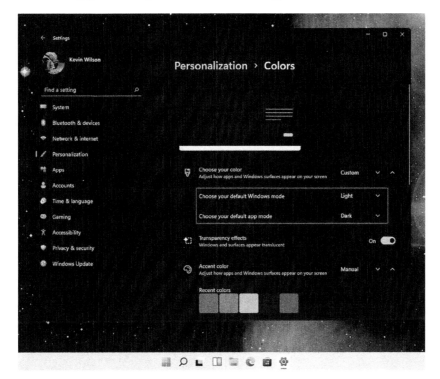

Chapter 3: Settings and Personalisation

Power Options

The power options allow you to set a time interval for windows to turn off your display or put your computer to sleep after a period of inactivity. If you need to change the power options, open your settings app, then select 'system' from the list on the left.

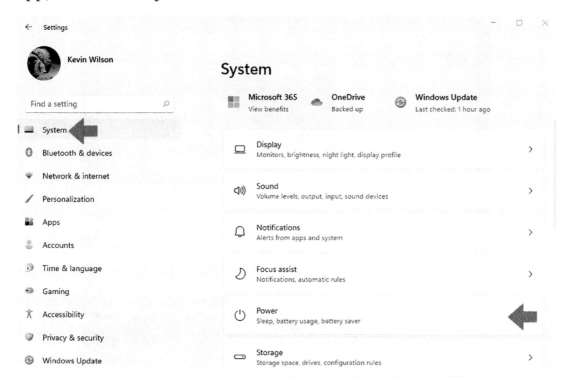

Here, you can set the amount of time before your computer turns off the screen and the amount of time before your computer goes into sleep mode. These times mean the length of time your computer is left unattended. Click the drop down box and select a time.

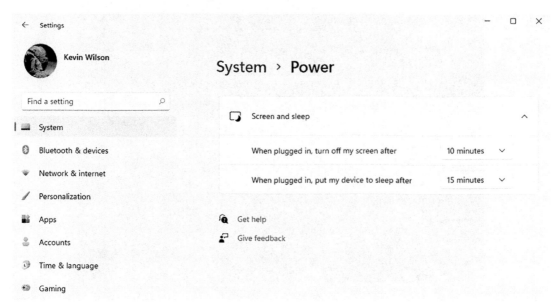

Additional Power Options

To change your power schemes, click 'additional power settings', click on the search icon on the taskbar, type in `control panel`.

Select 'system & security'. Then click 'power options'.

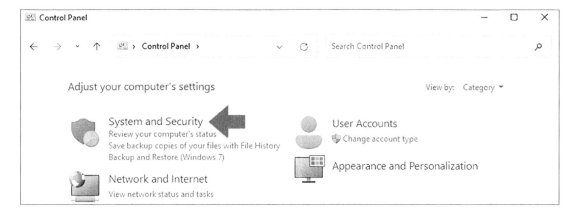

Here, you can select a power plan. The balanced plan is great for laptops and tablets as it gives you a balance between performance and power efficiency. Ultimate performance, and high performance plans are great for workstations and desktop PCs.

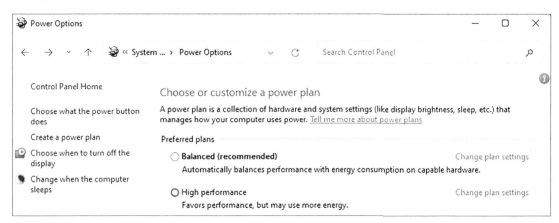

Click 'change plan settings' to further customise the plan.

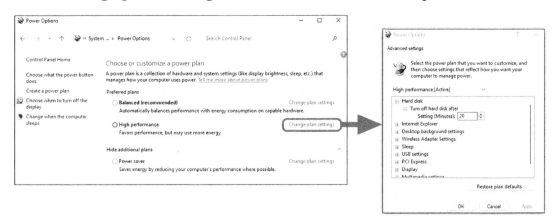

55

Chapter 3: Settings and Personalisation

Date and Time

To change the date and time, right click on the clock on the bottom right of the taskbar. Select 'adjust date and time' from the popup menu.

Here, you can select your time zone. Windows will automatically set the time when it connects to the internet.

Adjust for daylight savings time if your region observes this. You can select your time zone using the 'time zone' drop down menu - just select your country. You can also set your time zone automatically using your location - just turn on 'set time zone automatically'.

At the bottom you can manually sync your device with the time server to get the correct time.

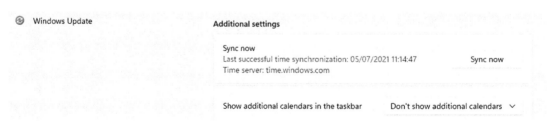

Regional Settings

If you need to change your language or the date/time format for your particular country, you can do that here. Open the settings app, then select 'time & language' from the list on the left. Select 'language & region' from the list on the right.

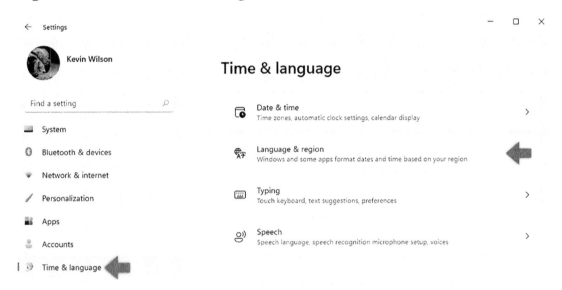

Here, you can select your country or region and regional format.

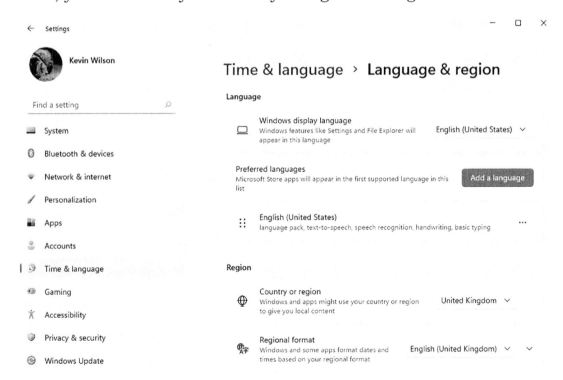

Regional format means the format of dates, times, and the calendar you use.

Keyboards

Most countries use a standard keyboard, however there are some regional differences with layouts and language.

Layout & Language

Open your settings app, then select 'time & language' from the list on the left. Select 'language & region' from the list on the right.

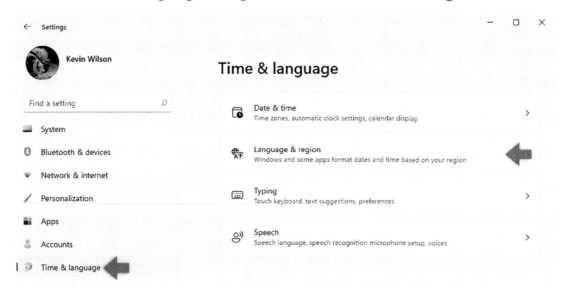

Click on the three dots icon on the right of your language, then select 'language options' from the drop down menu.

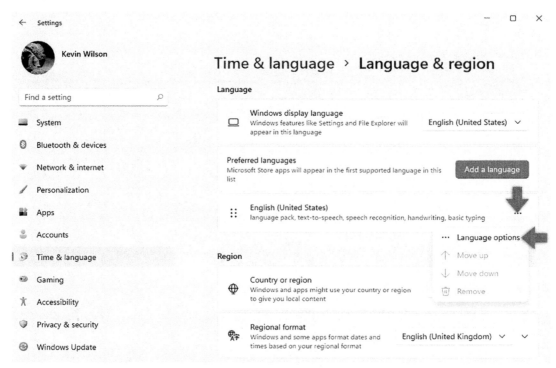

Scroll down to 'Keyboards' and then select 'Add a keyboard'. In the pop-up menu, select the keyboard language you want to add.

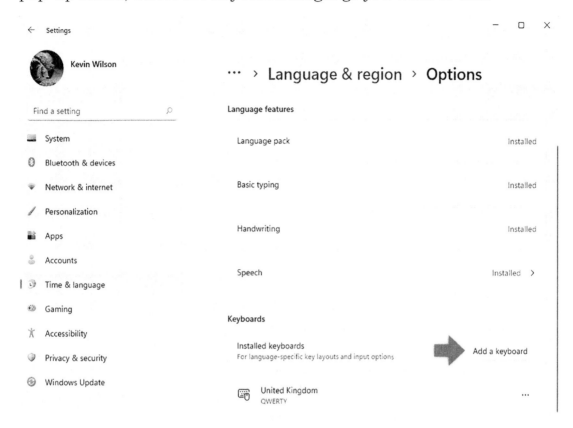

A language control popup box will appear above the taskbar on the bottom-right corner of the screen.

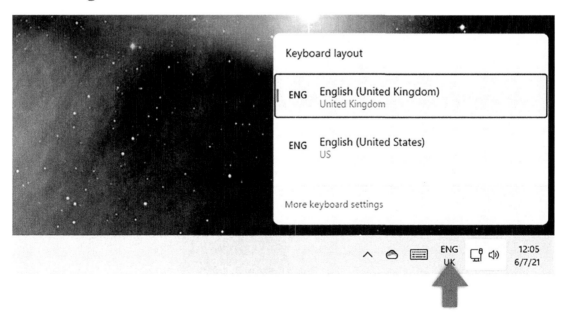

Here, you can switch between keyboards. Just click on the keyboard you just added.

Chapter 3: Settings and Personalisation

Touch Keyboard

On a touchscreen device such as a tablet, the touch keyboard appears along the bottom of the screen when you tap a text field, or need to start typing.

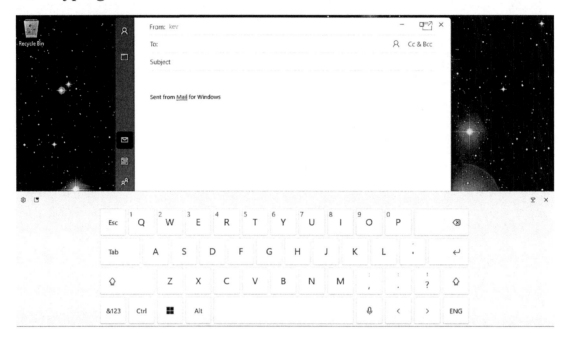

Open the settings app, select 'personalisation' from the list on the left, then click 'touch keyboard'.

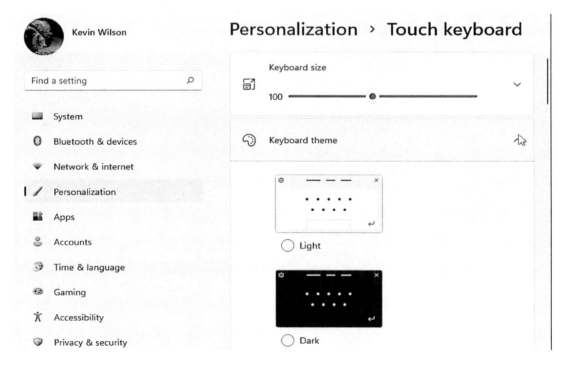

Here, you can change the keyboard size, and select a theme, or look, of your keyboard.

Mouse

To adjust mouse pointer speed and scrolling, open your settings app, then select 'bluetooth & devices' from the list on the left. Scroll down the list on the right, then select 'mouse'.

Here, you can swap the mouse buttons, change the mouse pointer speed, as well as how fast your scroll wheel scrolls pages - you can select how many lines at a time scroll by.

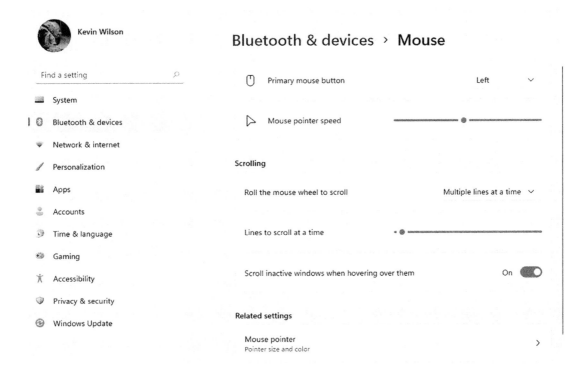

Down at the bottom of the window, you can change the mouse pointer size and colour.

Internet & Networks

You can connect to networks and the internet in a variety of ways. The most common is WiFi, but you can also connect using an Ethernet cable.

WiFi

To locate nearby WiFi networks, click the Network/WiFi icon on the bottom right of the screen then tap 'available'.

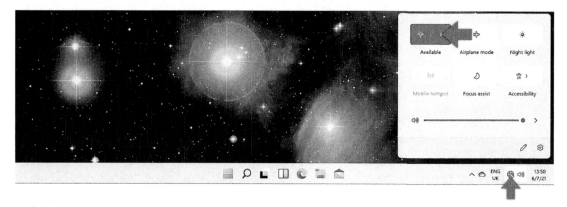

Tap the name of the network you want to join, make sure 'connect automatically' is selected, then click 'connect'.

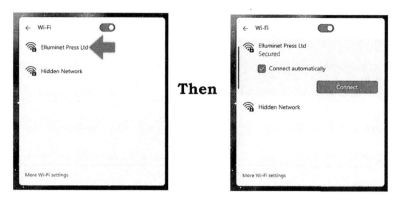

Enter the WiFi password or network password, then click 'next'.

For your home WiFi, the network key or password is usually printed on the back of your router. Sometimes the network name is called an SSID.

Use the same procedure if you are on a public hotspot such as in a cafe, library, hotel, airport and so on. You'll need to find the network key if they have one. Some are open networks and you can just connect.

When using public hotspots, keep in mind that most of them don't encrypt the data you send over the internet and aren't secure. So don't start checking your online banking account or shop online while using an unsecured connection, as anyone who is on the public WiFi hotspot potentially can gain access to anything you do.

Ethernet

To connect via Ethernet, you'll need an Ethernet cable. Plug one end into your laptop or PC. Plug the other end of the cable into your router or switch.

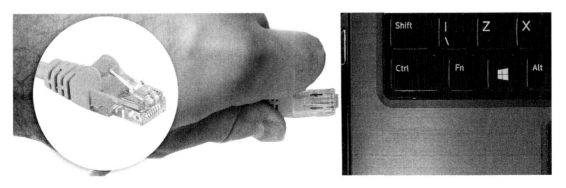

Most modern devices no longer include an Ethernet port. If this is the case, then you can buy a USB to Ethernet adapter.

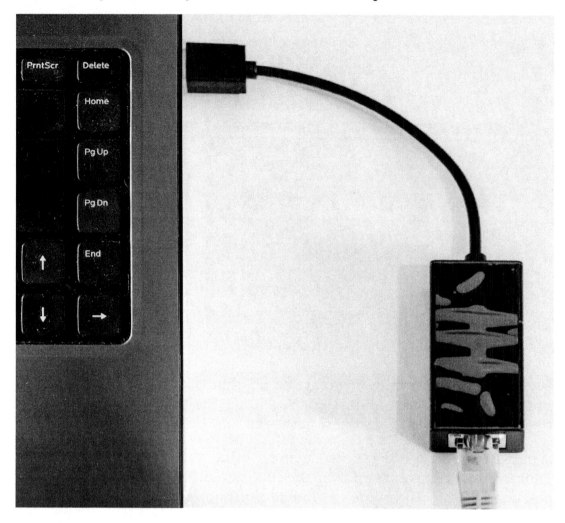

Mobile USB Modems

If you use your laptop on the go a lot or travel frequently, you should also consider using 3G/4G/5G LTE mobile data modem. You can get these from a phone provider such as AT&T, Verizon, O_2, T-Mobile, etc.

When you buy these from your phone provider, you can take out a contract or pay as you go in the same way you'd buy a cell/mobile phone.

VPN

If you're really concerned about security or use your devices on public hotspots for work, then you should consider a VPN or Virtual Private Network. A VPN essentially encrypts all the data you send and receive over a network.

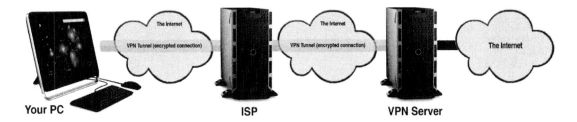

There are a few good ones to choose from, some have a free option with a limited amount of data and others you pay a subscription.

Take a look at
www.tunnelbear.com
windscribe.com
speedify.com

To set one up manually, right click on the network/WiFi icon on the bottom right of the taskbar, select 'network and internet settings'. Select VPN from the list on the right.

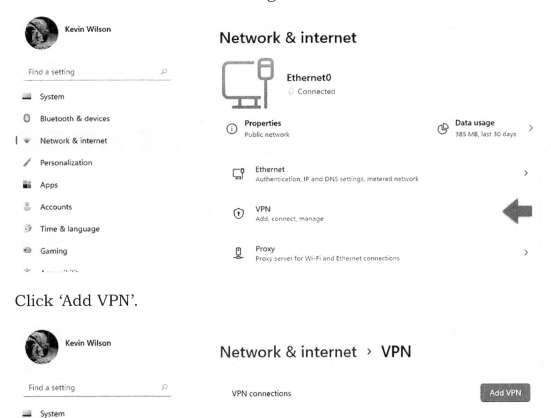

Click 'Add VPN'.

Enter the connection details. You'll need to get the connection information from your system administrator.

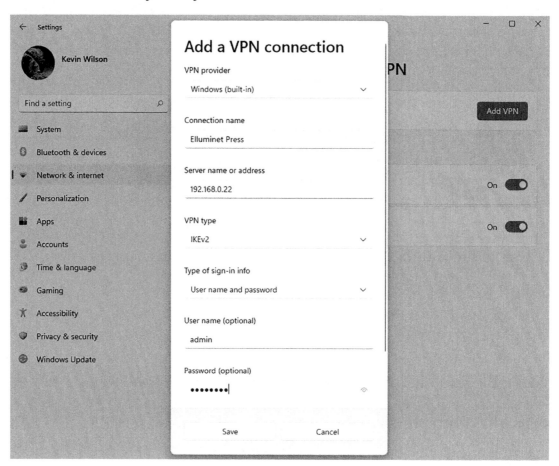

Network Settings

Network settings is where you'll be able to configure your WiFi or Ethernet settings. Right click on the network/WiFi icon on the bottom right of the taskbar, select 'network and internet settings' from the popup menu.

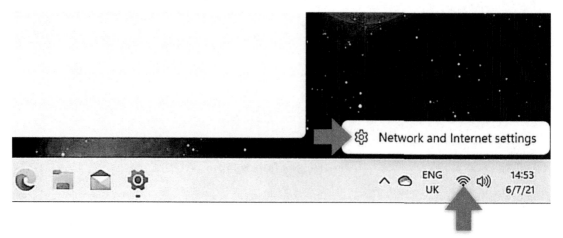

Here, you'll see your current network connections. Your active connection will be shown at the top - in this case we're connected to WiFi. Click on your connection to see settings

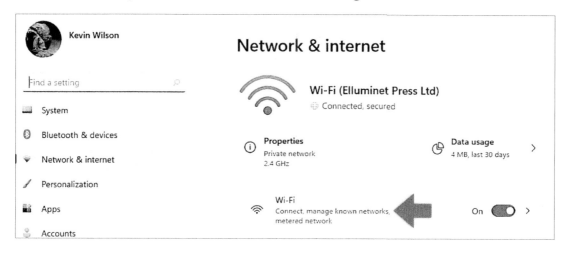

Properties

You can view your connection properties such as IP address, DNS and available WiFi networks.

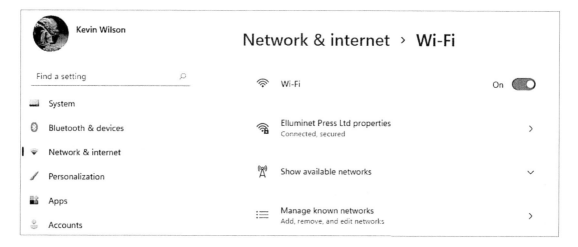

Available Networks will show you any WiFi networks that are in range. In 'manage known networks', you can add a network, or forget a network.

Chapter 3: Settings and Personalisation

DNS & IP Addresses

Open your network settings properties as in the previous section. Select your network connection, eg WiFi.

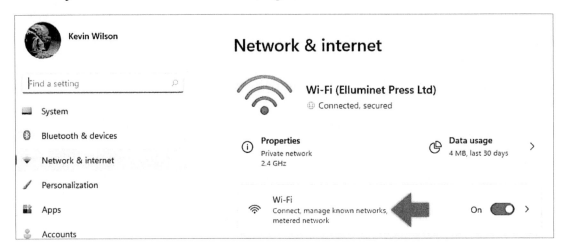

Select '...properties'.

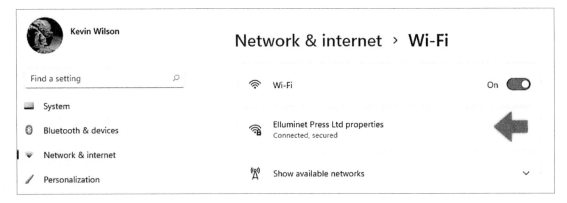

Scroll down the page, here you'll see assignments for your IP address and DNS server settings. Most of the time you can keep these on automatic (DHCP), but in certain circumstances you might need to change them.

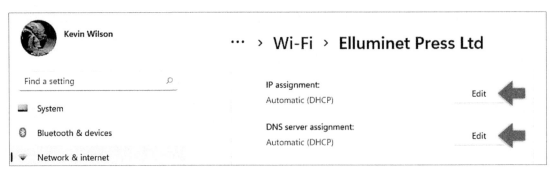

Your IP address is the unique address of your device that uniquely identifies it on the network. The DNS server converts website domain names into IP addresses.

To change the IP address, click 'edit' next to 'IP assignment'. Select 'manual', then enter the network details.

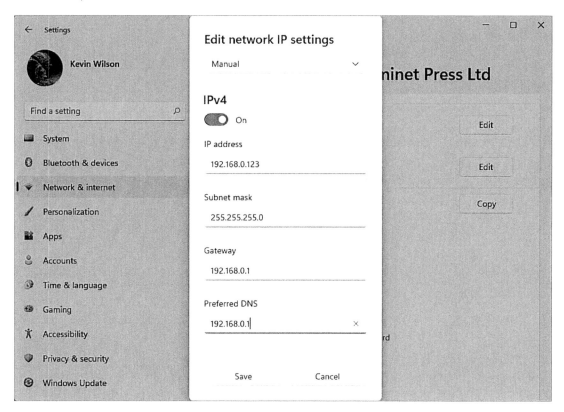

To change the DNS, click 'edit' next to 'DNS server assignment'. Select' 'manual', then enter the IP address of the DNS server. Try Cloudflare's DNS: 1.1.1.3 and 1.0.0.3

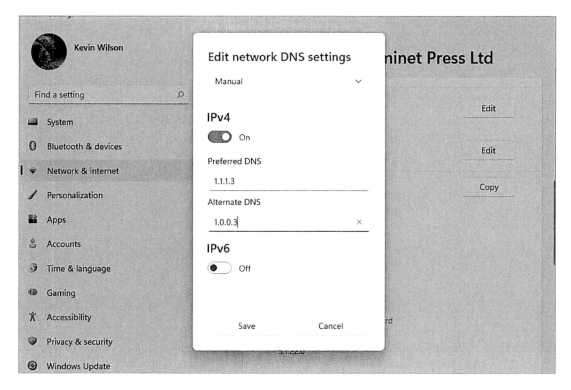

Printers

You can connect a printer to your computer with a USB cable as well as using WiFi.

WiFi

WiFi is definitely the way you'd want to connect to a printer if you are on a tablet or laptop. Unfortunately it is difficult to give specific instructions on printer setup as each model of printer and each manufacturer has their own method. However, I will provide some general guidelines you can use to get started.

If your printer is brand new, you'll need to connect it to your WiFi. Printers with LCD panels display step-by-step instructions for setting up the wireless connection when you first turn on the printer. So read the instructions for specifics on how to do this.

If your printer doesn't have an LCD panel, use the WPS method. You can use this method if you have a WPS button on your router - as shown in the photo below.

Refer to the printer's quick start guide to find the exact procedure for your printer model. Usually you have to press and hold the WiFi button on your printer for a few seconds, then go to your router and press the WPS button.

If your router doesn't have a WPS button, you'll have to select your WiFi network (SSID) and enter your WiFi password on your printer. You'll need to refer to the printer's instructions on exactly how to do that on your particular printer.

Your printer will let you know when it's connected to your WiFi - the WiFi light usually stops flashing and lights up.

Once connected, on your computer open the settings app, then click 'bluetooth & devices' in the list on the left. Select 'printers & scanners' from the panel on the right hand side.

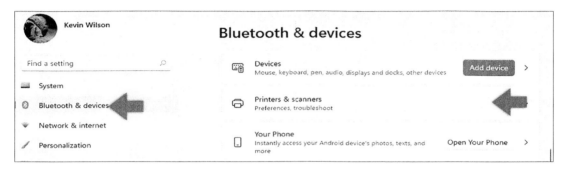

Click 'add device'.

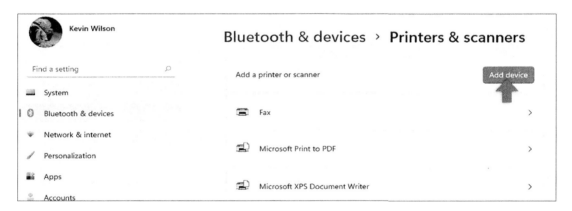

Windows will detect most modern printers, and display a list of any it finds. Click 'add device' next to your printer.

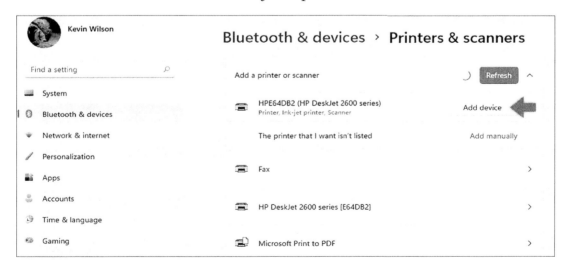

Windows will download and install the appropriate driver for your printer automatically.

USB

Using a USB cable, plug the square end into the back of the printer, then plug the other end into a USB port on your computer.

Turn on your printer, then open the start menu and click on the settings app icon. Select 'bluetooth & devices' from the list on the left.

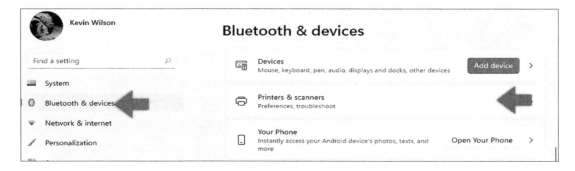

Select 'printers & scanners', then click 'add a printer or scanner'.

Windows will detect most modern printers. Select your printer from the list.

Manufacturer's Printer Setup Programs

Many printer manufacturers include a setup program to install the printer on your computer.

HP

HP have introduced a simplified setup method for their printers. To set up your printer, plug it in and turn it up. On your computer open your web browser and navigate to the following website

```
123.hp.com
```

Type your printer's model number into the search field.

Click 'download' or 'get the app'. Follow the instructions on the screen to download and install the drivers or the app.

Epson

To set up your printer, plug it in and turn it up. On your computer open your web browser and navigate to the following website

```
epson.sn
```

Type your printer's model number into the search field.

Click 'lets get started'. Scroll down the page.

Follow the instructions on the screen to download and install the drivers or the app.

Chapter 3: Settings and Personalisation

Canon

To set up your printer, plug it in and turn it up. On your computer open your web browser and navigate to the following website

    canon.com/ijsetup

Click 'setup', then type in your printer model number.

Follow the instructions on the screen to download and install the drivers or the app.

Brother

To set up your printer, plug it in and turn it up. On your computer open your web browser and navigate to the following website

    support.brother.com

Select 'downloads'.

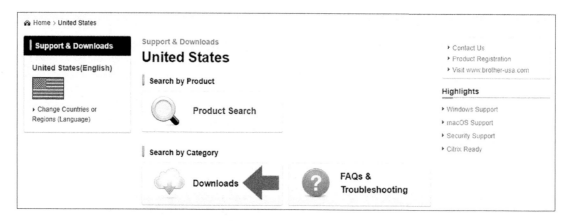

Type in your model number.

Select 'Windows 10' or 'Windows 11', then download the 'full driver & software package'. Follow the instructions on screen.

Downloading Printer Drivers

If Windows 11 has trouble installing your printer, you'll need to download and install the printer software.

To do this, you'll need to go to the manufacturer's website and download the software.

For HP & Samsung printers go to

    support.hp.com/drivers

For Canon printers go to

    www.usa.canon.com/support

For Brother printers go to

    support.brother.com

For Epson printers go to

    support.epson.com

Somewhere on the manufacturer's website, there will be a product search field. Type in the model name of your printer. Click 'OK' or 'find'

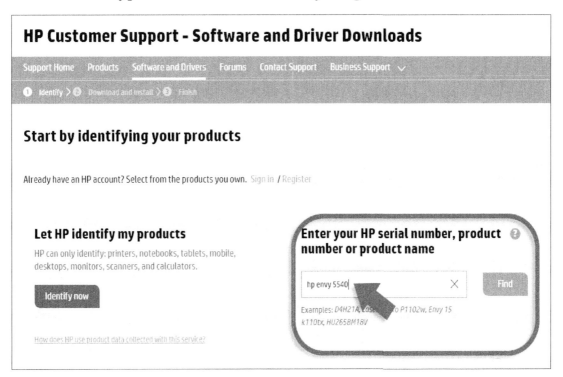

In the example above, I'm installing an HP printer. In most cases you'll need to download the driver software from the manufacturer's website.

Chapter 3: Settings and Personalisation

From the search results, select your Operating System if required, usually "Windows 10 (64bit)" or "Windows 11 (64bit)".

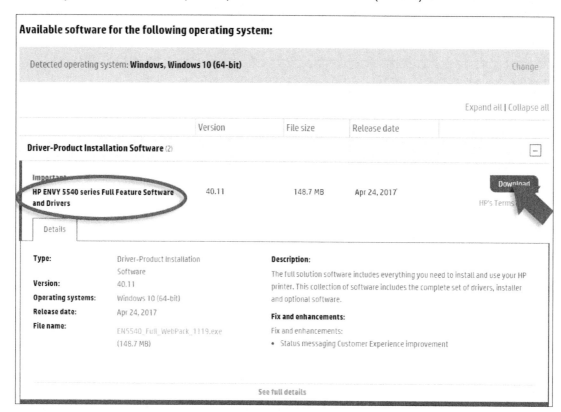

Click on the prompt at the bottom of your browser.

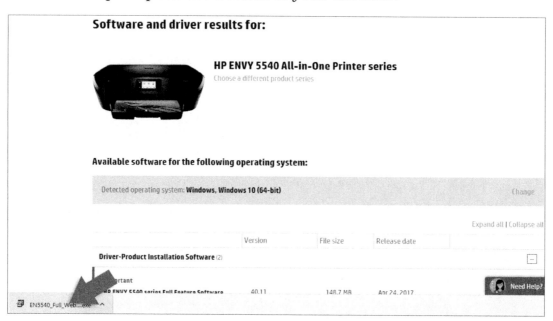

This will run the installation software. Click 'OK' or 'Yes' to the security prompt. If you don't see a prompt, go to your downloads folder in file explorer and double click on the EXE file you just downloaded. Follow the on screen instructions to connect to your printer.

Managing Printers

You can get to the print queue from the Settings App on the start menu. From the Settings App, select 'bluetooth & devices' on the left. On the right hand side of the window, click 'printers & scanners'.

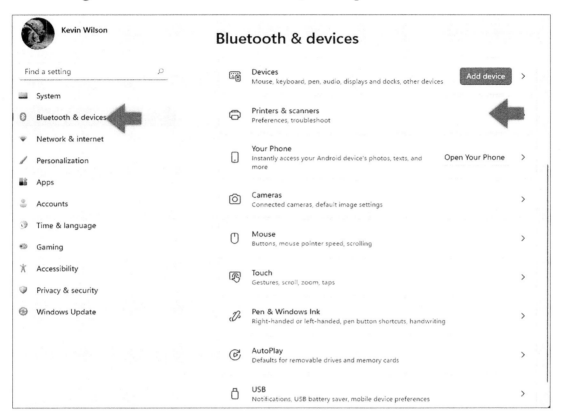

Select your printer. From the printer settings page, click 'open print queue'. This will open up the print queue for that printer.

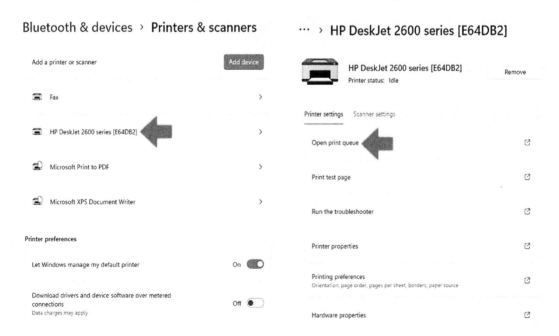

Chapter 3: Settings and Personalisation

Here you can see a list of documents that are queued for printing. If you right click on the print job in the list, you can cancel or pause the document.

You can also change global printer settings and preferences. From the printer settings page, select 'printer preferences'.

Use layout tab to change orientation to portrait or landscape. Use the quality tab to change quality settings and paper type.

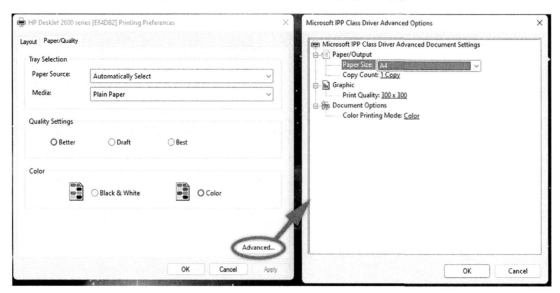

Use 'advanced' to change the paper size: letter, A4, A5 etc.

Bluetooth Devices

You can pair any bluetooth device such as a mouse, keyboard, headphones, pens and so on. To do this go to the settings app on the start menu, select 'bluetooth & devices'.

Pairing a Device

Shift the bluetooth slider to 'on'. Then click 'add device'.

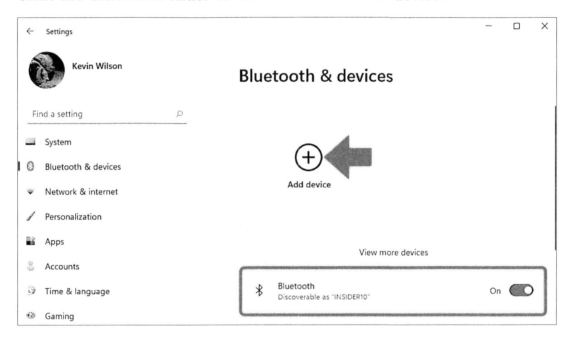

From the 'add a device' menu, select the type of device you're adding. In this example bluetooth.

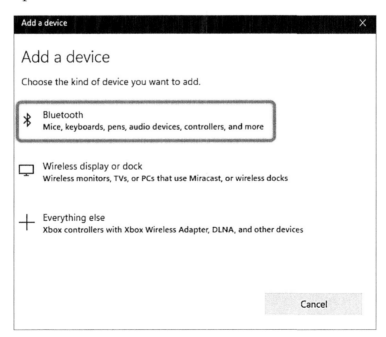

Chapter 3: Settings and Personalisation

Put your device into discover mode. How you do this depends on the device, so you'll need to read the instructions that came with it to find out. In this example, I'm going to pair a bluetooth mouse. To put the mouse into pairing mode, press and hold the button on the bottom of the mouse until the light underneath starts flashing.

Your laptop or PC will start scanning for bluetooth devices, and list them in this window. Select your device from the list. Windows will add and setup the device automatically. Click 'done'.

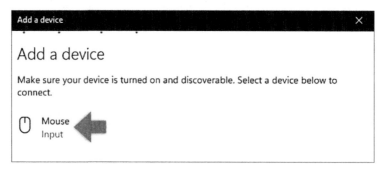

You'll see all your bluetooth devices appear along the top.

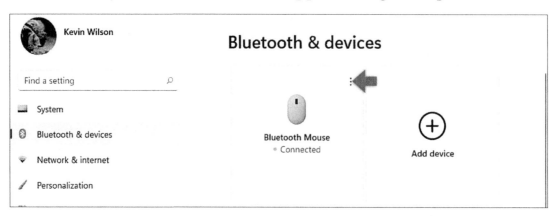

If you need to remove a device, click on the three dots icon on the top right of the device, then select 'remove device'.

80

Audio Settings

You can adjust settings and configure your audio in Windows 11.

Configuring a Microphone

To configure your microphone, make sure it's plugged into the pink 3.5mm jack on the back of your computer, or in the microphone jack.

Right-click the volume icon on the bottom right of your window, then select 'sounds' settings from the popup menu.

Here, you'll see your output - eg speakers, and your input - eg mics. Scroll down to 'input', then select your microphone.

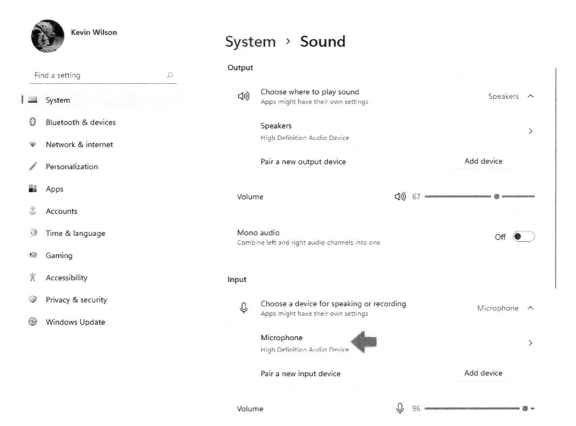

81

Chapter 3: Settings and Personalisation

Here, you can adjust the input volume - this is how sensitive your microphone is. You can also change the format which also adjusts the quality: CD quality, DVD quality, or studio quality.

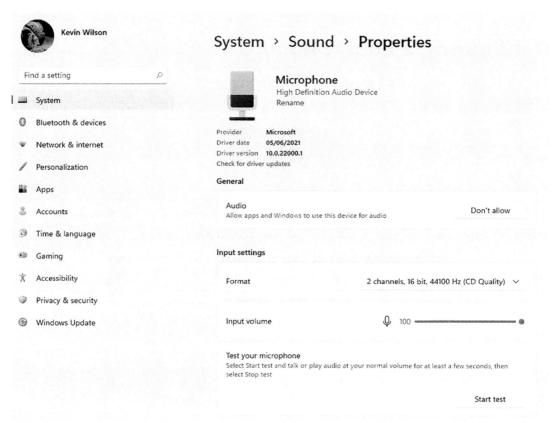

To test your microphone, click 'start test' at the bottom right of the screen.

Now, read the sentence displayed on your screen. Read the following paragraph into the microphone using your normal speaking voice.

Peter dictates to his computer. He prefers it to typing, and particularly prefers it to pen and paper.

You'll see the blue bar next to 'input volume' move as you speak. Windows 11 will adjust the input volume automatically depending on how loud you speak.

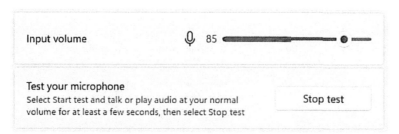

Once you're done, click 'stop test'.

Adjust Microphone Recording Volume

Right-click the volume icon on the bottom right of your window, then select 'sound settings' from the popup menu.

Scroll down to the bottom, then select 'more sound settings'.

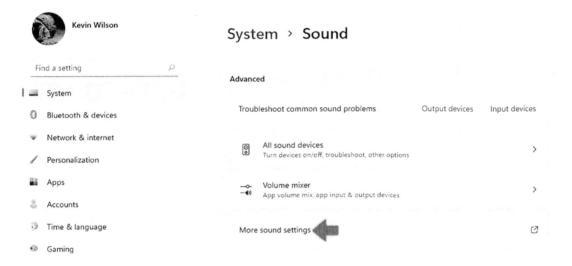

From the 'sounds' dialog box, select the 'recording' tab. Select your microphone, then click 'properties'.

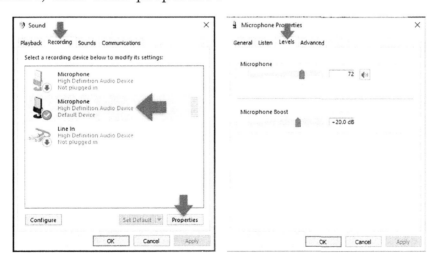

From the 'properties' window, select 'levels'. From here, set the microphone levels. Use the top slider to increase the recording levels of the microphone. Use the bottom slider to boost the microphone sensitivity - useful if your mic isn't picking up your voice clearly.

Attaching Speakers

Make sure your speakers are plugged into the green 3.5mm jack on the back of your computer.

Audio Levels

To adjust the audio volume, click on the speaker icon on the bottom right of the taskbar. Here, at the bottom of the popup box, you can adjust the overall volume. Click and drag the slider.

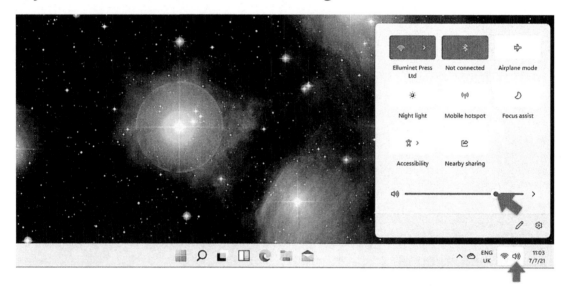

Click the 'side arrow' on the right of volume slider if you need to select a different device, such as speakers, headphones, etc.

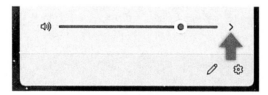

Select a device.

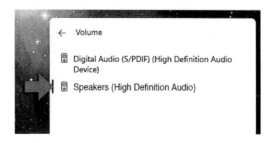

Volume Mixer

Each application that generates sound such as iTunes, Web browser, Spotify and so on, will have its own volume control. This allows you to adjust the volume for individual apps. For example, you can turn down the system sounds, but keep your music playing louder, or you can turn down your music in the background if you're on a video call.

To open the mixer, right click on the speaker icon on the bottom right of the taskbar. Select 'open volume mixer'.

You'll see a slider for each of your running apps. In this example, I have Groove Music playing in the background and I have a video running in Edge. Here, I can turn down the volume of the music in Edge without turning down the volume on Groove Music. Just use the appropriate slider on the mixer.

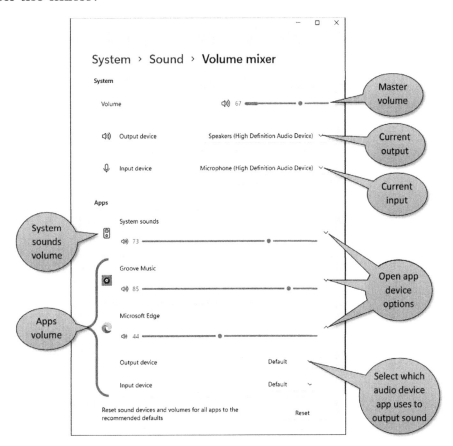

Display Settings

To adjust your display resolution, multiple monitor settings and so on, open your settings app.

Screen Resolution & Scaling

The screen resolution is the number of horizontal pixels by the number of vertical pixels on a screen. For example a full HD screen is 1920x1080. Windows 11 does its best to automatically select the correct screen resolution for any screens it detects.

Open the settings app, then select 'system' from the left hand side. Select 'display' from the list on the right.

Select the screen whose resolution you want to change. If you only have one screen you wont get this option.

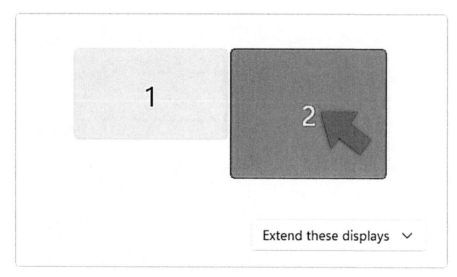

If you want to change the scale, eg to make the icons and text appear bigger, use the scale option at the top. 100% is normal size, 125% and higher, increases the size of the text, windows, and icons on the screen.

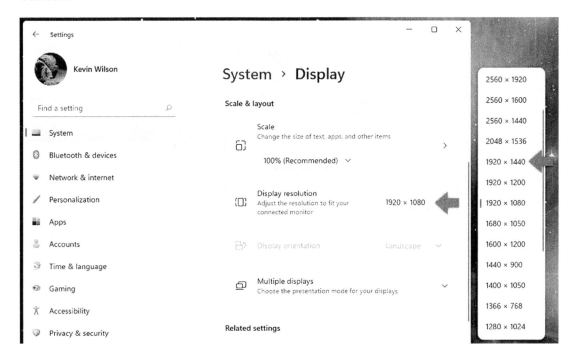

To change the resolution of the display, scroll down to 'display resolution', click the drop down box and select a resolution from the list. 1920 x 1080 is Full HD.

Multiple Screens

You can plug in more than one screen if your PC supports this.

Chapter 3: Settings and Personalisation

To set up your screens, open your settings app then select 'system' from the list on the left. Then select 'displays' from the list on the right.

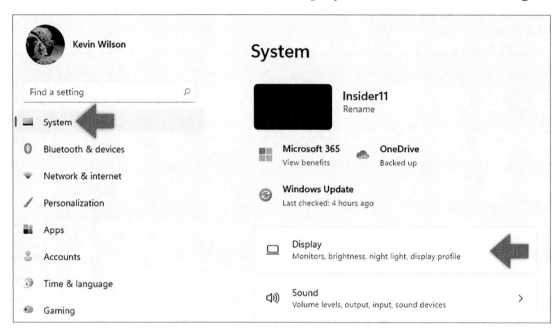

Here, you'll see a diagram with rectangles representing your screens. In this case, we have two screens, my main 24" screen (screen 1) and a smaller one (screen 2).

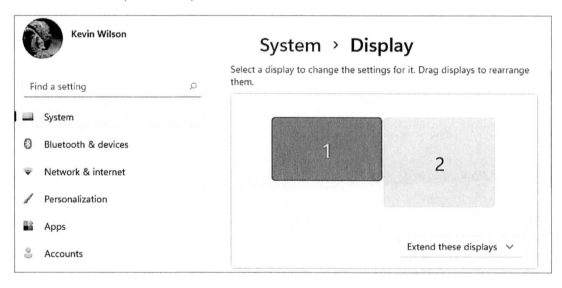

You can drag these rectangles in any order. It is useful to have them in the same order as the physical arrangement on your desk - as shown in the image opposite.

Click 'multiple displays' top expand the options.

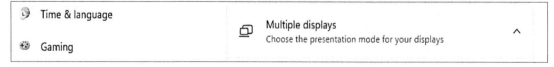

Here, you can force Windows to detect your displays. You can identify all your displays - this shows the display number on each screen: 1, 2, 3, etc depending on how many displays you have connected.

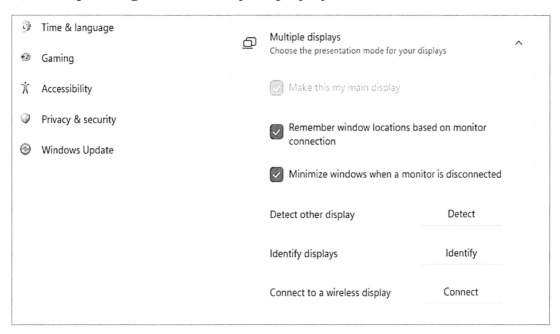

You can also connect to wireless displays using a feature called screen casting.

Wireless Displays and Screen Casting

You can connect to wireless compatible displays such as Smart TVs. Your TV will need to support screen mirroring or Miracast for this to work. On your TV look for settings or apps such as 'Miracast', 'Screen Casting', or 'WiFi Casting'. Make sure you enable them. Also enable bluetooth if it isn't already. Check your TV's documentation for details on how to do this for your model.

If your TV doesn't support screen mirroring, you can buy a Micracast dongle such as the one below. Or a Microsoft Display Adapter.

Chapter 3: Settings and Personalisation

To cast your screen, on your PC, press Windows K on your keyboard. Select your display or TV from the list of available displays.

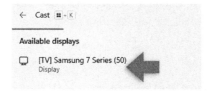

Once connected, your laptop screen will show on the wireless display

Note that at the time of writing, Miracast negotiates it's connection over WiFi using the 2.4GHz band. Some laptops and devices connect using the 5Ghz band, this may cause the connection to fail. To change this, on your laptop, right click on the start button, select 'device manager'. Click on network adapters to open it up, then right click on your WiFi adapter, select 'properties' from the popup menu.

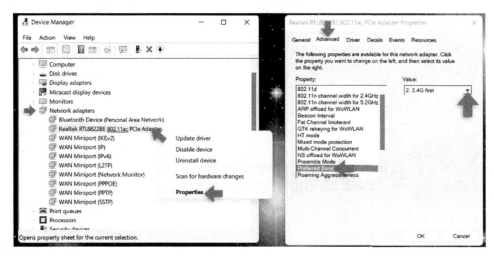

Select the 'advanced tab', scroll down to 'preferred band', change the value to '2. 2.4G first'.

User Accounts

You can set up multiple users for different people on your computer. This will allow them to sign into your computer with their own username and have access to their own OneDrive, calendar, and email.

Account Types

There are two different types of account: a local account and Microsoft Account.

Local

Local account is a username and a password you use to sign into your physical Windows 11 device only. Local accounts do not include online functions such as syncing between multiple Windows 11 devices or any of Microsoft's online services.

Microsoft

Microsoft account is an email address and a password used to sign in to services like Microsoft Store, Outlook, Microsoft 365, Office, OneDrive, and Xbox Live, as well as all your Windows devices.

User Types

There are three different types of user: administrators, standard users and child users.

Administrator

Administrators have complete access to your computer. They can install software and change settings. Administrator accounts should only be used to change settings and install software, not for everyday use.

Standard

Standard users can use apps and make limited changes to the system settings and are best for everyday use. This is the type of account you should be using for your every day tasks.

Child

Child users have restricted access to apps. Child user accounts are also monitored, allowing an adult user to check up on websites visited or apps used.

Chapter 3: Settings and Personalisation

It is considered best practice to have at least two accounts on your device: a local account set to an administrator type, and a Microsoft Account set to a standard user type. This allows you to use your standard Microsoft Account for every day activities, and the administrator account to change settings and install software.

Create a Microsoft Account

To set up a new Microsoft Account, open your web browser and navigate to the following address:

```
signup.live.com
```

Enter an email address you'd like to use for your Microsoft Account, click 'next'. Next, enter a password for the account. *Remember passwords must have at least 8 characters and contain at least one uppercase letter, lowercase letter, number, and a symbol (eg: *, $, #, etc).* Click 'next'.

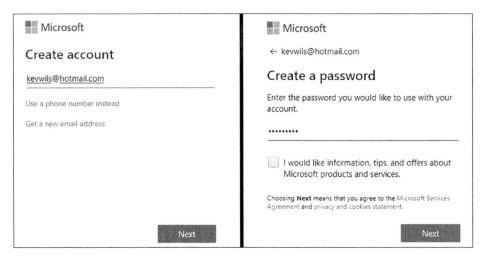

Enter your first and last names in the fields, click 'next'. Then enter the country you're living in and your date of birth.

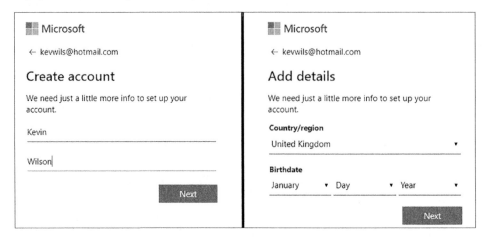

Enter the captcha code in the field at the bottom

Click 'next'. Your account will be created. Close the browser window and you're good to go.

Adding a New User with Microsoft Account

To add a new user, click the start menu, and select the settings app icon. Then select 'accounts' from the list on the left. Select 'family & other users'.

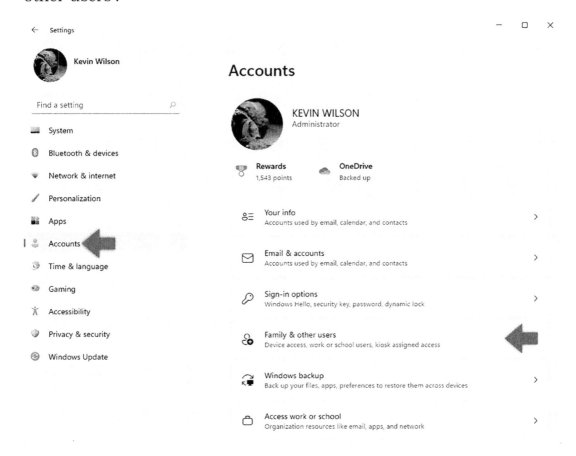

Chapter 3: Settings and Personalisation

Scroll down to 'other users', then click 'add account'.

Enter the new user's Microsoft Account email address and password.

Select the account type for this user: administrator or standard. For other users, it is best to set their account type to standard.

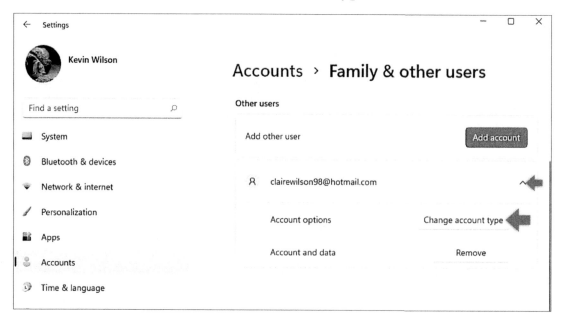

The new user will be able to log into Windows with their own account and can select it from the login screen.

Adding a New User with Local Account

A local account is an account you can log into your computer without having to sign up for a Microsoft Account email address and password.

To add a local user, click on the start menu, then select the settings app. Click on 'accounts' on the settings app home page. Select 'Family & other users'.

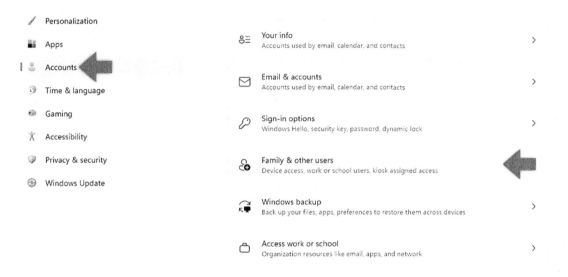

Scroll down the page, click 'Add account'.

Click 'I don't have this person's sign-in information. On the 'create account' screen, select 'add user without Microsoft account'.

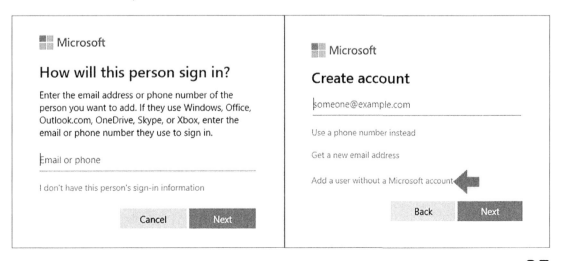

Enter the username and password for this user. Select three security questions - this is to verify your identity should you need to reset your password.

Click 'next'.

The new user will be able to log into Windows with their own account and can select it from the login screen.

Change an Account Type

As we mentioned earlier, you can change an account to either a standard user or an administrator. Click on the start menu, then select the settings app icon. Click on 'accounts' on the settings app home page. Select 'Family & other users' from the list on the left.

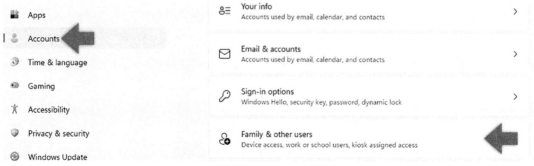

Scroll down to 'other users' select the user you want to change. From the options select 'change account type'.

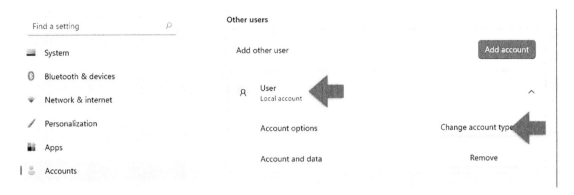

From the popup dialog box, select either 'administrator' or 'standard user', click 'ok'.

An administrator account allows complete control over the computer, which means an administrator can install apps and hardware, change system wide settings, or execute elevated tasks.

Standard user accounts can use apps, but they can't install new ones or change system settings without administrator approval. It is recommended that you have two accounts on your computer: an administrator account for changing settings or installing apps, and a standard account for everyday use.

This setup offers a more secure environment, any attempt to install new apps or change system settings while you are signed in with your standard account, will require the administrator account's password.

To remove the account, click 'remove'.

Windows Hello & Sign In Options

Windows Hello is Microsoft's biometric security feature built into some Windows 11 devices.

Windows Hello allows you to sign into your device and certain services, using a finger print or face scan instead of a password. You will need a compatible web cam or finger print scanner on your device/PC to do this. You'll be able to use this feature on Surface Laptops and Surface Pro Tablets, as well as certain laptops that include a finger print scanner or 'RealSense' webcam.

To find the Windows Hello settings, open the settings app. Select 'accounts' from the list on the left, then click 'sign-in options'.

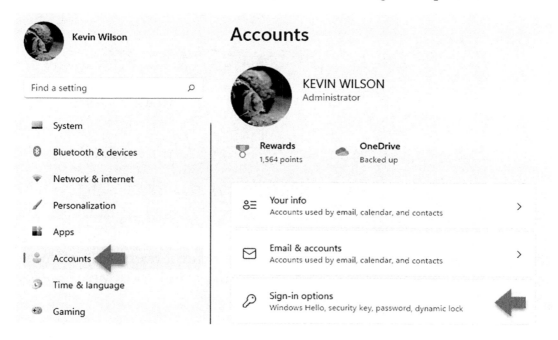

Fingerprint

To setup the finger print scanner, select 'fingerprint recognition' from the sign in options. Then select 'set up' under the fingerprint section of the 'sign in' options under 'fingerprint'.

Scan your finger using the fingerprint reader. Most people use their index finger

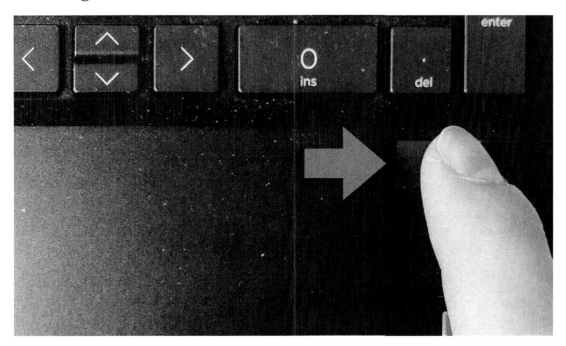

You may need to do this a few times. Keep going until Windows informs you the process is complete.

Select close on the bottom right.

You should now be able to sign in with your fingerprint from the lock screen. So instead of typing in a password, you can now just swipe my finger on the scanner to sign into my account.

Facial Recognition

To use this feature you will however need a webcam that supports this technology such as the Logitech Brio Ultra HD Pro Webcam shown below.

If you have a Microsoft device such as a surface studio, surface pro tablet or surface book laptop, the web cam is built in.

To set it up, select 'facial recognition'.

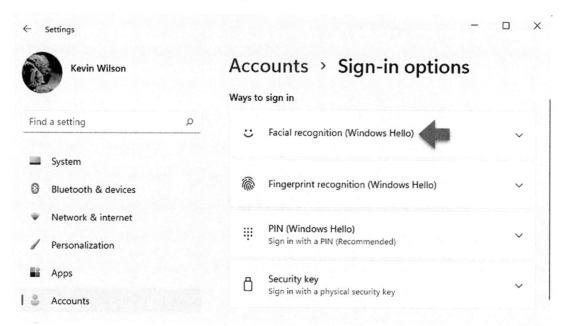

Under 'windows hello face' select 'set up'.

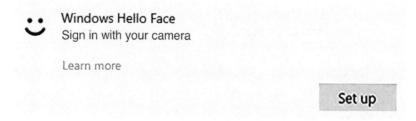

On your screen you'll see an image from your webcam. Make sure you can see your whole face and head in the image. Keep looking at the screen, until Windows has completed the scan. It will usually take a few seconds.

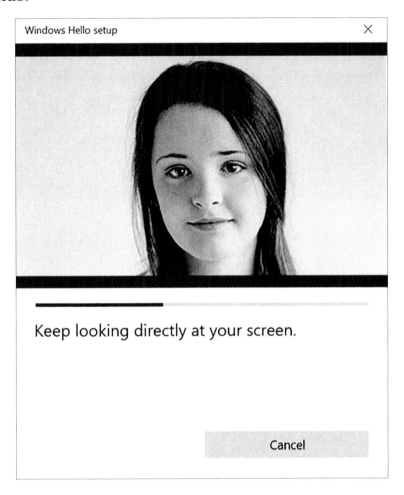

Make sure you turn on 'automatically unlock the screen if we recognise your face'.

Now when you turn on your computer, you won't need to sign in with a password, you just look at your screen and Windows will unlock your account for you.

PIN

A PIN is usually 4 - 8 numbers you can use to sign into windows instead of using a password.

From the 'sign in options', select 'PIN' from the sign in options.

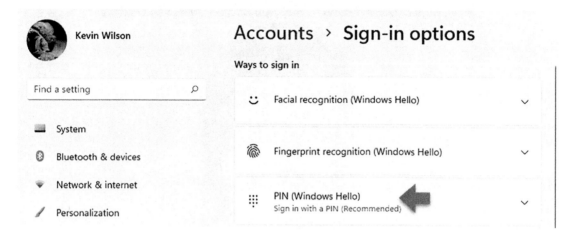

Tap 'add', then tap 'next'.

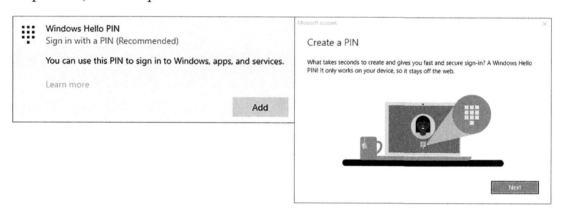

Enter your Microsoft account password if prompted. Enter your new PIN. Click 'ok'.

You can now sign in with a PIN instead of typing in your password.

Security Key

A security key is a physical device that you can use to sign into your PC instead of a password or PIN. A security key can be a USB device that you can keep on your keyring, or an NFC device like a smartphone or access card.

You can buy a key such as YubiKey or Thetis from Amazon or some other retailer.

To it set up, insert your security key into a USB port on your PC.

Select 'Security Key" from the sign in options.

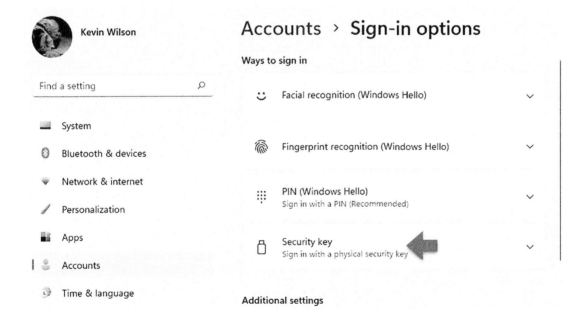

Click 'manage'.

Under 'security key PIN', click 'add'. Type in and confirm a security key PIN, then select OK.

The security key will be updated with the new PIN for use with your work or school account.

OneDrive

OneDrive comes with Windows 11 and is probably the safest place to store all your files as they are backed up in case your PC crashes.

The theory is, you work on the files on your local machine - you edit, update, create, save, and do the things you need to do. OneDrive automatically copies these updates onto your OneDrive Account in the Cloud. This is called synchronisation. This means you can access your files from any of your devices whether it is a tablet, phone, laptop, or on the web.

If you signed into Windows 11 with your Microsoft Account, then OneDrive is usually installed.

Setup

If OneDrive isn't already set up, click the OneDrive icon on the bottom right hand side of the screen.

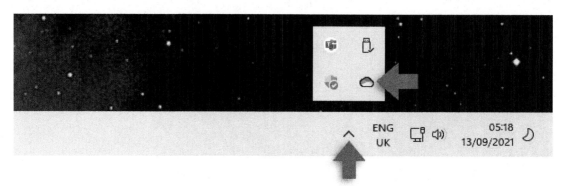

Enter your Microsoft Account email address and password then click 'sign in'.

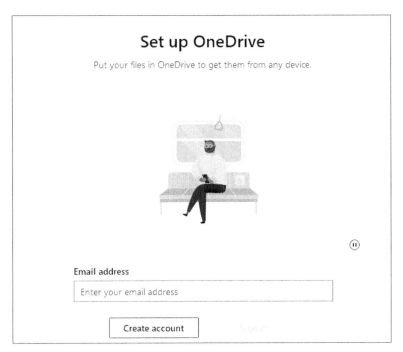

OneDrive will ask you where you want to store your OneDrive files on your computer while you work on them. Most of the time you can just leave it in it's default location.

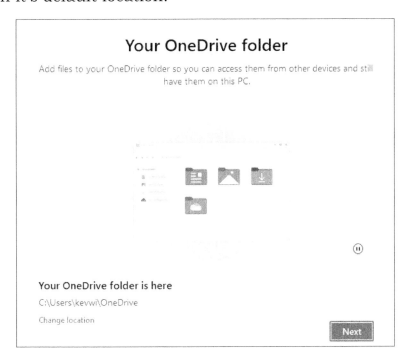

If you want to specify a different location click 'change location', then browse to the drive and folder you want OneDrive to use. .

Click 'next'

Chapter 3: Settings and Personalisation

Click 'not now' to use OneDrive free. You get 5GB of storage for free. If you need more space, click 'go premium' and select a payment plan.

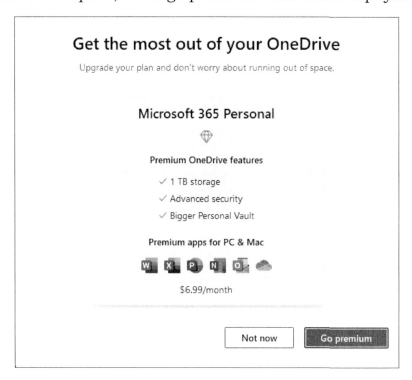

Run through the introduction... click 'next'.

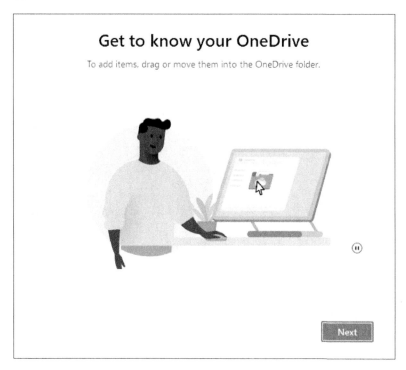

On the 'get mobile app' screen, click 'later'.

You can download this app on your other devices such as iPad, tablet, or phone using the app store.

106

You'll find your OneDrive files in File Explorer. To open File Explorer, click the icon on your taskbar.

You'll find your OneDrive listed in the left hand pane. This is where you should save all your files you work on, in your apps.

Changing Settings

To change OneDrive settings, click on the OneDrive icon on the bottom right of the screen. Click 'help & settings', then select 'settings'.

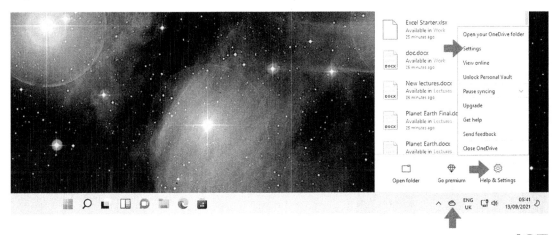

Chapter 3: Settings and Personalisation

You'll see a window appear. Along the top of the window, you'll see some tabs. Here you can change general settings.

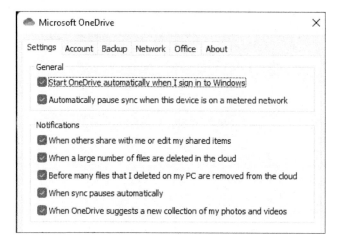

Account settings where you can add or remove a Microsoft account, unlink or remove your account, choose folders to include, and configure your personal file vault.

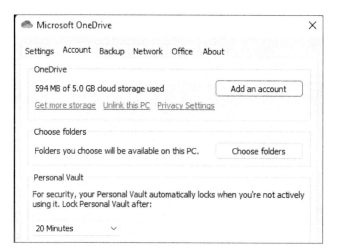

Backup settings where you can choose which folders to backup, and whether to backup photos/videos and screenshots.

Network settings where you can limit the bandwidth used to sync your files. Useful if you're using a slower connection.

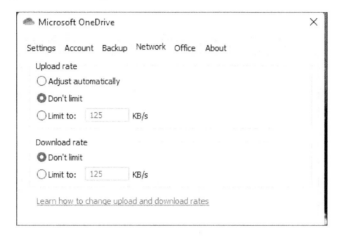

Files on Demand

Files On-Demand stores all your files on OneDrive Cloud and allows you to open them from Windows File Explorer.

Once you open your file, it is then downloaded to your device. This works with devices that have limited local storage such as tablets and smart phones, that do not have enough space to hold your entire OneDrive contents.

On the icons themselves or in the status column, you'll see some status indicators.

Lets take a look at what they mean.

Icon	Description
⊘	Files marked with this status icon are stored online and are downloaded to your device only if you open the file.
⊘	Files marked with this status icon will be download to your device, and will be available even when you are offline. Select "Always keep on this device".
☁	Files marked with this status icon indicate that the file is only available online.
☁ x	Files marked with this status icon indicate that the file has been shared with someone else.
⟳	Files marked with this status icon are currently being synchronised between your device and online.

Chapter 3: Settings and Personalisation

Enable and Disable Files On Demand

Open OneDrive settings, then select the 'settings' tab.

Under 'Files On-Demand', click the tick box next to 'Save space and download files as you use them' to enable the feature.

This will mark all your files as 'online', meaning they are stored on OneDrive Cloud not on your device. When you select a file to open, your file is downloaded to your device and then opened.

Making files available Offline

Having full access to all your files on OneDrive without having to download the whole contents to your device is great, but what happens if you don't always have an internet connection? Well, you can mark certain files as 'available offline', meaning OneDrive will download these files to your device.

To do this, select from your OneDrive the files you want to make available offline - hold down control and select your files, if you want more than one.

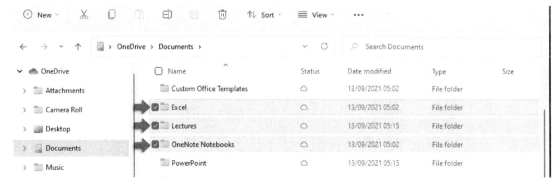

110

Right click on the selected files, and from the popup menu select 'always keep on this device'.

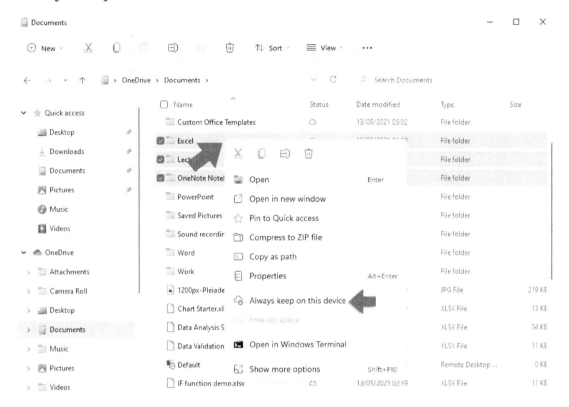

OneDrive will download the selected files to your device, so you can access them when you don't have a connection. If you change your files while offline, OneDrive will sync the changes once you re-connect to the internet.

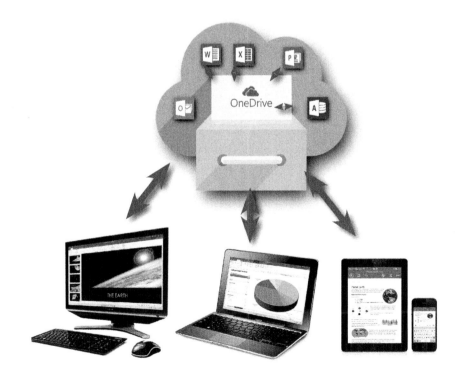

Linking your Phone

You can link to any Android Phone to your PC, where you can read and respond to text messages, see photos, sync contacts, and so on. This feature works best if you have a phone running Android 7 or later.

The first thing you'll need to do is open the 'your phone' app on your PC. Open the start menu, select 'all apps'. Scroll down to the bottom, then select 'your phone'.

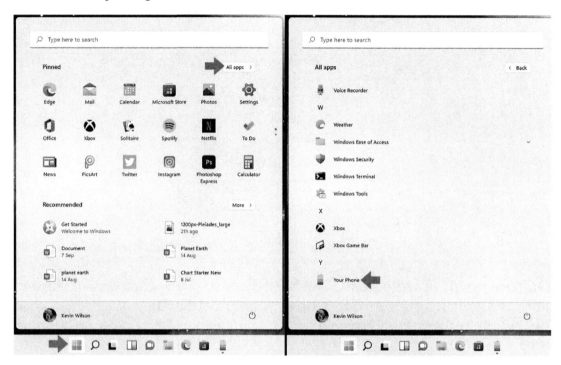

Click 'get started'.

Click 'pair with QR code'.

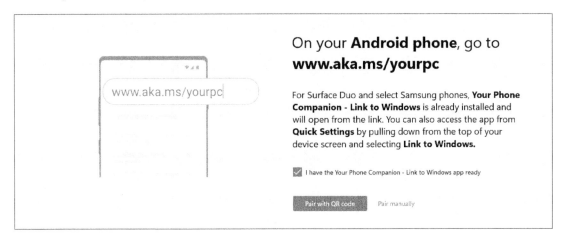

You'll see a QR code appear on your screen.

On your phone, open your web browser and navigate to the following website

```
www.aka.ms/yourpc
```

The phone companion app will appear in the Google Play Store. Tap 'install'. Once installed, tap 'open' to start the app.

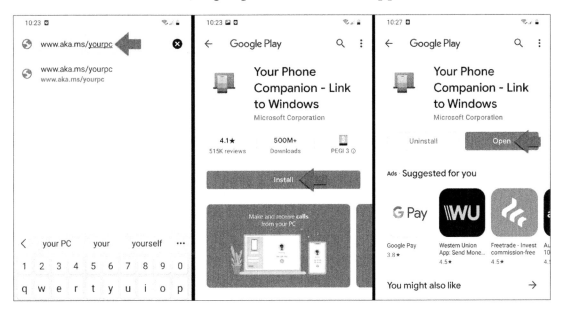

Chapter 3: Settings and Personalisation

Tap 'link your phone and pc'.

Scan the code on your PC's screen with your phone.

Tap 'continue', then tap 'allow' on any permission or access prompts.

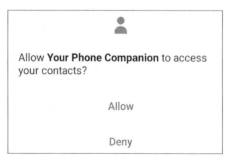

Tap 'done' to finish.

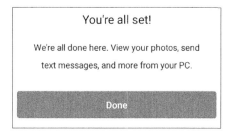

Now, on your PC, click 'continue';

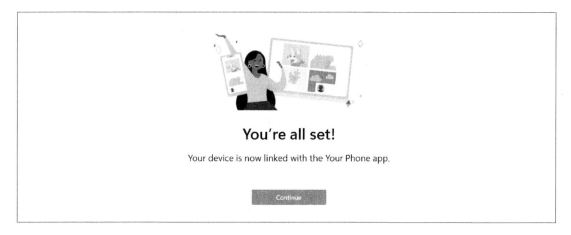

When the setup is complete, you'll land on the phone home page.

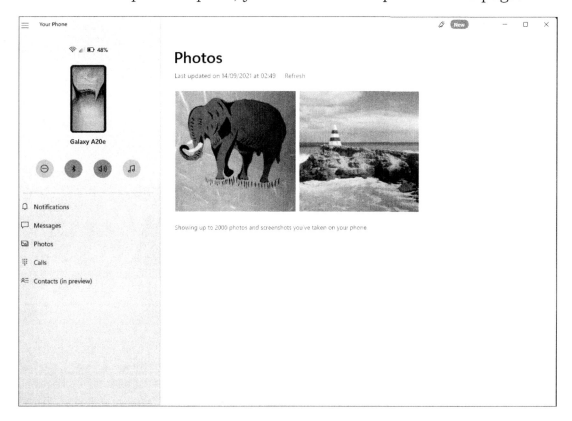

See page 339 for details on how to use the phone app.

Dynamic Lock

Dynamic lock allows you to automatically lock and unlock your PC using a paired bluetooth device - usually an Android phone. For this to work, you first need to pair your phone with your PC using bluetooth.

Pair your Phone

Before activating the dynamic lock, you will first need to pair your device or phone with your PC or laptop via Bluetooth. To do this open your settings app and select 'bluetooth & devices'. Then in the right hand side, click 'add device'.

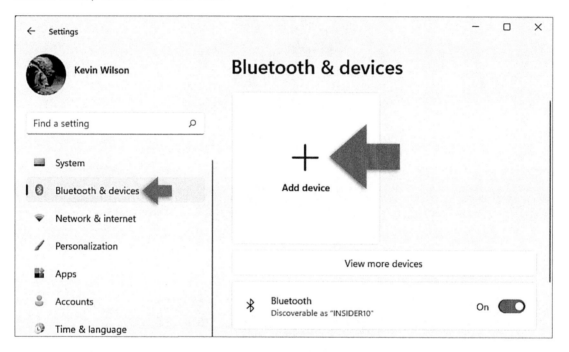

From the 'add a device' dialog box, select 'bluetooth'.

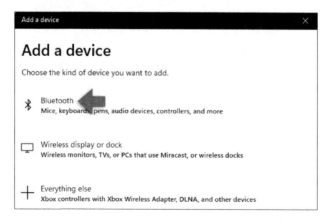

Windows will scan for your phone. Make sure your phone is turned on and unlocked. Open the bluetooth settings on your phone.

Give your PC a minute to detect your phone. Select the device from the list.

Windows will generate a code once your phone has been detected. Enter this code into your phone and tap 'pair'. .

If you're having a bit of trouble connecting, try rebooting both devices.

Enable Dynamic Lock

To enable dynamic lock, open the settings app, select 'accounts' from the list on the left, then click 'sign-in options'. Scroll down to 'dynamic lock'

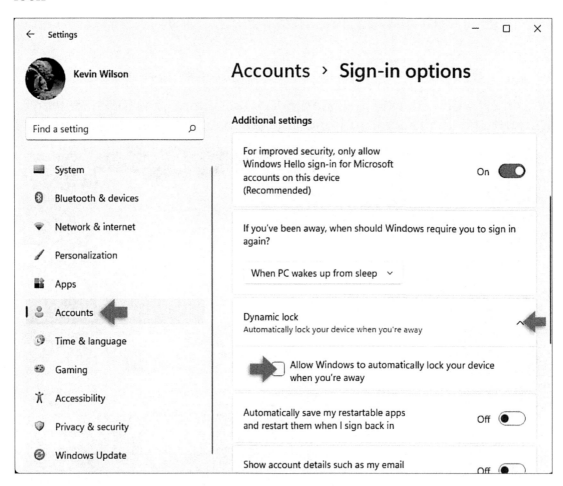

Tick the box next to 'Allow Windows to detect when you're away and automatically lock the device.'

When you move your phone away from your PC, it will automatically lock a minute or so after you're out of range.

118

Focus Assist

Focus Assist allows you to silence notifications during a period of time, so you can focus on your work without distraction.

Change Focus Assist Mode

You can change focus assist from action center. To do this, click on the action center icon on the bottom right of your screen.

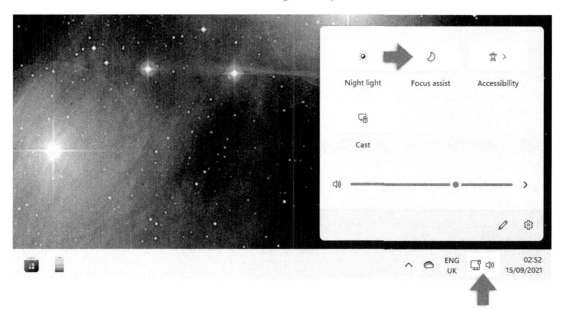

Click the 'focus assist' icon. When you click the icon, you can toggle between three different settings. Click once to set it to 'priority only', click again to show alarms only, click again to turn off completely.

Priority only mode, silences all notifications except those from the apps in your priority list, or messages from people in your priority list.

Alarms only mode, ie do not disturb mode, silences all notifications except for an alarm from the Alarms & Clock app.

Open Priority List

Open settings app and select 'system' from the left hand side. Then select 'focus assist'.

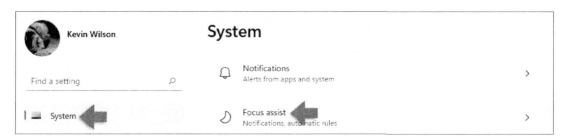

119

Chapter 3: Settings and Personalisation

Now, select 'customise your priority only', then click 'customise your priority list.

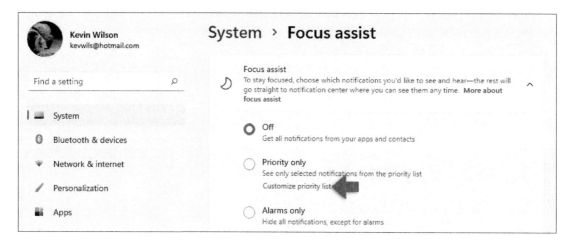

Add People to Priority List

Open your priority list, Scroll down to 'people', click 'add contacts'.

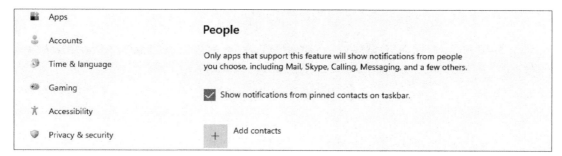

Select the contacts from the list, or search for them using the search bar at the top of the dialog box. You'll receive notifications when these people send you a message using email, skype, or messaging.

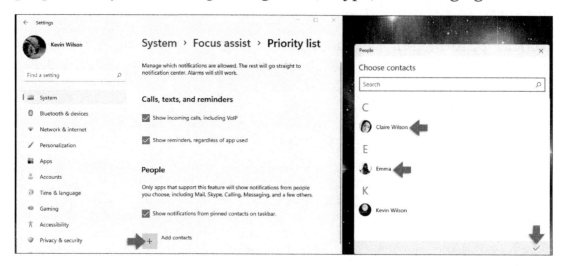

Click the back arrow on the top left of the window. Select 'priority only' to enable.

Add Apps to Priority List

Scroll down to 'apps', click 'add app'.

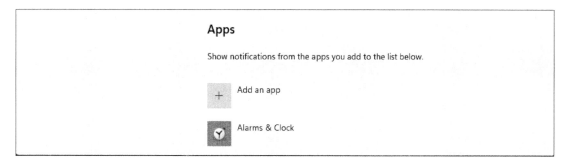

Then select the apps you want to receive notifications from.

Click the back arrow on the top left of the window. Select 'priority only' to enable.

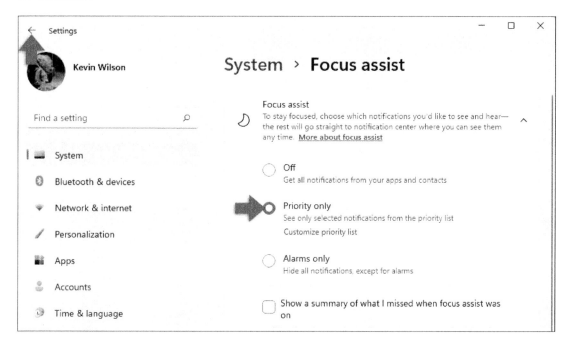

Configure Automatic Rules

Open settings app and select 'system' from the list on the left. Then select 'focus assist'.

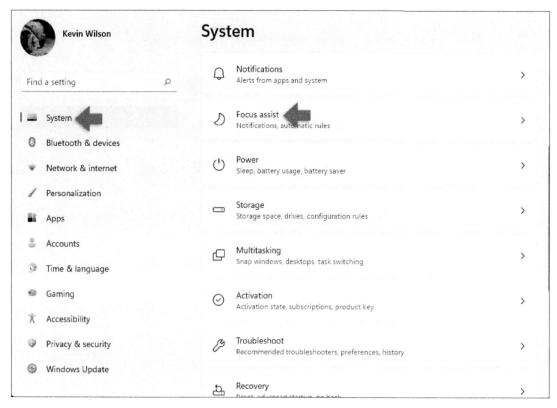

Scroll down to 'automatic rules'. Click the slider next to 'during these times' to turn it on, if it isn't already. Here, you can configure the hours you don't want to be disturbed. You can set a start time and an end time.

For example, you could set the start time to the beginning of your working hours, and the end time to the time you finish. Click the times, then select the time you want from the popup menu. Set 'repeats' to daily, this repeat setting every day.

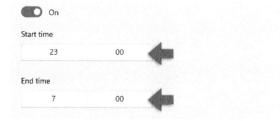

Set focus level to 'priority only' if you want to receive notifications from apps or people on your priority list. Select 'alarms only' if you don't want to be disturbed by any notifications during this time.

Click the back arrow on the top left of the screen to return to the focus assist settings.

Turn on 'when I'm duplicating my display', 'when I'm playing a game', and 'when I'm using an app in full screen mode' to stop notifications during these events.

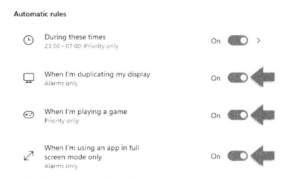

Click on each of them to set the priority level. For example, when duplicating a display, the priority is set to 'alarms only'. Click on the drop down box under 'focus level' to change the setting.

This means that when you are duplicating your display on another screen or projector - when giving a presentation or watching a movie, only important notifications will show up.

Notification Settings

Open the settings app, then select 'system' from the list on the left hand side. Click on 'notifications'.

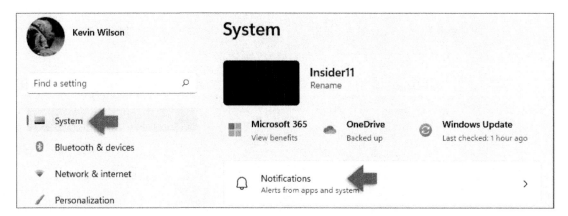

Here you can turn on/off notifications from apps.

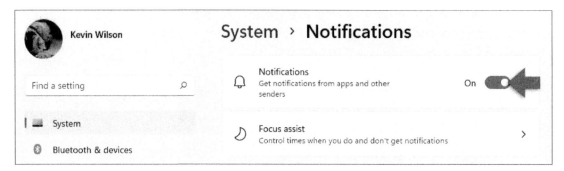

Scroll down to turn on/off individual apps. To do this, click the on/off switch.

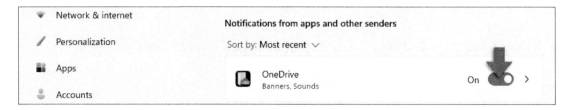

Click on the individual app to change the notification settings for that app. For example Mail.

Here, you can turn on/off notifications for this app.

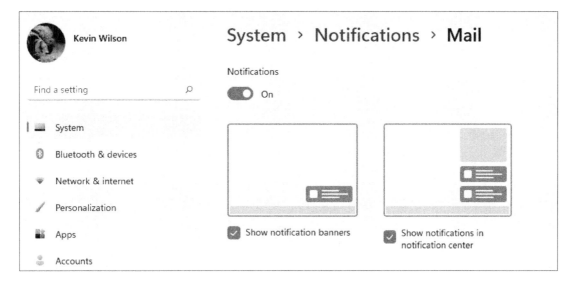

Underneath you can allow the app to show notifications on the bottom right of the desktop: "show notification banners".

Or on the notification center: "show notifications in notification center.

At the bottom, you can hide/show notifications from this app on the lock screen. Or play a sound when a notification arrives from this app. Just click on the switches to turn the features on or off.

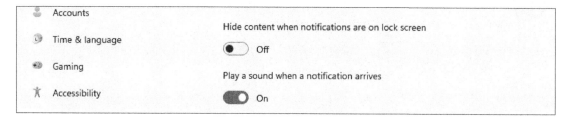

Underneath, you can set the priority for this app. Top priority will always show notifications from this app at the top of the notifications, so they always appear first in the list. Useful for important apps such as reminders, email, or message.

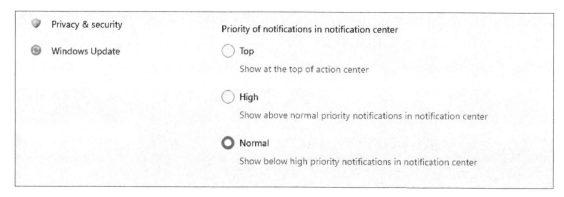

Apps set to 'normal' show at the bottom of the list in notification center. Apps set to 'high' show above any apps set to 'normal'.

Storage Sense

Over time, temporary files, caches and files in the recycle bin start to accumulate. Storage sense monitors and deletes these files, keeping your system running smoothly. To find storage sense, open the settings app and select system on the left hand side. Click on 'storage'.

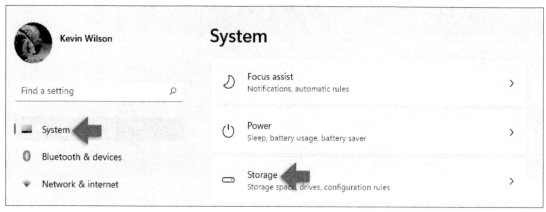

Scroll further down the page and you'll see your hard disk drive and various categories. This is a breakdown of how your storage is being used. You'll see space allocated to 'system & reserved' such as system files. You'll also see space allocated to 'apps & features', temp files and so on. For example, click 'temporary files'

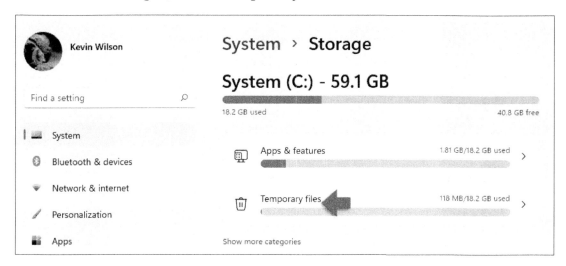

From here, you can clear out any temp files. Click 'remove files'.

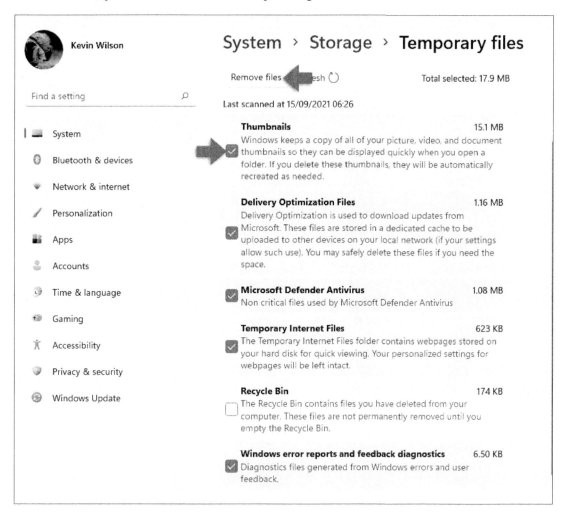

Configure Storage Sense

Open the settings app and select system.

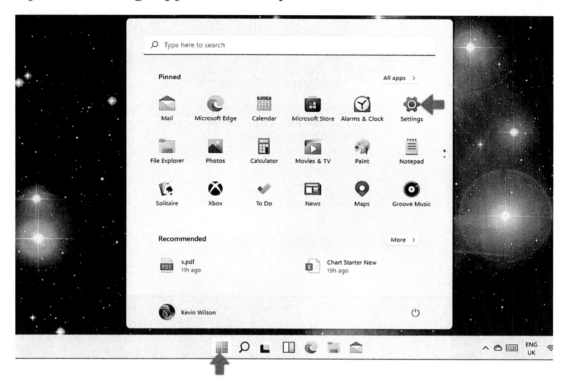

On the left hand panel select 'storage'. Click 'configure storage sense or run it now'.

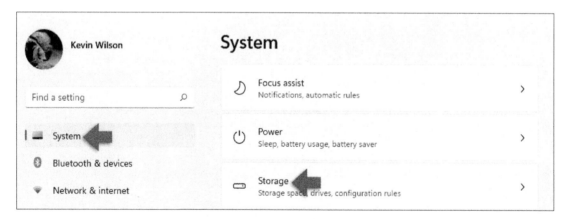

Click the switch to turn on 'storage sense', then click on 'storage sense'.

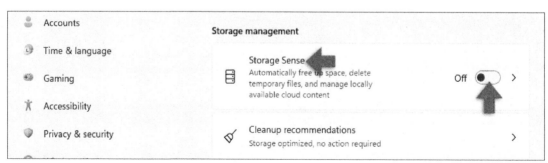

Under the 'temporary files' section, make sure there is a tick next to 'keep windows running smoothly'. This helps to automatically clean up system files

Under 'automatic user content cleanup', set 'run storage sense to 'once a month'. This will help to clear up temporary files.

Set 'delete files in my recycle bin' to '30 days'. This will ensure your recycle bin is cleared once a month. You can also set this to 'never' if you prefer not to clear the bin, or want to clear the bin yourself.

Set 'delete files in downloads folder' to 'never'. I don't usually allow Windows to delete files in my downloads folder, as sometimes I like to reuse or keep things I have downloaded from the web. However if you don't do this, then you can allow Windows to delete files in your downloads folder after a certain number of days - usually 30 days is a good setting.

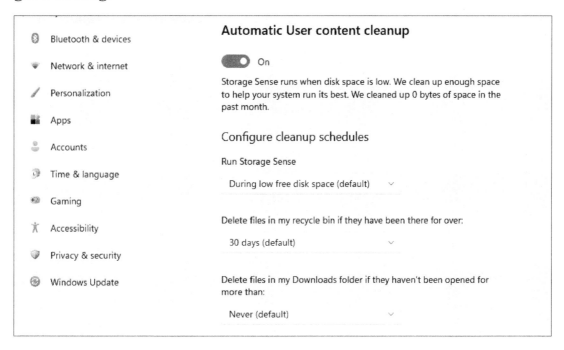

I have found this strategy works well for me. You can tweak the settings to find what works best for you.

Scroll down to the bottom of the page. Locally available cloud content is usually used when OneDrive's 'Files on Demand' feature is enabled. This allows storage sense to remove files from your device that have not been used in a while. These files are however still available on OneDrive - just not physically on your device. To be safe, set this feature to 'never'.

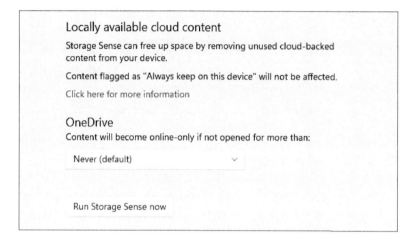

Once you're done, click 'run storage sense now'. Windows will automatically clear temporary files.

Cleanup Recommendations

Cleanup Recommendations is feature designed to automate the process of identifying unused files, uninstalling unused apps, and clearing temporary files in order to free up hard drive space on your PC.

To view these recommendations under the 'storage management' section.

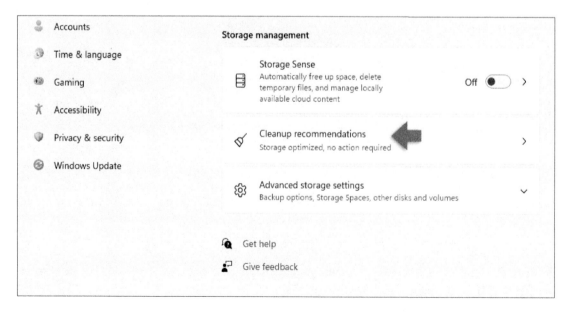

Here, you'll see a list of temporary files you can clean up. To see all the options click 'see advanced options'.

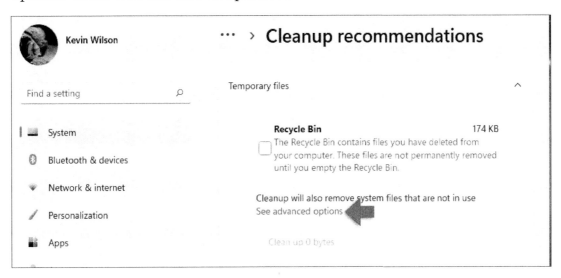

Select all the options, click 'remove files' to clear them.

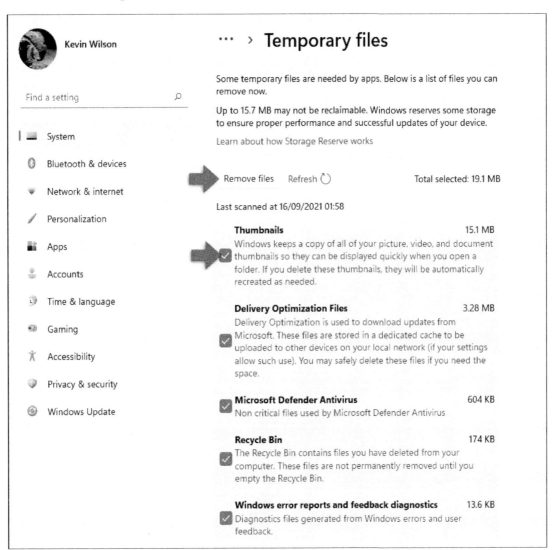

Chapter 3: Settings and Personalisation

Click the back arrow on the top left of the screen to return to cleanup recommendations.

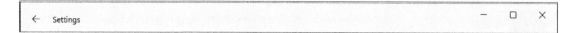

Further down the page, you'll see recommendations for removing large or unused files, synced files, and unused apps.

Click on 'large or unused files'. Look at the dates to see when you last used the file. Click the tickbox next to the filename. *Warning! This will delete these files, make sure you don't need them. If in doubt, leave the file un-ticked.* Click 'clean up' to remove selected files.

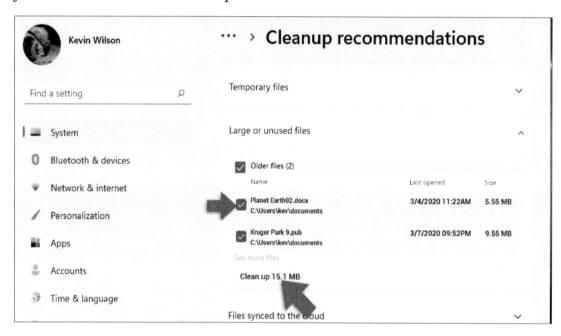

Click on 'unused apps'. Look at the date to see when you last used the app. Click the tickbox on the apps you don't use. Click 'clean up'.

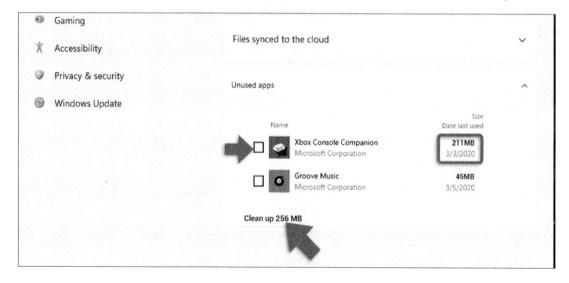

Search Settings

You can customise the search settings. To do this, click the search icon on the taskbar.

Click the three dots icon on the top right. Select 'search settings' from the drop down menu

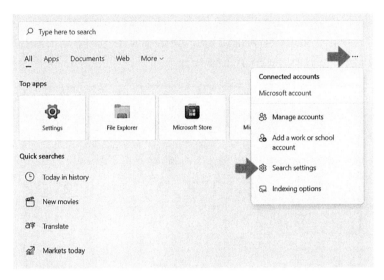

You'll land on the permissions and history settings page.

Under 'SafeSearch' you can filter out web search results. This means you can remove adult images and text from web sites that appear in windows search results. This is set to 'moderate' by default, and only filters out images, but you can also set it to 'strict' if you have children or don't want to see any adult content including text.

SafeSearch

In Windows Search, web previews will not automatically load web results if they may contain adult content. If you choose to preview web results, we'll apply the following setting:

○ Strict — Filter out adult text, images, and videos from my web results

◉ Moderate — Filter adult images and videos but not text from my web results

○ Off — Don't filter adult content from my web results

Cloud content search

Windows Search can personalize your search results by including your content from OneDrive, SharePoint, Outlook, Bing, and other services.

Microsoft account

Allow Windows Search to provide results from the apps and services that you are signed in to with your Microsoft account.

◯● On

Work or School account

Allow Windows Search to provide results from the apps and services that you are signed in to with your work or school account.

◯● On

If you have a Microsoft Account, or an account supplied by your company, school/college, then you can control whether windows search can search files on your OneDrive, email, photos, or messages linked to your accounts.

Further down the page, you'll see search history. You can turn this on or off using the switch. To clear the search history, click 'clear device search history'.

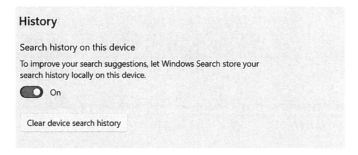

The search history allows windows search to save previous searches. You'll see these on the search screen.

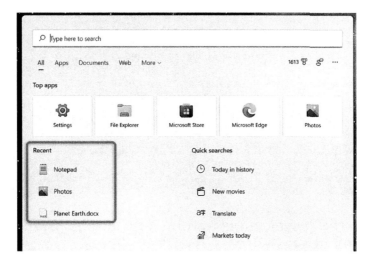

Search Indexing Options

You can change how Windows indexes files on your machine. You can add network locations, other drives, folders and so on. To adjust the indexing options, click the three dots icon on the top right of the search screen.

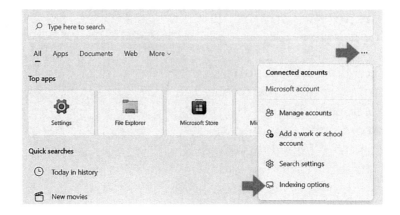

Under 'find my files' you'll see two modes. Classic mode is the default and will only index files in your own profile folders such as documents, desktop, as well as apps on your start menu. Enhanced mode turns on indexing for all files and apps on other drives and on other folders but doesn't search the content of the files.

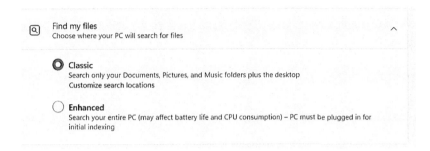

For most situations, classic mode is best. You can add locations to this search if you want to include other drives. To do this click 'customise search locations' under the 'classic' option.

Here, you'll see a list of folders windows search will index. Click 'modify' to add or remove folders.

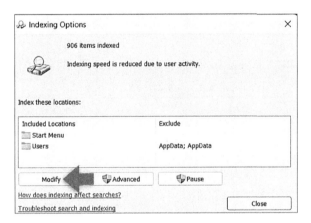

On the 'indexed locations' dialog box, select the folders to include. Click 'ok'.

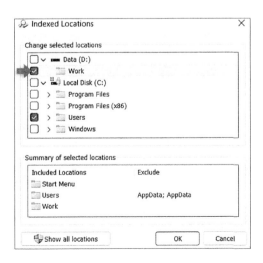

Fonts

You can download and install new fonts. This is useful if you are a designer or want a different font for a document you are working on.

You can download endless types of fonts from various websites on the internet. Many of these are free, but there are one or two you'd have to pay for. Here are a few useful sites offering fonts to download.

```
fonts.google.com
www.dafont.com
www.fontsquirrel.com
```

To install fonts you have downloaded, open File Explorer, then select your 'downloads' folder from the left hand side.

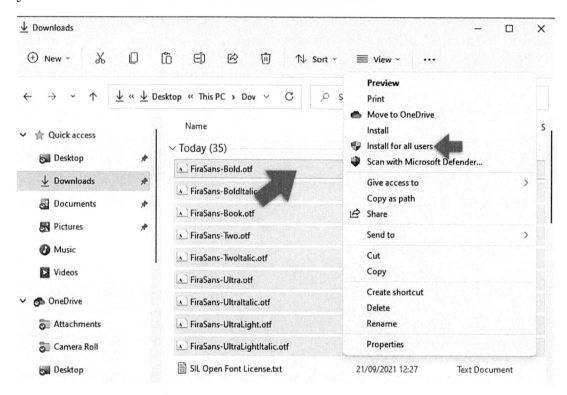

Select all the font files you have downloaded, right click on the selection, click 'show more options', then select 'install for all users'.

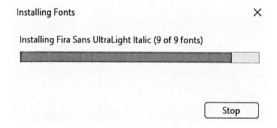

Allow the fonts to install.

136

You can see all your installed fonts using the settings app. Click the settings app icon on your start menu and select 'personalisation'. Select 'fonts' from the list.

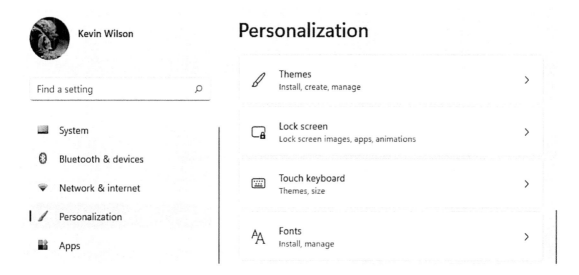

Here, you can drag and drop font files to install them, or you can download some from the Microsoft store. Just click 'Microsoft store'

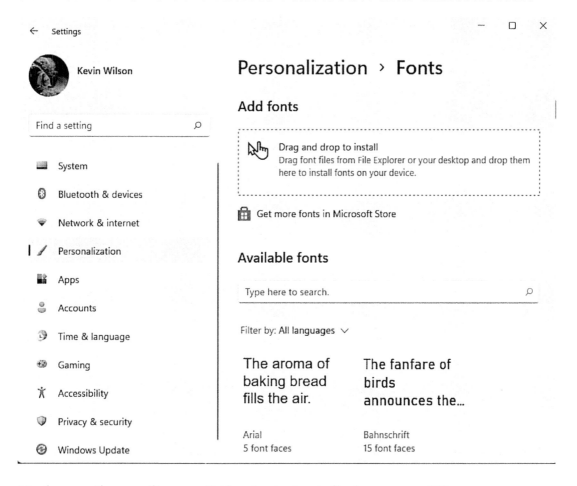

Underneath, you'll see all the fonts installed on your PC.

Windows Subsystem for Linux

Windows Subsystem for Linux (WSL) allows you to run native Linux command-line tools natively on Windows, alongside your Windows apps and is primarily aimed at developers.

Enable WSL

To enable this feature, click the search icon on the taskbar then type 'turn windows features on or off'. Click 'turn windows features on or off'

Scroll down the list, select 'windows subsystem for linux.

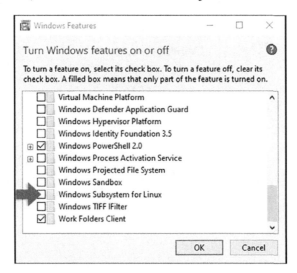

Click ok. Restart your machine when prompted.

Installing a Linux Distribution

Now that you have the system enabled, you need to install a linux distribution. To do this, open up your Microsoft Store and search for linux. Eg 'ubuntu linux'.

Click the distribution in the search results

Click 'install', on the info page.

Now, find the distribution on your start menu, and run the app. It will take a few minutes to install. Run through the setup wizard, enter a username and a password. This will be used to log into linux.

```
user@insider: ~                                                          —  □  ×
Installing, this may take a few minutes...
Please create a default UNIX user account. The username does not need to match your Windows username.
For more information visit: https://aka.ms/wslusers
Enter new UNIX username: user
New password:
Retype new password:
passwd: password updated successfully
Installation successful!
To run a command as administrator (user "root"), use "sudo <command>".
See "man sudo_root" for details.

Welcome to Ubuntu 20.04 LTS (GNU/Linux 4.4.0-19628-Microsoft x86_64)

 * Documentation:  https://help.ubuntu.com
 * Management:     https://landscape.canonical.com
 * Support:        https://ubuntu.com/advantage

0 updates can be installed immediately.
0 of these updates are security updates.


This message is shown once once a day. To disable it please create the
/home/user/.hushlogin file.
user@insider:~$
```

Family Safety

You can create child accounts for your children either on your devices or their own devices. These are special, restricted accounts you can monitor and tailor to your child. It is not a good idea to allow a young child to use your account. Child accounts are used for children under 13.

Child Accounts

On your child's computer or tablet, sign in as an administrator (your own account). Open the Settings App and click 'accounts'. Select 'family & other users'.

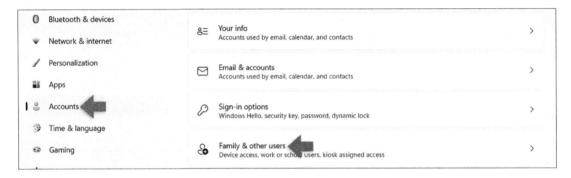

Under 'add a family member', click 'add account'.

Click 'create one for a child'.

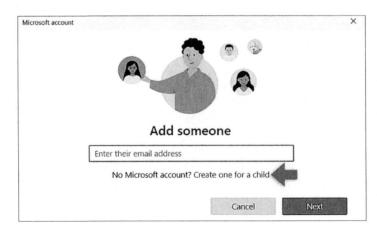

Enter an email address for them, click 'next'. Then enter a password, click 'next'.

Enter the child's name, click 'next'.

Enter your country and the child's date of birth

Click 'next'.

Chapter 3: Settings and Personalisation

Sign in with the account you just created. If the child is under 13, you'll need to give parental consent. To do this, click 'I'm a parent or guardian', then click 'continue'.

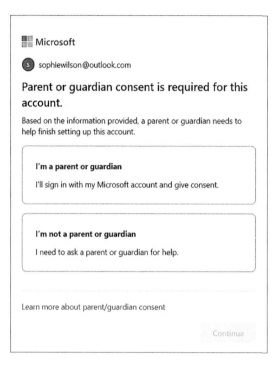

Sign in with your Microsoft Account email address and password.

On the 'give consent' screen. Scroll to the bottom, click 'I agree'.

142

Do you want to allow your child to access all games and apps, or only those published by Microsoft?. Tick the box to allow all apps, click 'continue'.

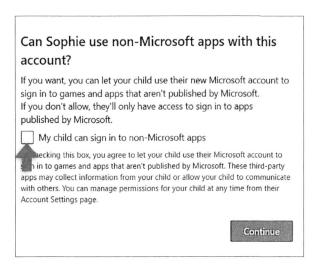

Adjust the safety settings if you need to. You can age limit apps - just click the drop down box and select an age.

You can monitor their activity, filter their web search results, or use 'ask to buy' which alerts you when your child attempts to make a purchase.

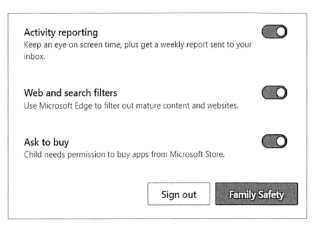

Leave them all on, then click 'sign out' to sign out of your account.

Now you can sign out of your account. On the lock screen allow your child to sign in using the account you just created. Select the child's account from the bottom left, click 'sign in'. Follow the on-screen prompts to finalise the account.

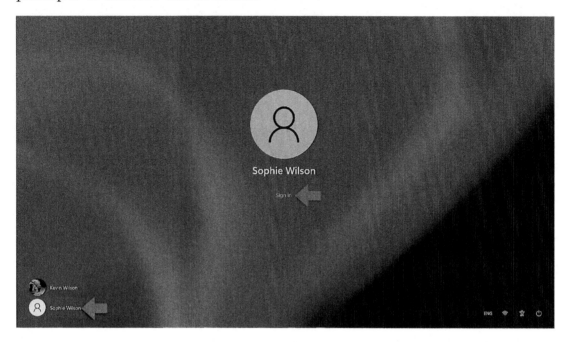

Monitoring Activity

You can log on to your family safety website by opening your web browser and navigating to the following address. Click 'sign in' and enter your Microsoft Account email address and password.

```
account.microsoft.com/family
```

On the main family screen you'll see a list of child accounts.

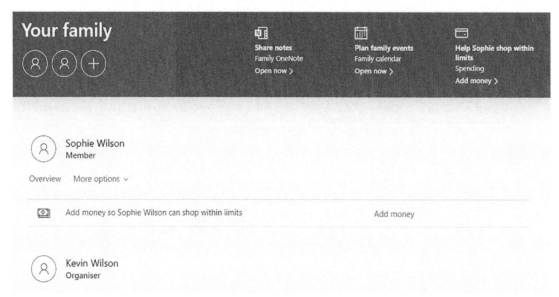

Under their name, click 'overview'.

You'll see the overview page. Down the left hand side, you'll see a menu. Screen Time, allows you to set limits and curfews to control how long your child uses the computer and times they are allowed access.

Content filters allow you to block types of apps, and restrict content according to age. You can also monitor your child's spending, as well as add some money for your child to spend in the Microsoft Store. Find your child allows you to track your child's physical location.

Screen Time

You can set curfews and limits to the amount of time your children can use their devices. To do this select 'screen time' from the menu on the top left.

Select 'devices' from the top left.

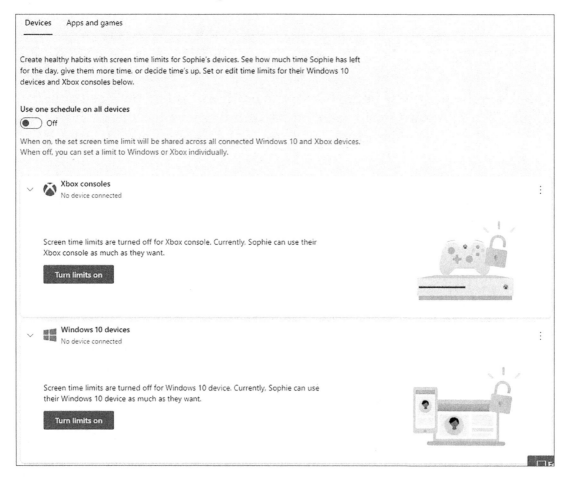

Under 'windows 10 devices' click 'turn on limits'.

Click the days you want to allow your child to use the computer.

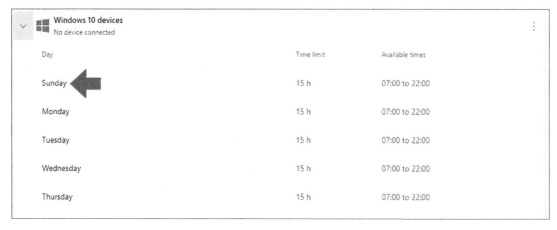

Change the day at the top to 'every day'. Drag the slider to select the amount of time. Then set the time window you want to allow your child to use the computer. *The example below shows the child can use the computer for two hours each day, between 4pm and 8pm.* Click 'finish.

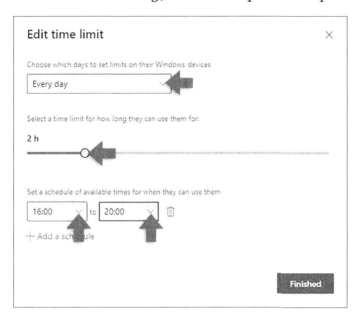

Click on a day to edit the times etc.

To remove the restriction, click the three dots icon on the top right, select 'turn limits off'.

Content Filters

You can view your child's web activity and what apps they've been using. You can also filter out websites, or block certain apps.

To see this, select 'content filters' from the menu on the top left of the screen.

Chapter 3: Settings and Personalisation

Web Activity

Select 'web and search' from the two options along the top. Here, you'll see web activity.

Select the date on the top right, then scroll down to the 'activity' section where you'll see a list of websites and web searches. Click the small side arrow to the left of the site to view all pages visited. If you want to block the site click 'block'.

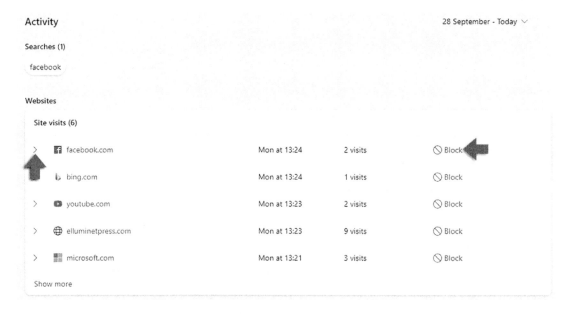

Scroll down to 'filter settings'. Block mature content using the 'filter inappropriate websites' switch.

At the bottom you can allow only certain websites and block all others. To use this, turn on 'only use allowed websites'.

Only use allowed websites

⚫◯ Off

Sophie will only be able to visit websites that you've allowed. Anything else, and they'll need your permission first.

148

Under 'allowed websites', click 'add a website', then type the URL, eg facebook.com

If you want to block a particular website, under 'blocked websites', type in the URL, eg youtube.com

Spending

You can add money or a credit card for your child to use in the microsoft store. To see this, select 'spending' from the menu on the top left of the screen.

Select 'add money' in the 'microsoft account balance' section.

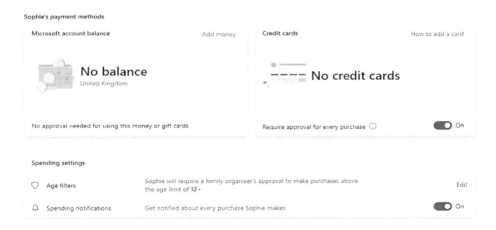

Follow the instructions on the screen to add the funds.

Find your Child

You can track your child's physical location. To use this feature, you'll need to install the family safety app on the device the child uses. Currently this only works with iPhones/iPad or Android phones and tablets.

On your Phone/tablet, open the app store, search for Microsoft Family Safety, then download and install the app. Once installed, open the app, then sign in with your Microsoft Account.

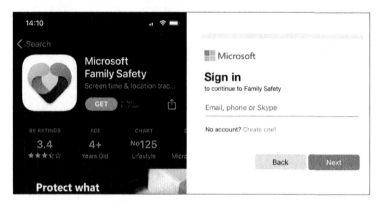

On your child's phone/tablet, open the app store then search for Microsoft Family Safety. Download and install the app.

Once the app is installed, open it, then sign in with your child's Microsoft Account.

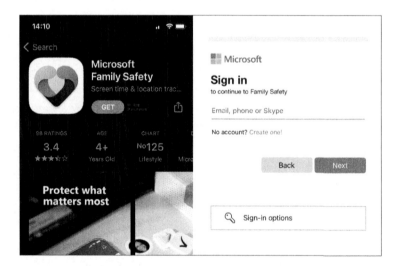

Click the profile icon on the top left to open the settings.

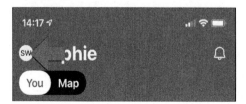

Select settings, then turn on 'share your location'.

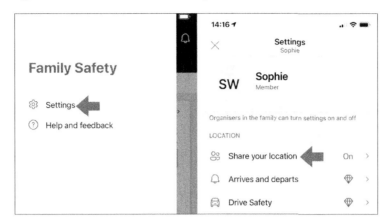

Now on your Phone, you'll be able to track your child's device. Tap 'map' on the top left. You'll see the members of your family appear on the map.

Basic Navigation

With a PC and a laptop, you'll be using a keyboard and mouse or touchpad for navigating around Windows.

There are various different types of mice and keyboards available on the market.

Pens are also available for hybrid devices with touch screens such as the surface book and tablet.

In this chapter we'll take a look at

- Using the Mouse
- Left click, right click & scrolling with your mouse
- Using the Touch Pad
- Left click, right click & scroll with a touch pad
- Keyboards
- Keyboard Function Keys
- Keyboard Modifier Keys
- Pens

To help you better understand this section, take a look at the video resources. Open your web browser and navigate to the following site:

elluminetpress.com/win-11-nav

Mouse

Computer mice come in various different shapes, however most of them have two click buttons and a scroll wheel. Some have other buttons you can assign various functions to. You'll want to find a mouse that fits comfortably in your hand allowing you to use both buttons and the scroll wheel without straining your wrist. Mice can be wired or wireless. Wireless mice are nice to use as they don't have a wire hanging out the side which can get in the way. These mice either need batteries or recharged.

Using the Mouse

When using your mouse, make sure it fits securely into the palm of your hand. This will allow you to use both mouse buttons comfortably and reduce wrist strain. When you move the mouse, try keep wrist movement to a minimum.

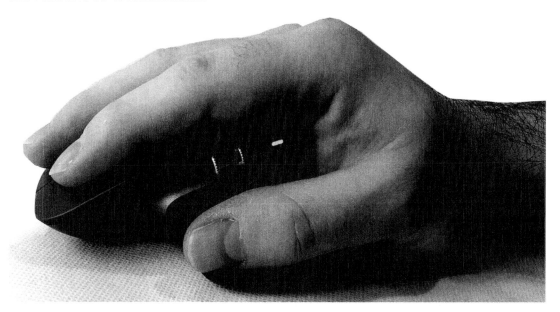

Move the mouse along your desk, while keeping an eye on the mouse pointer on the screen.

Left Click

The most common function of your mouse is the left click. This is used to select something on the screen. You can select an icon, file, button, or text field.

Move your mouse pointer to the object on the screen, then click once with the left mouse button.

Double Click

To start an app, application, or open a file, you need to double click. This means clicking the left mouse button twice in quick succession.

Right Click

The right mouse button opens a context menu on an object such as a file or app. This provides in context functionality for that file or app.

Here, in the screen on the right, you'll see I've right clicked on a file in File Explorer. This brings up the context menu with additional functions you can perform on that file.

Scroll Wheel

The scroll wheel allows you to scroll up and down pages in a document, a window such as File Explorer, or a web page in Chrome or Edge. Move your mouse pointer over the page you want to scroll, use your index finger to move the wheel up or down.

Touch Pad

The touchpad is usually found on laptop devices and allows you to control the mouse pointer using your finger. Slide your finger left, right, up, or down on the touchpad to move the mouse pointer on screen.

Left Click on Something

Use one finger to tap on the touch pad. Tap on the touch pad to select something, double tap to open an app or file.

Right Click on Something

To right click on something - to open a popup menu, move the mouse pointer to an icon, then tap with two fingers.

Scroll

Use two fingers up and down the touch pad to scroll up and down web pages, documents or emails.

Keyboards

Computer keyboards come with the standard QWERTY layout. There are other layouts for other regions and languages but we'll concentrate on the QWERTY design. Here is a common example

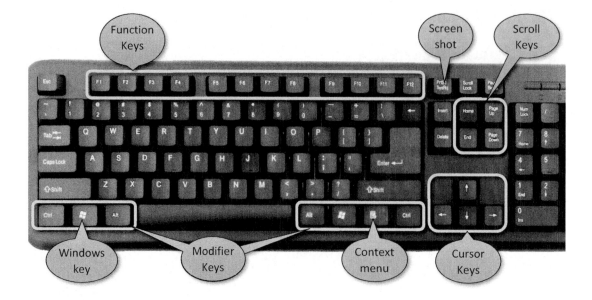

Function Keys

Along the top of the keyboard you'll see some function keys. These are usually assigned a standard function within windows.

Lets take a look at what each key does.

Key	Function
F1	Used to access the help screen
F2	Renames a selected icon, folder or file
F3	Often opens a search
F4	Open the address bar in file explorer
F5	Refresh document, page or window
F6	Jumps to address bar in browser
F7	Spell/grammar check in Word
F8	
F9	Refreshes a document in Word or sends and receives emails in Outlook
F10	Activates the menu bar of an open application.
F11	Full screen mode
F12	Save as in most windows programs. Also opens developer tools in web browser

Modifier Keys

Modifier keys are used when executing a keyboard short cut, such as CTRL C to copy text. CTRL, or control is the modifier key. Here are some useful keyboard shortcuts.

Windows + Tab	Opens thumbnail list of open applications
Windows + A	Open Windows 10 notification centre
Windows + D	Show Windows desktop
Windows + E	Open Windows Explorer
Windows + K	Connect to wireless displays and audio devices
Windows + P	Project a screen
Windows + R	Run a command
Windows + X	Open Start button context menu
Windows key + Arrow key	Snap app windows left, right, corners, maximize, or minimize
Windows key + Comma	Temporarily peek at the desktop
Windows Key	Show windows start menu
Alt + Tab	Switch to previous window
Alt + Space	Reveals drop down menu on current window: Restore, move, size, minimize, maximize or close.
Alt + F4	Close current app
Ctrl + Shift + Esc	Open Task Manager
Ctrl + Z	Undo Command
Ctrl + X	Cut selected text
Ctrl + C	Copy selected text
Ctrl + V	Paste selected text at cursor position
Ctrl + P	Print

Chapter 4: Basic Navigation

Modifier keys live at the bottom of the keyboard next to the space bar.

Some keyboard will have special keys on the right hand side such as insert or home, page up and page down. 'Home' moves the cursor to the beginning of the line, 'end' moves it to the end. You can use these when typing a document as they help when moving around the page.

Below that, you'll see some cursor keys. These are useful when moving up and down a page, or moving your cursor around a word document.

On the far right you'll see a numeric pad. These keys are useful if you work with numbers as the keypad makes it easier and faster to enter numbers.

Pens

You can buy pens and styluses to use with your tablet or laptop with a touchscreen. These come in useful for Windows Ink & OneNote, as well as any art apps out there that you can find in the Microsoft Store.

You can pick these up quite cheaply in any electronics store.

You can use the pen to draw on your screen, or select apps and icons on the taskbar, start menu, or within an app.

See page 387 for information on using pens and touchscreens.

5

Getting around Windows 11

In this chapter we will take a look at the different parts of Windows 11, as well as

- The Desktop
- Start Menu
- Task Bar
- Widgets Panel
- Windows Search
- Virtual Desktops
- Quick Settings (Action Center)
- Notifications
- Windows Ink
- Arranging Windows on the Desktop
- Multiple Screens
- Cloud Clipboard
- Character Map & Symbols
- Taking Screenshots
- Task Manager
- File Explorer
- Managing your Files
- External Drives

To help you better understand this section, take a look at the video resources. Open your web browser and navigate to the following site:

elluminetpress.com/using-win-11

Lets begin by looking at the desktop.

The Desktop

The desktop is the basic working area on your PC. It's the equivalent of your workbench or office desk, hence why it is called a desktop.

Desktop Anatomy

On the desktop itself you can save files such as documents or photos - these will appear as file icons. On some devices you may see other icons such as the trash can for deleted files or network connections.

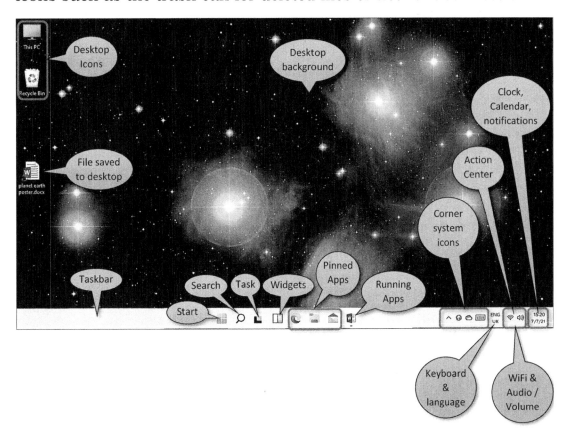

If you've come from using Windows 10, you'll notice some differences. First, the start button and the other icons on the taskbar are now centred.

Action center, now known as quick settings has been stripped down and only includes volume controls, Wi-Fi, bluetooth, airplane mode, and focus assist, as well as battery life and screen brightness if you're using a laptop.

Windows search has been reduced to an icon on the taskbar.

There is a new widgets panel, virtual desktops, and notifications sidebar.

Start Menu

The start menu is the central launch point for apps, changing settings, as well as system shut down, reset, hibernate, and sleep.

Have a look at the video resources. Open your web browser and navigate to the following site:

`elluminetpress.com/win-11-start`

Opening

To open the start menu, click the start button on the bottom of the screen.

Lets take a closer look at the different parts of the menu.

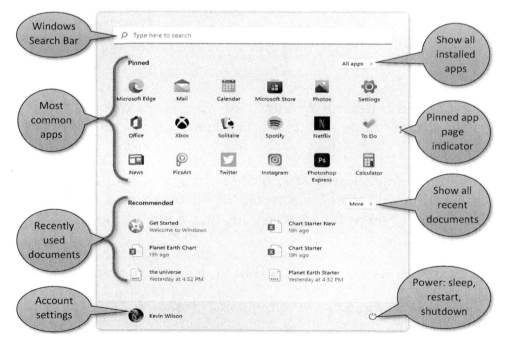

Pinning Apps

In the top section of your start menu, you'll see your pinned apps. This is usually your most used apps. To pin an app, click on the 'all apps' icon on the top right.

Right click on the app you want to pin - eg 'groove music'. Select 'pin to start'.

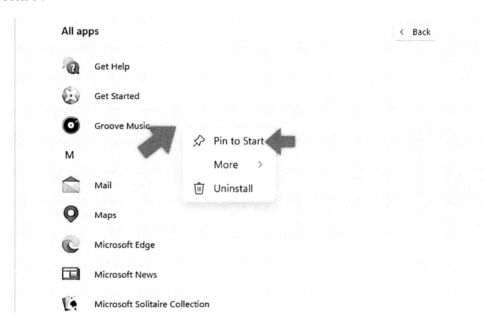

You'll see the app appear in the 'pinned apps' section.

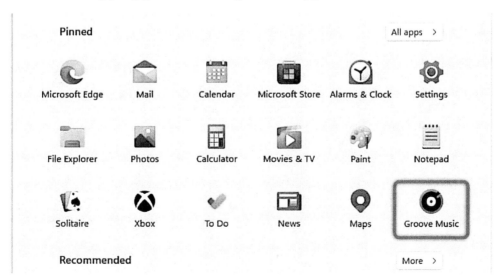

App Pages

If you have a lot of apps pinned to your start menu, Windows 11 will split your apps into pages. If you have multiple pages of apps, you'll see a page marker on the right hand side of the start menu.

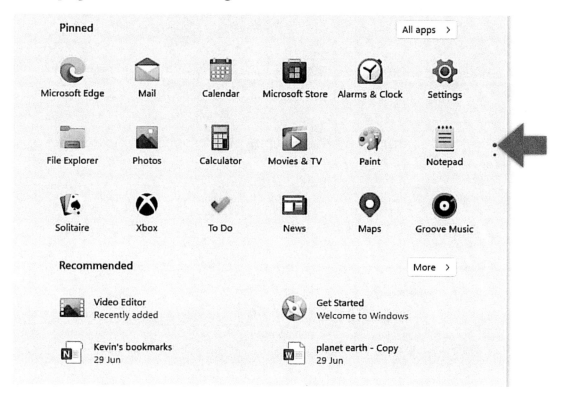

Click on the small dot, or use the scroll wheel on your mouse to move between pages.

Moving Pinned Apps

You can rearrange the apps on your start menu. To do this, click and drag the icon to it's new position.

The other icons will move out the way so you can drop the app icon where you want it.

Remove App

Right click on the app you want to remove, select 'unpin from start'.

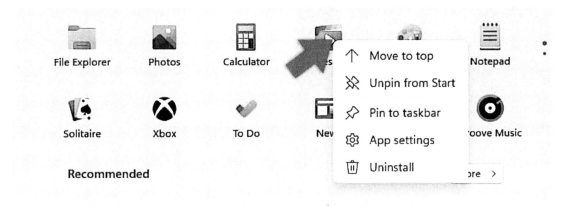

Search Bar

At the top of the start menu, you'll see a shortcut to Windows search.

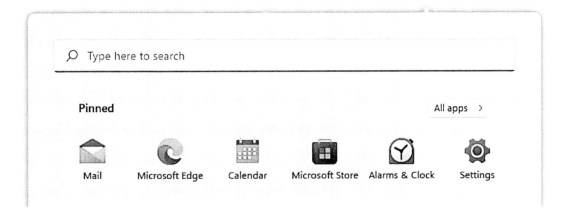

See windows search on page 172.

Hidden Start Menu

To open the secondary start menu, right click on the start button on your taskbar.

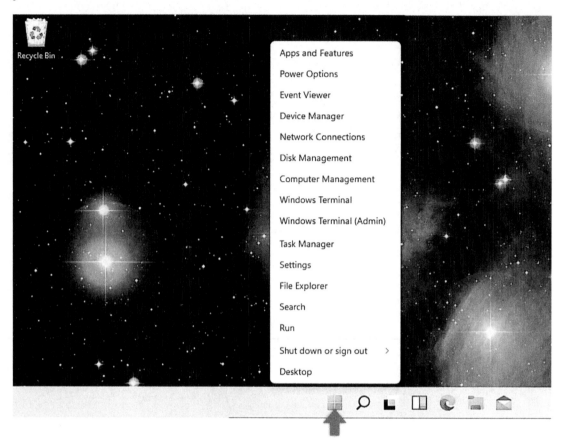

Here, you can quick access:

- 'Apps and features' and 'power options' in the settings app.
- You can open 'Event viewer' which allows you to view various event logs and is useful for troubleshooting.
- You can use Device manager to view all the hardware devices on your computer
- Network connections takes you to the network settings in the settings app.
- Disk management is useful for partitioning and formatting disk drives.
- Computer management takes you to the computer management console with task scheduler, shared folders, local users, device & disk manager, and services.
- Terminal opens up powershell command line terminal. You can also access Task manager, Settings App, File Explorer, Search, and Run.

Task Bar

The taskbar runs along the bottom of your screen and houses various icons to help you navigate around the system.

Anatomy

In the middle of the taskbar, you'll see your main icons. On the left, is the start button that is used to open the start menu.

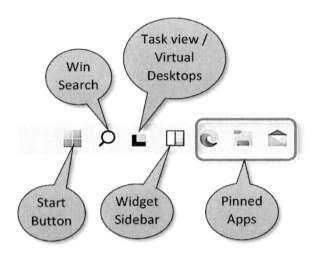

The search icon is used to search for apps and files. The virtual desktops and taskview icon shows currently running apps and virtual desktops. Last is the widgets icon. Next to these, you'll see pinned and currently running apps. As you open apps, the icons appear along the taskbar with a line underneath indicating that the app is running.

The taskbar also serves as a shortcut bar so you can pin apps you use most often and switch to other apps running in the background.

Over on the right hand side you'll see your system clock, click on this to open up the notifications and calendar sidebar.

Next to that, you'll see the action center icon (quick settings), click on this to open Wi-Fi/Network settings, focus assist, nearby sharing, bluetooth, volume control, and settings.

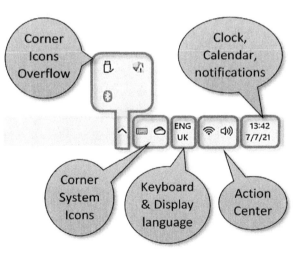

The next icon will allow you to change the keyboard settings or select a keyboard layout if available.

The other icons are called corner system icons, and these are usually system apps such as OneDrive, Windows Security, Touch Keyboard, Pen, etc. The small up arrow to the left of these is called the corner icons overflow area. These are icons that don't appear in the corner system icons.

Jump Lists

Apps that appear on the taskbar have a recent files list called a jump list. To open a jump list, right click on the app's icon on the taskbar.

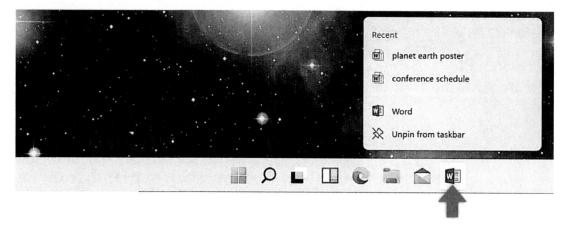

Here, you'll be able to re-open any of your recently accessed files for that particular app. As well as pin the icon to the taskbar so it doesn't disappear when the app is closed.

Pin Icons to your Task Bar

For more convenience, you can pin all your favourite apps to your task bar along the bottom of your screen. To do this, open the start menu, then right click on an app. If your app isn't there, click 'all apps' on the top right of the menu. From the menu that appears, select 'pin to taskbar' (select 'more' if it isn't there).

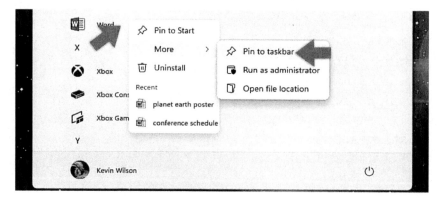

You'll see the icon has been added to your taskbar.

If you want to remove the icon, right click on the icon, select 'unpin from taskbar'.

168

Widgets Panel

The widgets panel opens up on the left hand side of your screen and contains small applets called widgets for web search, weather, stock, news, photos and so on.

Opening

To open the widgets panel, click on the widgets icon on the taskbar, or press **Win W** on your keyboard. You can also swipe inwards from the left hand side, if you're using a touch screen device.

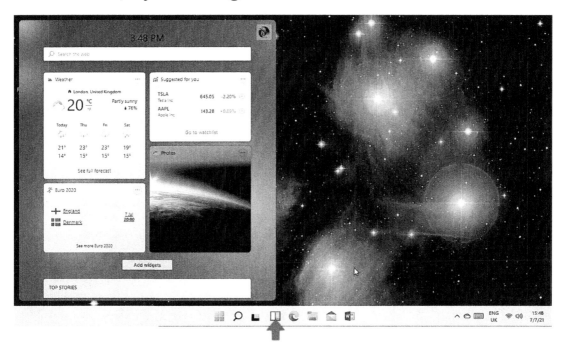

Add Widget

To add a widget, open the widget panel, then click 'add widgets'.

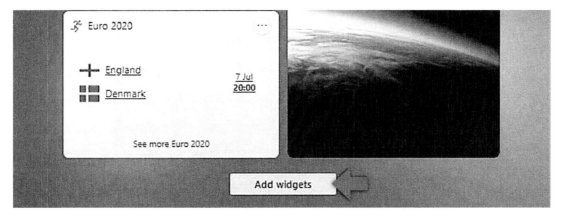

Select a widget from the options. Click on the plus sign to add a widget.

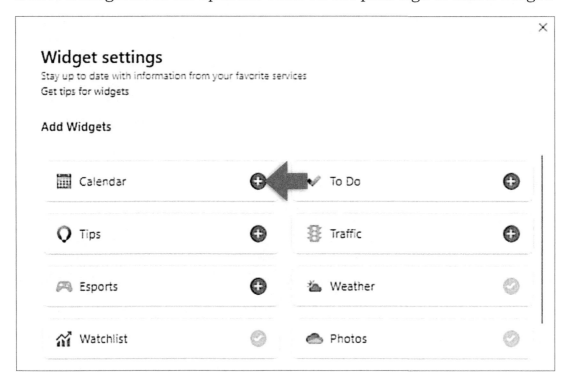

Click the 'x' on the top right to close the 'widget settings' dialog box.

Customise Widget

Open the widgets side panel, click on the three dots icon next to the widget you want to customise. Here, you can change the size - select small, medium, or large. To customise the settings, click 'customise widget'.

Here, you can customise the widget. The actual settings will depend on the widget you're customising, but in this case, the weather app, I can search for my location.

Remove Widget

To remove a widget, open the widget side panel, click on the three dots icon on the top right of a widget. Select 'remove widget'.

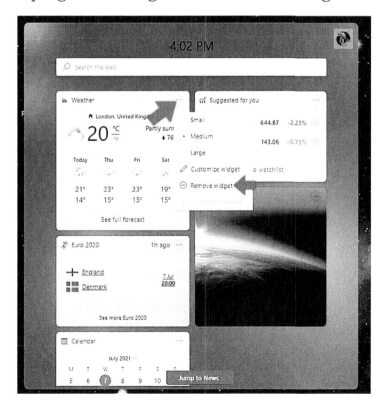

Windows Search

With Windows search you can search for files, apps, email, music, people, and settings on your PC, as well as a web search.

You'll find the search icon on the taskbar next to the start button.

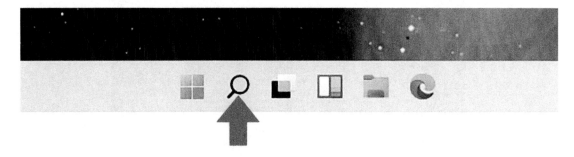

When the search window opens, you'll see a search field at the top. Here, you can type in your search.

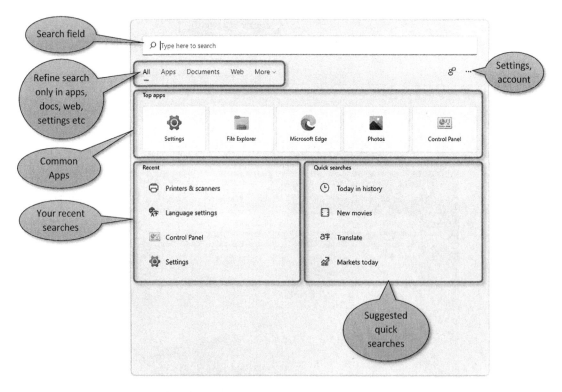

On the next line, you can refine your search to search only for apps, documents, or the web. Click 'more' and you can refine your search to search for settings, email, folders, people, photos and videos. This is useful if you want to search only for documents, email, or apps, rather than your whole PC. This helps to narrow down your search.

Underneath, you'll see your most recent searches and suggested quick searches.

Searching for Files

Click on the search icon on your taskbar, then type in your search into the field at the top of the window. This could be the name of an app, a document, email, or website.

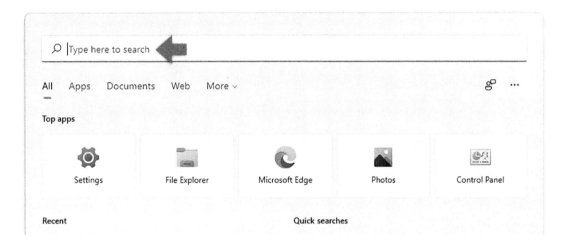

On the left hand side of the search results, you'll see a list of files, apps, and web search suggestions.

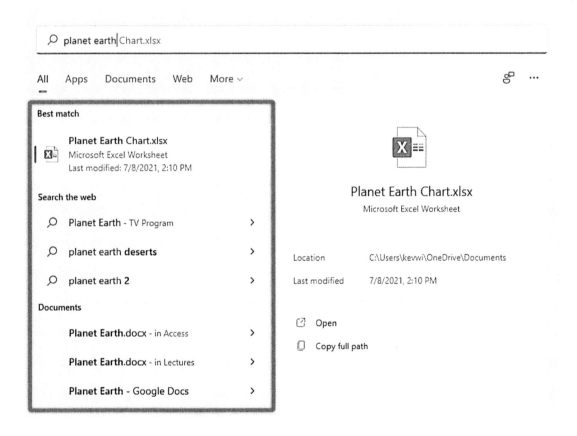

Press the down arrow key on your keyboard to scroll down the list to see some details about the search result.

173

These details will appear in the right hand half of the window.

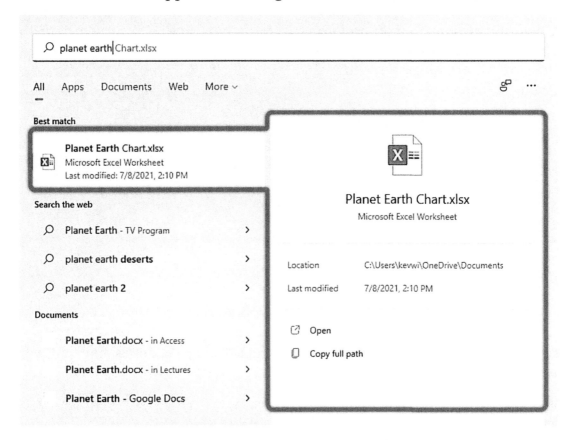

Click on a match from the search results. In this case I was searching for my 'planet earth' chart which happens to be the 'best match' at the top.

Searching for Apps

You can also search for apps. Click on the search icon on the taskbar next to the start button, then type the name of the app into the search field at the top of the search window.

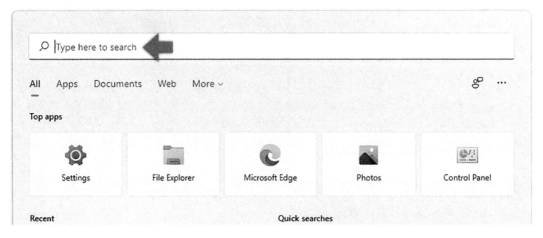

In the search results, you'll see the app name appear under 'best match' on the left. On the right, you'll see some options. Here, you can open the app normally, or run it as an administrator - useful if you need the app to edit system files or change settings. You can pin or unpin it on the start menu or taskbar, and you can edit the app settings - useful if you want to reset the app or repair it. You can also share the app or uninstall it. Most apps, you can just open normally. To do this click on 'open'.

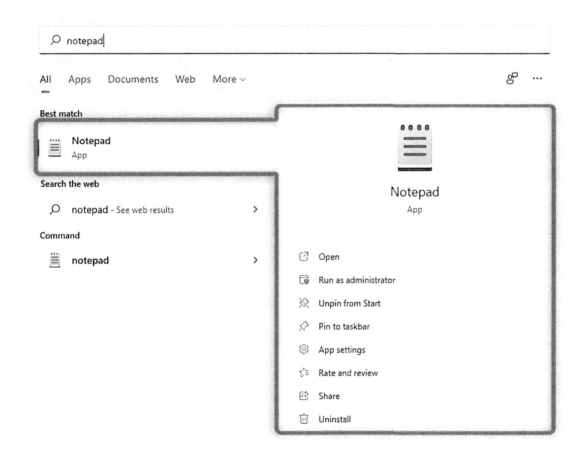

Searching for Windows Settings

You can search for settings. To do this click on the search icon on the taskbar next to the start button. Type the setting into the search field at the top of the window. For example, you can search for printer settings, Wi-Fi, BlueTooth, display settings and so on.

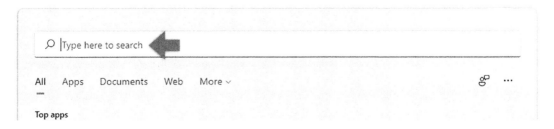

Select the setting from the search results.

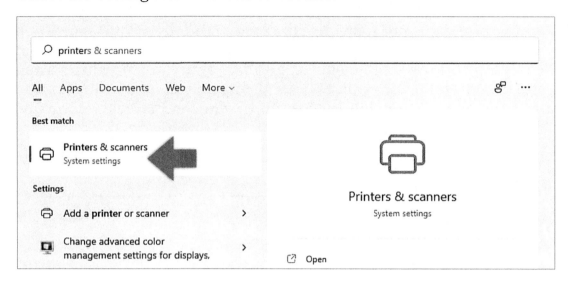

Narrowing Down the Search

Along the top of the window, under the search field, you'll see a bar with some options. These allow you to refine your search to apps, documents, email, web, folders, music, people, photos, settings, or videos (click 'more' to see the rest of the options).

So, if I was searching for my 'planet earth' documents, I'd type 'planet earth' into the search field.

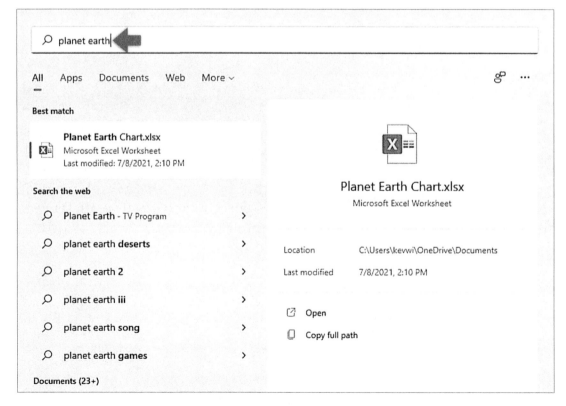

176

Then from the options, I'd select 'documents'.

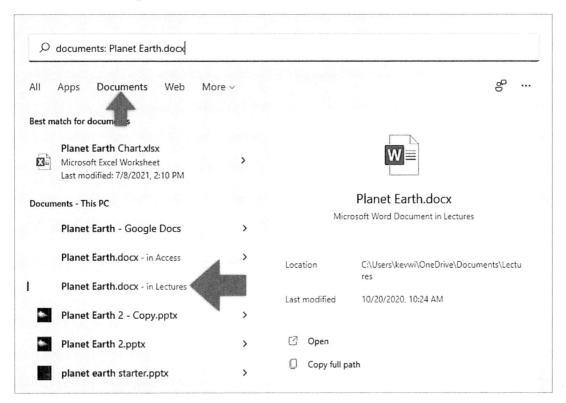

If I just wanted to search my email, I'd select 'email' from the options.

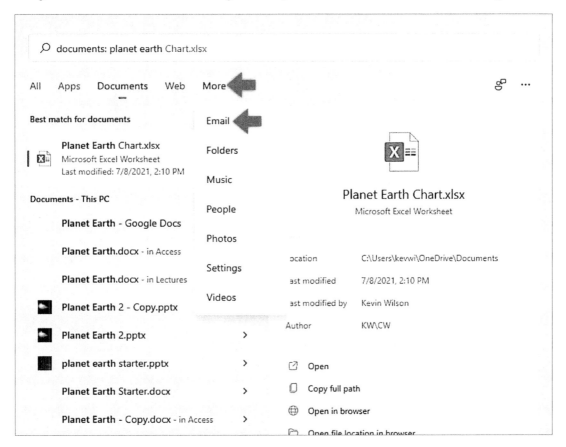

Virtual Desktops

Using 'Multiple desktops' is almost like having two or more desks in your office, where you can do your work. You could have a desktop for your web browsing and email, another desktop for your word processing, another desktop for your photo editing and sharing and so on. Multiple desktops help to organise your tasks, so you can keep things you are working on together.

Task View

To access your virtual desktops, click the task view icon on your taskbar, or press Win Tab on your keyboard.

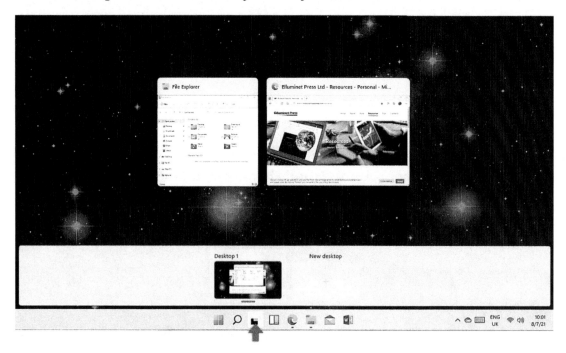

Creating a New Desktop

To create a new desktop, click the task view icon on your taskbar, then click 'new desktop' from the thumbnails along the bottom of the screen.

Click on the desktop thumbnail icon to switch to the new desktop.

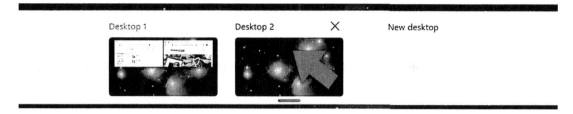

Now, you can open apps as you would on any desktop.

Change Background

You can set different backgrounds to help you distinguish between your desktops. To do this, open the taskview, then right click on the thumbnail of the desktop you want to change. Select 'choose background' from the popup menu.

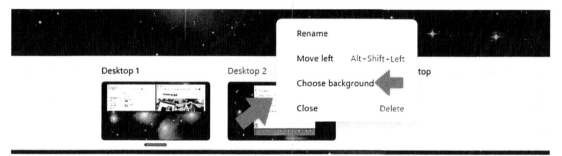

Here, you can select a background, or choose one from your photos.

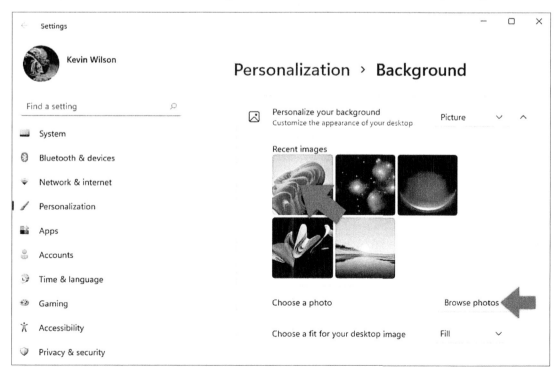

Renaming

You can name your desktops. To do this, open your taskview, then click on the name of the desktop you want to change.

Type in a meaningful name.

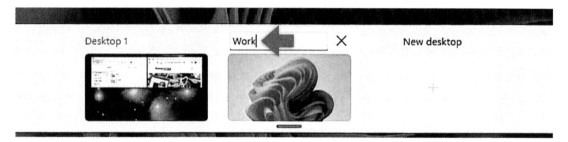

Reordering

You can reorder your desktops. Just click and drag the thumbnail icon.

Quick Access

For quick access to your desktops, hover your mouse over the taskview icon on the taskbar.

Quick Settings (Action Center)

This was known as action center in Windows 10. In Windows 11, the action center has been stripped down and renamed 'quick settings'. Quick settings allows you to access commonly used PC settings quickly and easily, such as Wi-Fi, Bluetooth, volume control, screen brightness, focus assist, and media controls for music or video apps.

To open quick settings, click the icon on the bottom right of the screen.

Here, you'll see some buttons for Wi-Fi, bluetooth, airplane mode, night light, mobile hotspot, focus assist, accessibility settings, and nearby sharing.

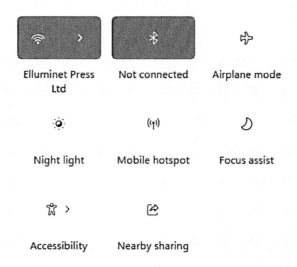

Along the bottom, you'll see a slider to control your audio volume.

On the bottom right of the window, you'll see some icons. One allows you to add or remove buttons from the quick settings window, the other opens the settings app.

Notifications

You'll see notifications and messages. These could be email message that have just arrived, system messages or status alerts from applications. *See page 124 for settings and configuration.*

To open notifications, click on the clock on the bottom right of the taskbar.

Along the top section of the sidebar you'll see all the notifications from apps and system events such as antivirus, etc.

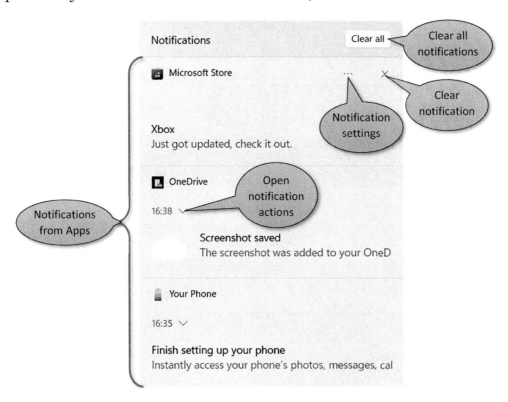

Click the down arrow under the app name to view actions to deal with the notification.

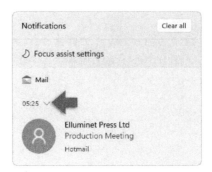

Here, you'll see a preview of the notification from the app, with some action buttons along the bottom.

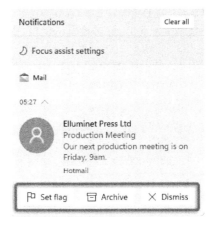

Click on the notification message to open it up.

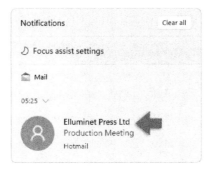

Underneath the notifications, you'll see a quick view of your calendar.

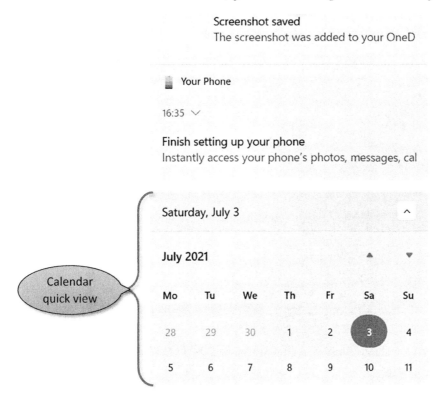

Windows Ink

Windows Ink is a feature in Windows 11 that contains app and features that are designed to make use of a touch screen and a pen.

The windows ink icon will appear on the bottom right of your screen when a pen is paired with your device.

A small popup pen menu will appear. Here, you can open Whiteboard, the snipping tool and edit pen menu, change pen settings.

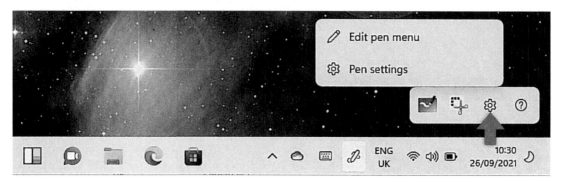

If you select 'edit pen menu', you can add or remove icons from the menu.

Arranging Windows on the Desktop

It's useful when working in Windows 11 to arrange the windows on your desktop, especially when you're using more than one application at a time. For example, you could be browsing the web and writing a Word document at the same time - perhaps you're researching something, you could have Word open and your web browser next to it on the screen.

Take a look at the 'resizing and moving windows' demo in the video resources. Open your browser and navigate to the following website:

```
videos.tips/win-11-nav
```

Moving a Window

Move your mouse pointer to the title bar at the top of the window.

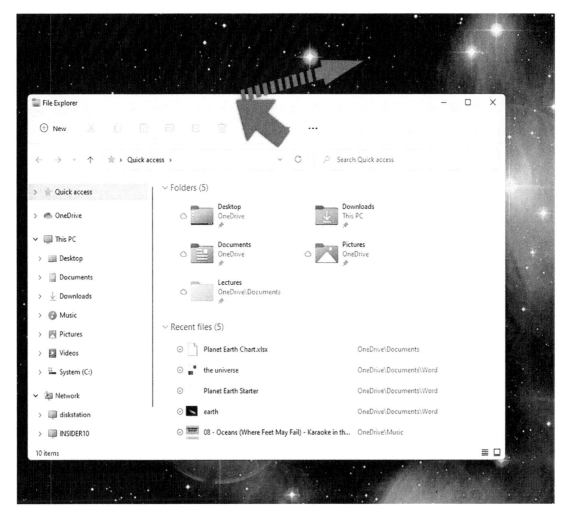

Now click and drag the window to your desired position on the screen.

Resizing a Window

To resize a window, move your mouse pointer to the bottom right corner of the window - your pointer should turn into a double edged arrow.

The double edged arrow means you can resize the window. Now click and drag the edge of the window until it is the size you want.

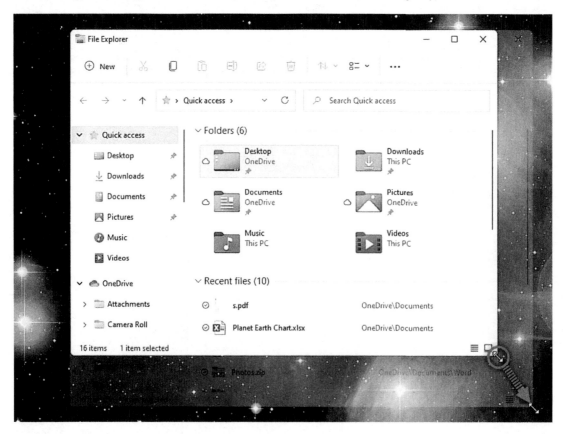

You can drag any edge of the window - left, bottom or right edge, but I find using the corner allows you to freely resize the window much more easily.

If you're on a touch screen, tap and drag the corner of the window.

Minimise, Maximise & Close a Window

On the top right hand side of every window, you'll see three icons. You can use these icons to minimise a window, ie reduce it to the taskbar essentially hiding the window from the desktop. With the second icon, you can maximise the window so it fills the entire screen, or if the window is already maximised, using the same icon, restore the window to its original size. The third icon you can use to close a window completely.

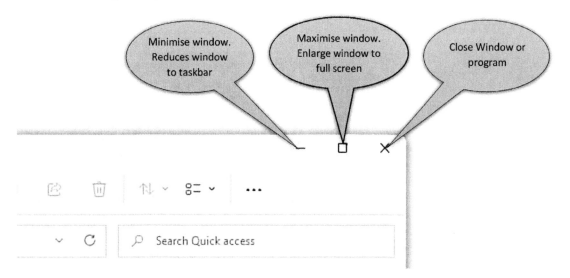

Snap Layouts

Snap layouts allow you to quickly arrange applications and other windows on your screen according to pre-set template (called a layout) such as the layouts shown below. You can snap two apps side by side, with both the same size, or the left app larger then the right app.

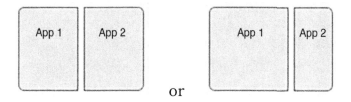

Or you can snap three apps - one large down the left, and two underneath one another on the right. Or you can snap four apps, one in each corner.

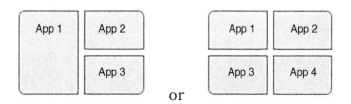

Snapping Windows

To snap a window, hover your mouse over a window's maximize button, then select a zone on one of the layouts to snap the window to. Or press **Win Z** on your keyboard.

The window will snap to the zone you selected.

If you have any other apps open, snap assist will ask you to snap the rest of the windows to the layout of the zone you selected earlier. Remember we selected the left zone on the two apps side by side layout.

So, if I had Edge and Word running, the snap assist will ask me to snap Word to the second zone on the layout I selected.

If you want to snap the app to the other zone, click on it.

Snap Groups

Snap groups are a way to easily switch back to your snapped windows. Hover over one of the open apps on the taskbar, you'll see a snap group. Click on the group to switch back.

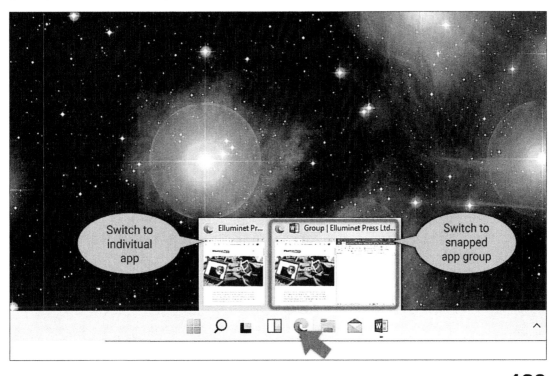

Multiple Screens

You can plug in more than one screen into most modern computers or tablets if you have the correct adapters.

To set up multiple monitors, open your settings app, select 'system' from the list on the left, then click 'display'.

At the top of the display settings, you'll see two rectangles. If you don't, set the drop down box to 'extend these displays'.

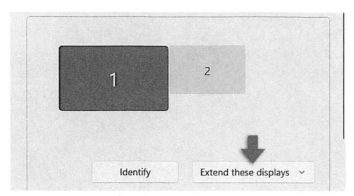

These rectangles represent your screens. The idea is to arrange these so they match the physical layout. In the image at the top of the page, screen 1 is the one on the left, screen 2 is on the right. *Click 'identify' if you don't know which is which.*

Now, click and drag these rectangles and move them so they match.

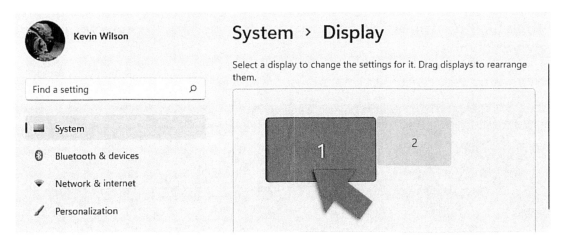

The blue rectangle is your main screen (the one you use most often), the grey rectangle is your secondary screen. Make sure your main screen is selected (blue). In this demo, the main screen is screen 1.

This allows you to extend your main screen onto another - which can be another monitor, TV, or projector. If the screens are extended, you can drag windows onto your second screen. In the demo below, I'm dragging Microsoft Edge onto the second screen on the right.

Your main screen is the one you use most often. With the second screen, you can drag other apps. So for example, you could have Microsoft Word open on your main screen (Screen 1), and a web browser open on screen 2.

Using Projectors

Much like using multiple screens, you can also use a projector as your second display.

Press **Win P** on your keyboard.

From the options panel, select the display you want.

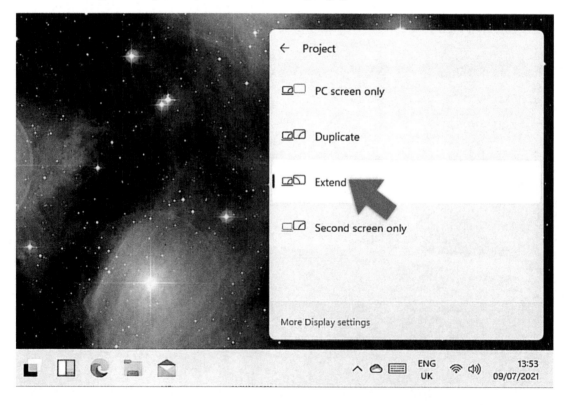

Here, you can project to your PC screen only, you can mirror or duplicate the screens so they both display the same thing, or you can extent the screen making the projector or second screen an extension to your PC screen. Or you can project to the second screen or projector only, leaving your PC screen blank.

Duplicate PC screen onto Second Screen

Everything you do on the laptop screen (PC Screen) will be duplicated on the second screen (eg projector). So both screens will show the same image.

Second Screen Only

This disables your PC's monitor and allows the display to only appear on the second screen.

PC Screen Only

This disables the projector and allows the information to be seen only on the PC's monitor.

Extend PC screen onto Second Screen

The second screen (such as a projector) acts as an extension to your laptop screen (PC Screen), rather than just a duplicate. So you can have something on your laptop screen and show different images on the projector as shown below.

This allows you to move windows from the laptop's screen (PC Screen 1) to Screen 2 (eg projector) and vice versa.

PC Screen   Screen 2

Screen 2 becomes an extension of the PC Screen. Ideal for using presentation software such as Pro Presenter or PowerPoint.

194

Docking

If you use a laptop or a windows tablet, sometimes you want to connect it to a larger monitor with an external keyboard and mouse. This could mean you simply plug in an external monitor, keyboard and mouse, or use a docking station. In the image below, you can see my laptop is docked with a docking station. There is a large external monitor connected to the docking station, as well as a keyboard and mouse.

When you un-dock the laptop, the windows on your external monitor will be minimized. Here, below on the laptop's screen, you can see the two apps I had open on my external monitor have been minimised.

This is indicated with a small dot under the icon. You can click on these icons to open the apps you were working on.

When you re-dock your laptop, Windows returns the apps you had open on the external monitor, as shown below.

To find the settings of this feature, open your settings app then select 'system' from the list on the left. Click on 'display', then select 'multiple displays'.

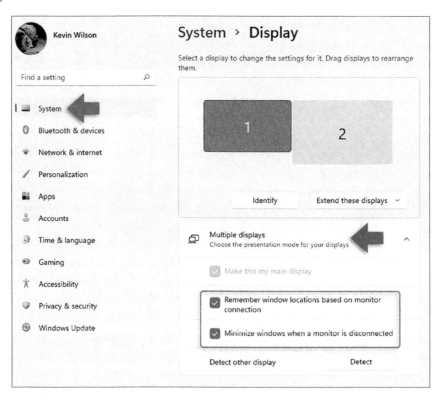

Here, you can enable/disable the 'remember window locations' on your external monitor. You can also enable whether you want the apps to be minimized when you un-dock your laptop, or you can disable 'minimize windows' to have the apps you had on your external monitor, simply transfer to your laptop screen when un-docked.

196

Cloud Clipboard

Cloud clipboard allows you to copy & paste multiple items across all your devices. So for example, you could copy a paragraph off a Word document on your laptop, and paste it into a document on your surface tablet.

To open cloud clipboard, hold the windows key, then tap V.

You'll see a small window appear on the right hand side of the screen. When you do this for the first time on your device, Windows will ask you to turn on clipboard history.

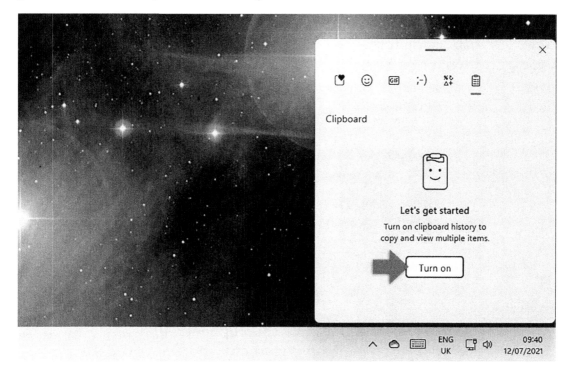

Click 'turn on' to enable clipboard history.

Copying Multiple Items

If you are doing something that requires you to copy and paste different images or text, you'll find yourself re-copying the same piece of text or image multiple times. Cloud clipboard allows you to copy multiple images or blocks of text, so you can store them on your clipboard, then select and paste in what you need.

You can see below, as we've copied the paragraph, it has been added to the clipboard.

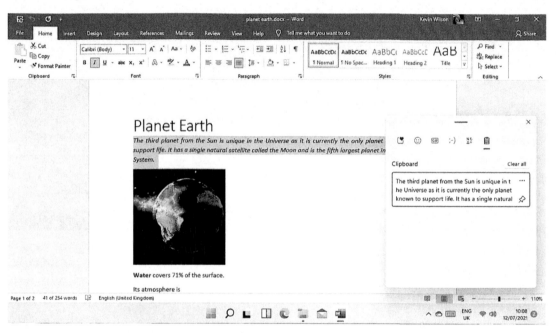

Now, lets copy something else. You can see in the clipboard panel on the right, there are now two items.

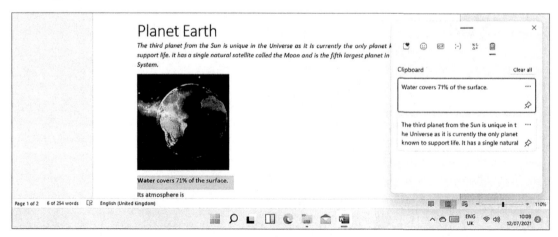

You can select any of the items in the clipboard and paste them in. Just position your cursor in the document and select the item in the clipboard you want to paste. Remember press windows key & V to open the clipboard panel, if it disappears.

Copying Across Devices

To sync your clipboard across all your devices, first check that this feature is enabled and you are signed into your device using your Microsoft Account. To check, open your settings app, click 'system', then select 'clipboard' from the list on the right hand side.

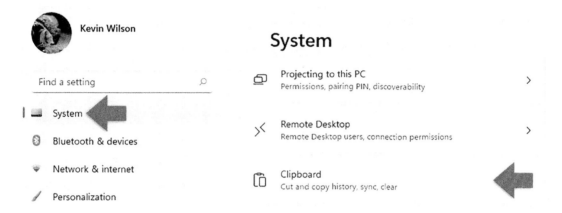

Turn on 'sync across your devices'.

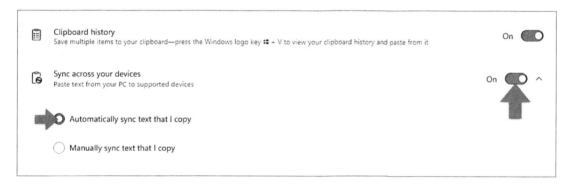

Do this on all your devices.

Now that we have enabled cloud clipboard, in this demo we're going to copy a paragraph from a Word document on a laptop, and paste it into another document on a surface tablet. You can see this setup in the photograph below.

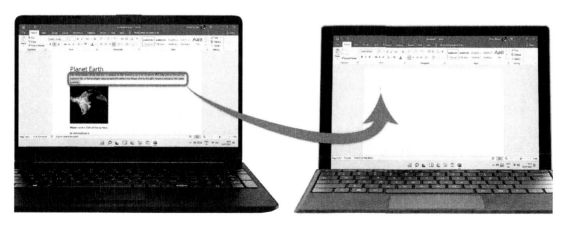

On the laptop, select and copy the text using normal copy and paste.

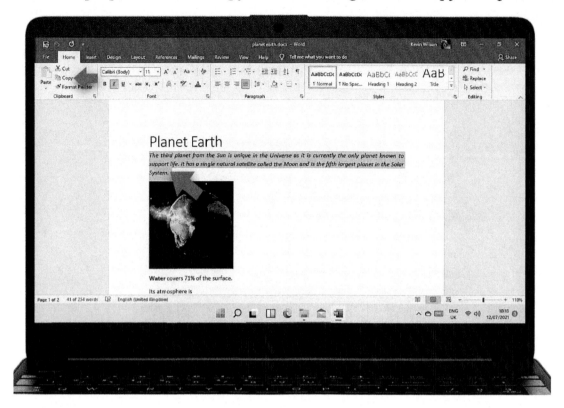

Now go onto the other device - the surface tablet. Hold down the windows key, then press V.

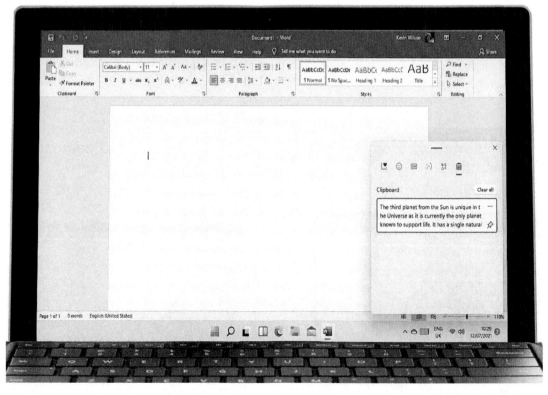

You'll see the clipboard window open up.

Click on the clipping from the clipboard window to paste it into the word document.

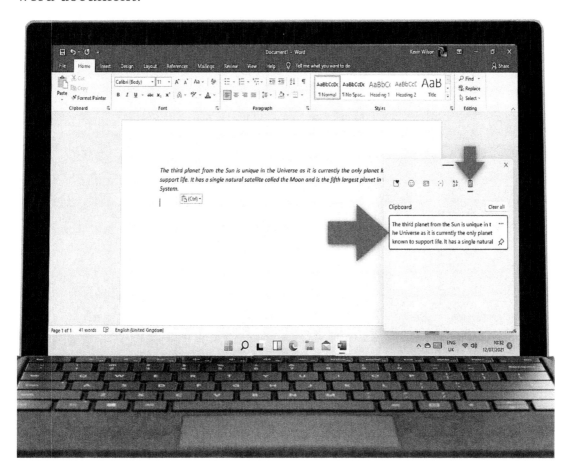

You can do this with text and images. Anything you can copy and paste, you can now paste to any device you've signed into with your Microsoft Account.

Note that all your devices must be running Windows 11, or the October 2018 Update (1809) of Windows 10 or later for this feature to work.

Character Map & Symbols

The character map is useful for inserting symbols that do not appear on your keyboard. These could be mathematical symbols or emojis.

To open the character map, hold down the windows key on your keyboard, then press ;

Along the top of the panel, you'll see six icons.

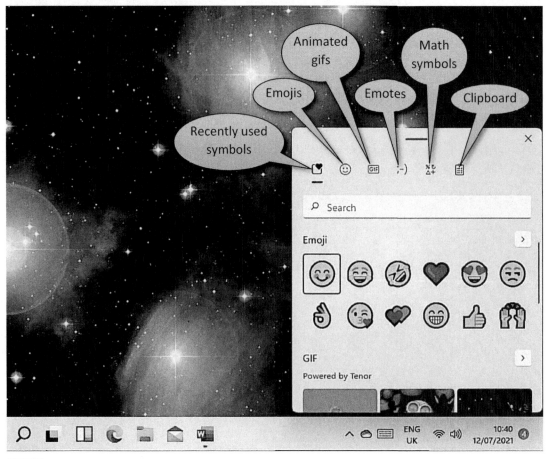

Here, you can add currency, mathematical and language symbols. Select the symbols icon from the top of the panel, then select a symbol group from the list along the top

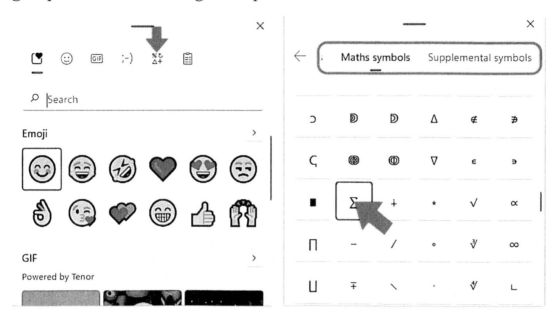

You can also add emojis, select the emoji icon from the icons along the top

Select an emoji from the icons.

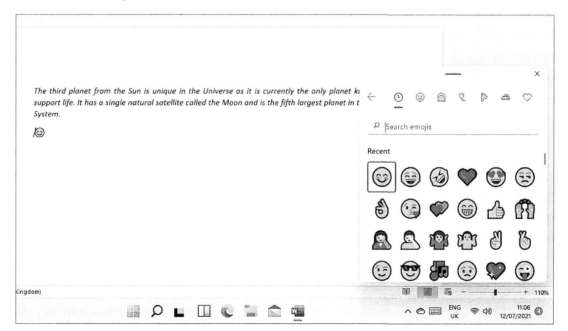

Taking Screenshots

You can take screenshots using the screen snip feature. Use it to save and share recipes, stories, articles and so on. Screenshots are saved to your clipboard. You can then paste them into an email, message, Word document, or graphics application.

To take a full screen screenshot, press print screen on your keyboard.

To take a screenshot of only part of the screen, hold down the Windows Key and the Shift key, then press S.

Along the top of your screen you'll see a toolbar with some options.

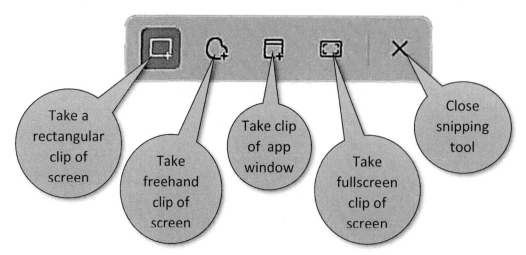

Select which type of clip you want to capture. The rectangular or fullscreen clips are the most useful. You can also take a freehand clip or capture a window.

To take a rectangular clip of the screen, click and drag the rectangular box highlight around the area that you want.

To take a freehand clip of the screen, select the freehand slip icon, then click and draw around the section of the screen you want.

You'll be able to find the clips of the screen on your clipboard. Press Windows V to view your clipboard. Here, you'll be able to paste into a message, document, image editor or email.

Task Manager

The task manager shows you all the processes, services and apps that are currently running on your machine, as well as some performance statistics of your processor, memory, hard drives and graphics cards. The task manager is also useful if a program stops responding and freezes up - you can terminate the program from the task manager.

To open task manager, press **control-shift-esc** on your keyboard

If you see the reduced task manager as shown below, click 'more details'.

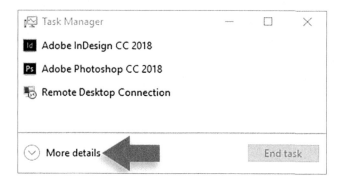

Here you will see some tabs along the top of the window. This will show you running processes, computer performance, a history of apps, apps that run at start up, apps used by a specific user, details of apps and services running.

Name	Status	9% CPU	43% Memory	2% Disk	0% Network	1% GPU	GPU Engine
> Task Manager		4.5%	17.9 MB	0 MB/s	0 Mbps	0%	
> Service Host: Remote Desktop S...		1.3%	49.7 MB	0 MB/s	0.6 Mbps	0%	
Windows Explorer		1.1%	26.9 MB	0 MB/s	0 Mbps	0%	
RDP Clipboard Monitor		1.0%	1.5 MB	0 MB/s	0 Mbps	0%	
CTF Loader		0.4%	2.1 MB	0 MB/s	0 Mbps	0%	
> Antimalware Service Executable		0.2%	67.9 MB	0.1 MB/s	0 Mbps	0%	
Desktop Window Manager		0.2%	34.0 MB	0.1 MB/s	0 Mbps	0%	
System		0.1%	0.1 MB	0.1 MB/s	0 Mbps	0%	
System interrupts		0.1%	0 MB	0 MB/s	0 Mbps	0%	
> Windows Shell Experience Host		0%	28.4 MB	0.1 MB/s	0 Mbps	0%	GPU 0 - 3D
> wsappx		0%	1.0 MB	0 MB/s	0 Mbps	0%	
System Settings Broker		0%	1.3 MB	0 MB/s	0 Mbps	0%	
Microsoft Windows Search Filte...		0%	0.6 MB	0 MB/s	0 Mbps	0%	
Microsoft Windows Search Prot...		0%	0.9 MB	0 MB/s	0 Mbps	0%	
Client Server Runtime Process		0%	0.7 MB	0 MB/s	0 Mbps	0.8%	GPU 0 - 3D
> Service Host: Superfetch		0%	31.2 MB	0 MB/s	0 Mbps	0%	
Application Frame Host		0%	4.0 MB	0 MB/s	0 Mbps	0%	
Client Server Runtime Process		0%	0.6 MB	0 MB/s	0 Mbps	0%	
COM Surrogate		0%	1.3 MB	0 MB/s	0 Mbps	0%	

You can also terminate some of these apps - to do this click the service/ app then click 'end task'. You should only do this if the particular app/ service is causing a problem. Don't start terminating services as it can cause your machine to become unstable.

Task manager is useful to terminate apps that have crashed or 'not responding'.

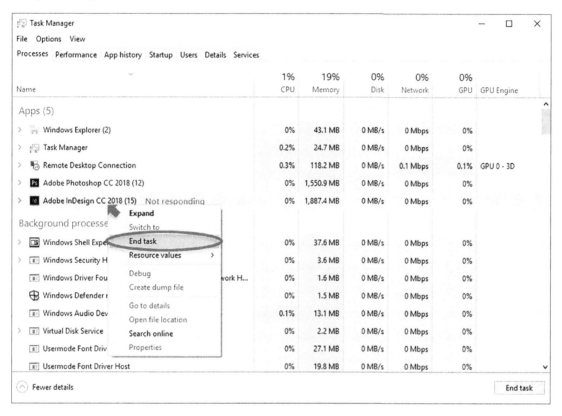

To do this, find the app in the 'processes' tab. The app that has crashed is usually marked with 'not responding'. Right click on the app then from the popup menu, select 'end task'.

You can also sort the processes according to the resources they are using. For example, if you want to see what processes are hogging all the CPU resources, click the CPU column. As you can see, the photos app is using a lot of the CPU.

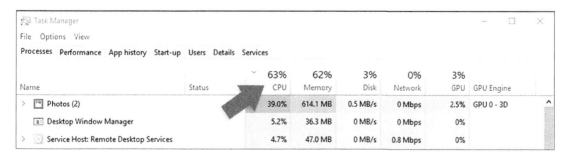

You can do the same for memory, disk, network and GPU.

You can also check the performance of your machine. To do this select the 'performance' tab.

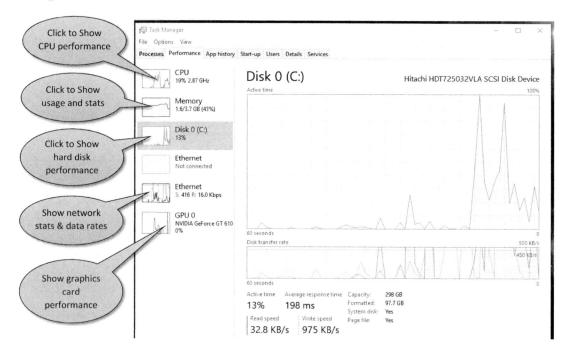

Here we can see the CPU time. On the right hand side you'll see the cores of the CPU and the graph indicates the activity - how much each core is being used to execute various tasks.

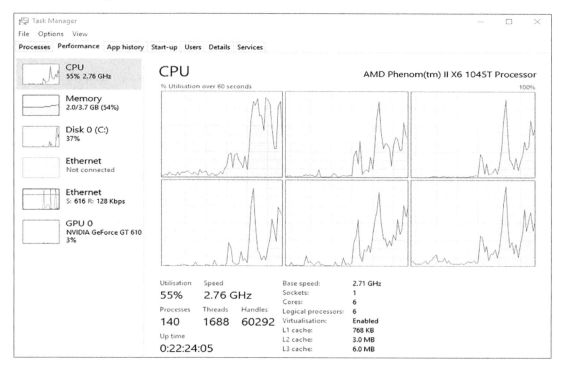

Underneath you'll see some stats for clock speed in GHz, cache sizes, cores and sockets, the up time, as well as the number of processes currently running.

File Explorer

File explorer can be used to find your files on your computer, access your OneDrive, network resources, and external hard drives or flash drives.

Launching

You'll find file explorer on your taskbar, or on your start menu.

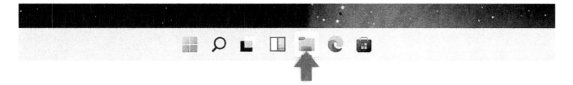

Anatomy

Down the left hand side of the main window, you will find a list of all file locations on your computer. Quick access lists the folders and documents you've most recently used. OneDrive contains all your files saved to OneDrive. This PC lists all the local file resources such as local disk drives and folders. Network lists all the other devices and machines on your current network.

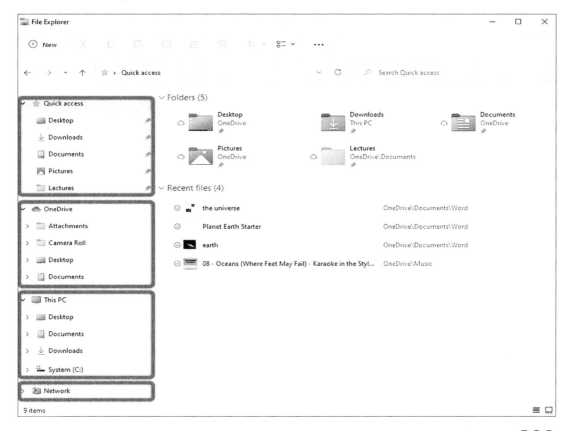

Along the top of the window, you'll see the toolbar. Here, you'll find tools to cut, copy, and paste a selected item (a file or folder). You can also rename, share and delete the item. You'll also see icons to sort your files, and display them as a list or icons. With the three dots icon on the far right, you can burn the selected items (or files) to a CD/DVD, or you can compress them into a Zip file.

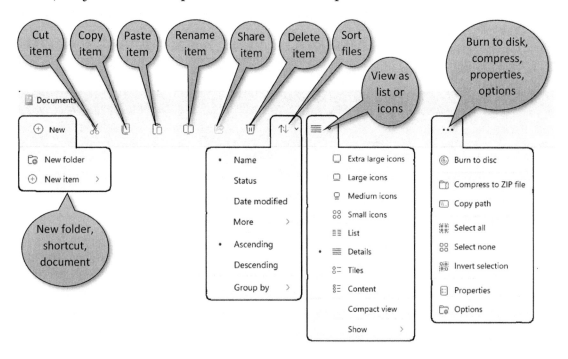

Underneath you'll see an address bar and search field. Here, you can type in a network path to a shared folder, a drive, or folder.

You can also search for files and folders using the search field.

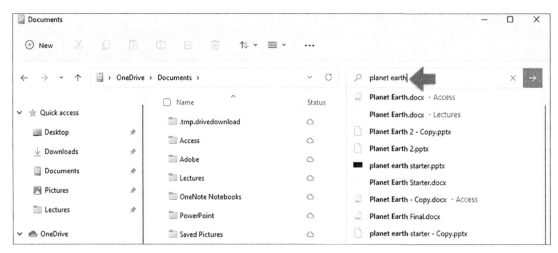

Managing your Files

Windows 11 stores data in files and organises the files into folders. Files and folders are saved onto a Drive which is allocated a drive letter such as C, D, E and so on. C is usually reserved for the system drive - ie the drive Windows itself is installed onto.

Windows Folder Structure

Windows stores files in folders (sometimes called directories). Here is a typical folder structure on the C drive.

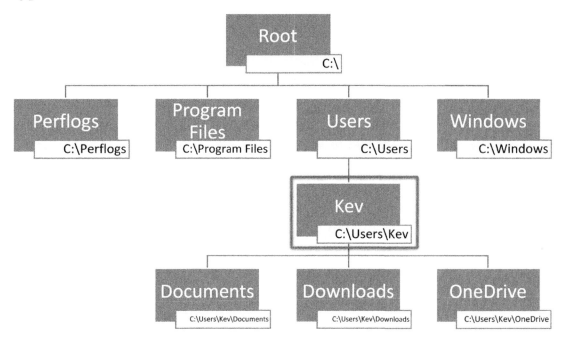

The top of the drive structure is called the root directory. All other files, folders/directories are created in the root directory.

Perflogs contains performance related reports and system logs and is a folder you usually never have to worry about.

Program Files contains all the apps and programs you've installed on your device. *One some systems you'll also see another folder called Program files (x86), this is for older 32bit software.*

Users folder contains all the personal folders for each user you've created an account for.

Windows is a folder that contains all the system files and folders required to run Windows. This is a folder you don't normally have to worry about and should keep clear of unless you know what you're doing.

Files & Folders

There are many different types of file types; files for photos, videos, documents, speadsheets, presentations and so on. These files are identified by a file extension.

```
filename.extension
```

So for example...

A photograph is usually saved as a JPEG or JPG. Eg **photo-of-sophie.jpg**. This could be from a graphics package or a camera.

A document is usually saved as a DOC or DOCX. Eg: **production-resume.docx**. This is usually from a word processor such as Microsoft Word.

The 3 or 4 letters after the period is called a file extension and it is what Windows uses to identify the application needed to open the file.

It's best to save all your files into your OneDrive.

Windows stores your files in a hierarchical tree like structure.

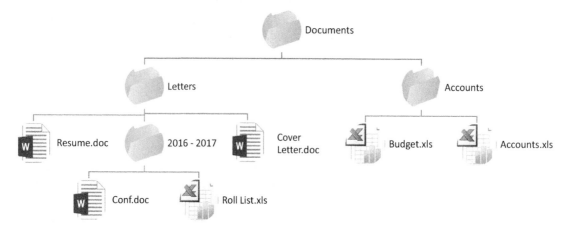

You can create yellow folders to store files of the same type or for the same purpose.

In the example above, letters to various recipients are stored in a 'letters' folder. This can be further divided into year folders, so you have one for each year.

Similarly, all files to do with the accounts are stored in an 'accounts' folder.

Storing files in this fashion keeps them organised and makes them easier to find.

Creating Folders

It's a good idea to create folders to help organise all your files. You could have a folder for your personal documents, work documents, presentations, vacation/holiday photos, college work and so on. To do this open your File Explorer.

On the left hand side of your screen, navigate to the place you want to create a folder. In this example, I'm going to create a folder in my 'OneDrive' 'Documents' folder.

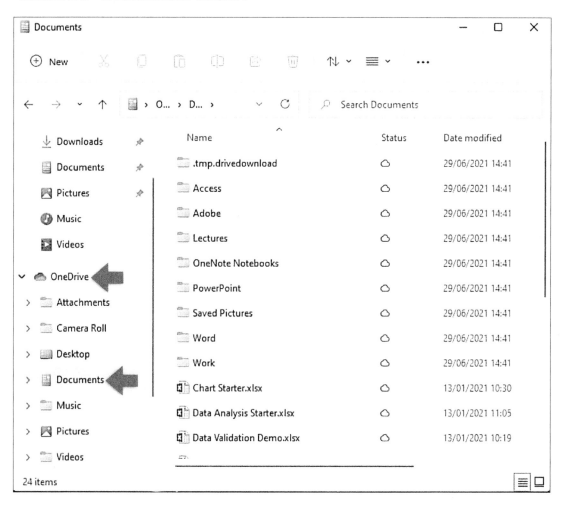

From the toolbar along the top of your screen, click 'new'. Select 'new folder' from the drop down menu.

You'll see a new folder appear called 'new folder'. Delete the text 'new folder' and type in a meaningful name - ideally the name of the group of documents you are saving into this folder.

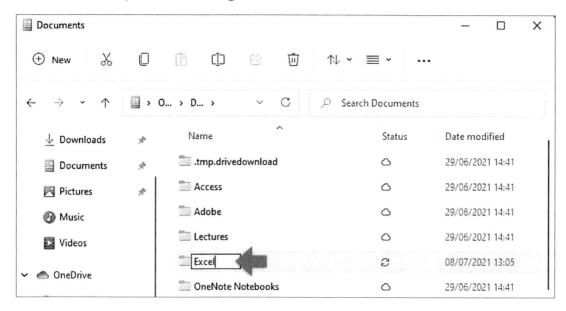

Moving Files

Moving files is a bit like cut and paste. To move files, open your File Explorer. In the left hand pane, click the folder where the file you want to move is saved, eg documents. Then click on the file(s) you want to move to select them. Hold down the ctrl key while you click to select multiple files.

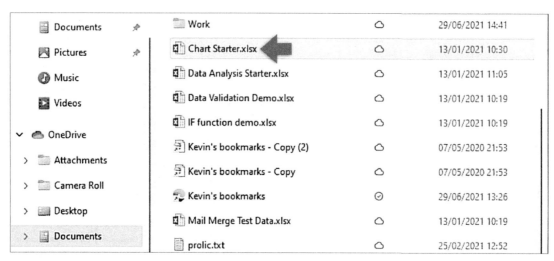

From the toolbar select 'cut'.

Using the left hand pane, navigate to the folder you want to move the file to, eg documents > excel. Click the small side arrows on the left of the folder names to open the folders. Click the folder you want to move the files to.

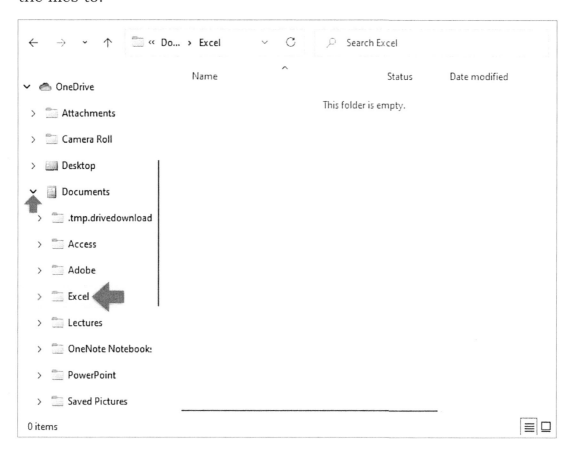

Select 'paste' from the toolbar.

Windows will move the file into the folder.

Copying Files

Copying files is a bit like copy and paste. To copy files, open your File Explorer.

In the left hand pane, click the folder where the file you want to copy, is saved, eg documents. Then click on the file(s) you want to copy to select them. Hold down the ctrl key while you click to select multiple files.

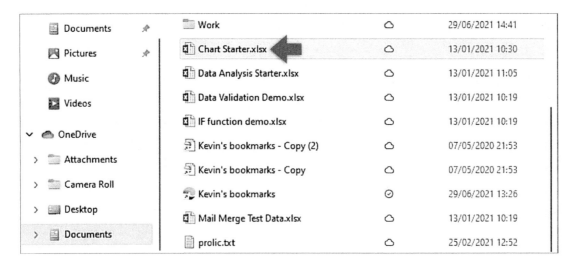

From the toolbar select 'copy'.

Using the left hand pane, navigate to the folder you want to move the file to, eg documents > word. Click the small down arrows to open the folders. Click the folder you want to move the files to.

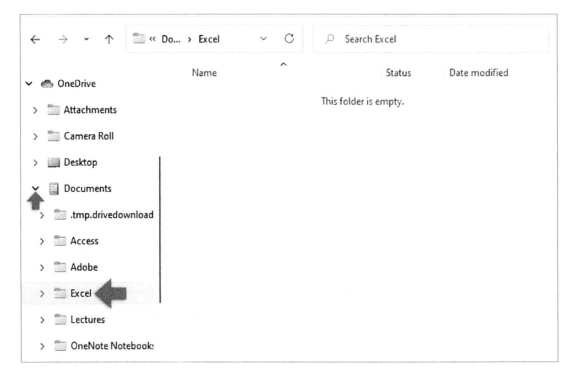

Select 'paste' from the toolbar.

Windows will copy the file into the folder.

Renaming Files

To rename a file, open up your File Explorer and find the file you want to rename. Navigate to the folder your file is saved in. In this demo it's in the OneDrive > documents folder. Click on the file to select it.

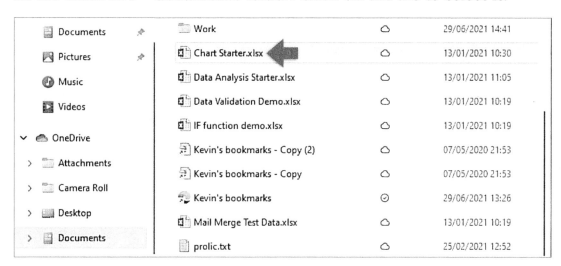

From the toolbar click 'rename'.

You'll see the name of the file highlighted in blue. Now type in a name for the file. Press 'enter' on your keyboard when you're done.

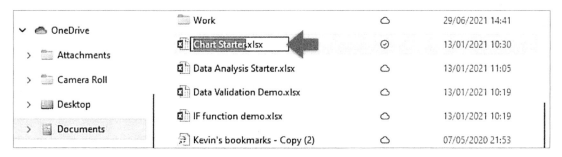

Deleting Files

Deleting files is fairly straight forward. In File Explorer, click on the files you want to delete. Hold down the CTRL key on your keyboard while you click to select multiple files.

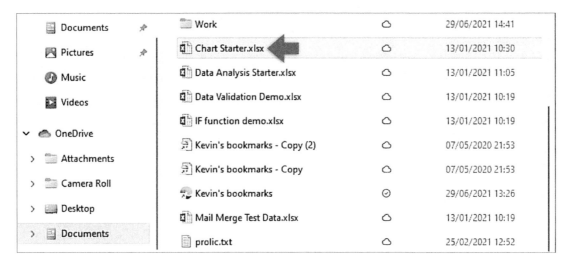

Click the 'delete' icon on the toolbar in File Explorer. You can also press the DEL or DELETE key on your keyboard. Any files you delete will be moved to the recycle bin.

Restoring Files

When you delete a file, Windows moves the file to the trash (or recycle bin). You'll find the recycle bin icon on your desktop - double click the icon to open it up.

Click 'empty recycle bin' to permanently delete all files in recycle bin. Click 'restore all items' to put all the files back where they were deleted from. Or select a file and click 'restore the selected items' to restore individual files. *If you don't see these icons, click the three dots icon on the far right on the toolbar.*

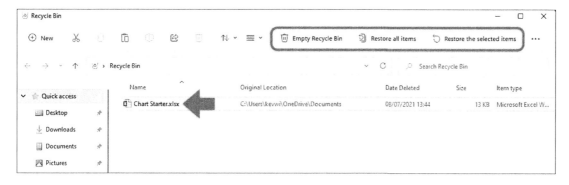

Compressing Files

You can compress files into a zip archive using File Explorer. To do this, select the files you want to compress. Hold down the CTRL key on your keyboard while you click to select multiple files.

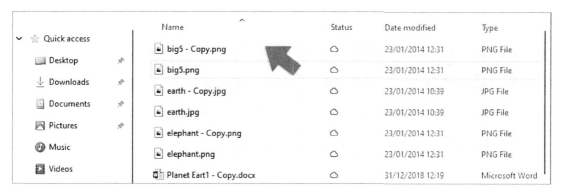

From the three dots icon on the right of the toolbar, select 'compress to zip' from the drop down menu.

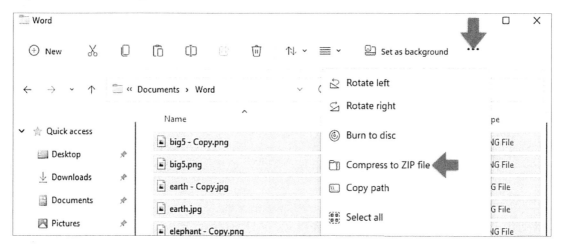

Give the zip file a meaningful name.

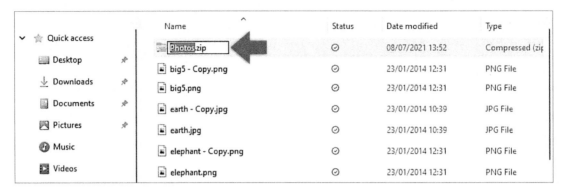

Sorting Files

Within File Explorer, you can sort files alphabetically by name, or by size and date created. This makes it easier to find files especially when you have a lot of them in one folder. To sort your files, select the folder from the left hand side of File Explorer, eg, 'documents'.

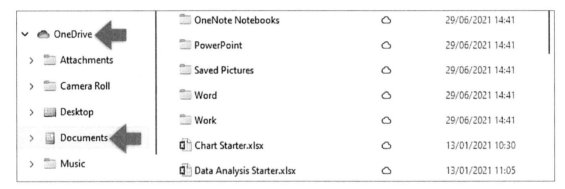

To sort the files, select 'sort by', then select what you want to sort your files by. This could be date modified - so the latest files appear at the top. Or by name - so your files appear in alphabetical order by file name.

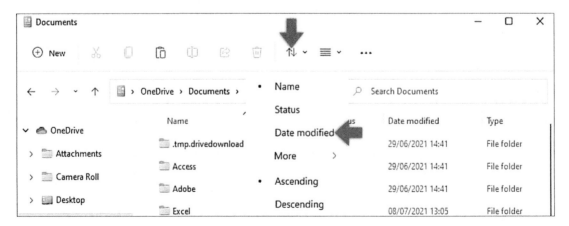

At the bottom of the menu, select ascending or descending order.

Searching for Files

You can search for files within File Explorer using the search field on the top right of the window. First, select the location to search from, eg OneDrive, This PC. Then type your search keywords into the search field. You'll see a list of suggestions appear, to select, click on one in the list.

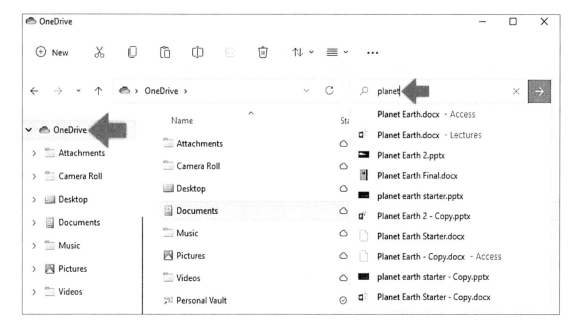

To perform a full search, click the blue arrow icon to the right. A list of matching files will be listed. From here, you can refine your search. - just click 'search options'.

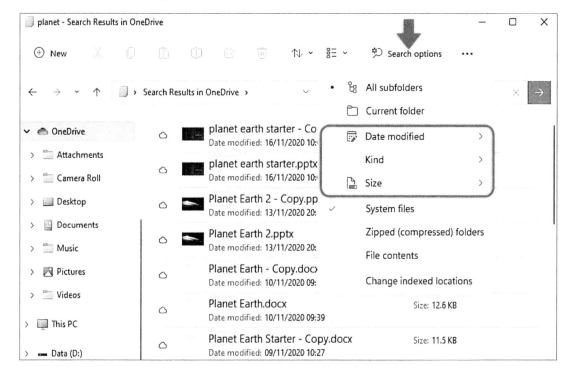

You can search by date modified (eg files you've used today, yesterday, or in the last week. Just select an option from the 'date modified' option on the drop down menu.

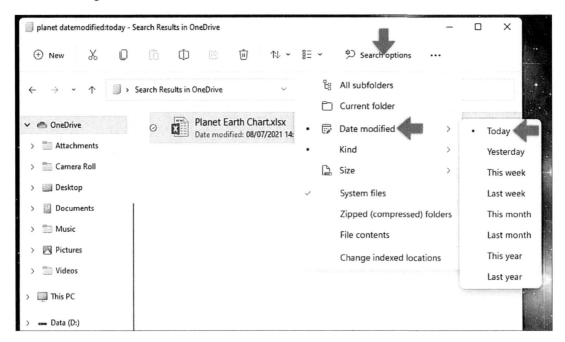

You can search by file type (kind), so you can search through all documents, or images. Just select an option from the 'kind' section of the drop down menu.

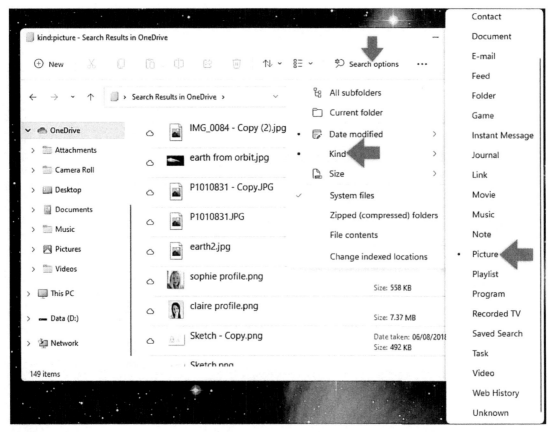

Address Bar

The Address bar is located at the top of File Explorer and displays the path of the currently selected folder.

To view the folders at the same level as the current folder (eg in OneDrive), click on the right pointing arrow to the right of that folder in the Address bar. You'll see a drop down menu appear. This lists all the folders at that level.

Click in the address field, you'll see the full path to the currently selected folder. In this example, the documents folder on OneDrive.

You can type in a folder path, eg if we had a downloads folder on drive E, we'd type `E:\downloads`

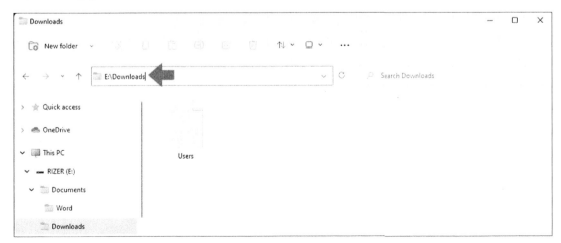

Remember the address bar follows the folder structure of the drive. Here, we can see the downloads folder on drive E.

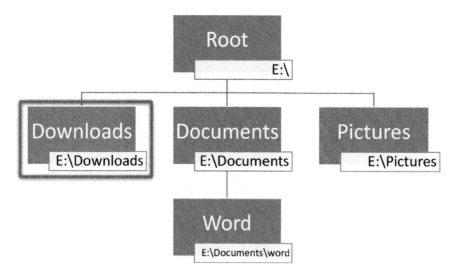

If your folder is on Drive C, the folder structure is different. Your personal files will be stored in the 'users' directory under your username (my username is 'kev'.

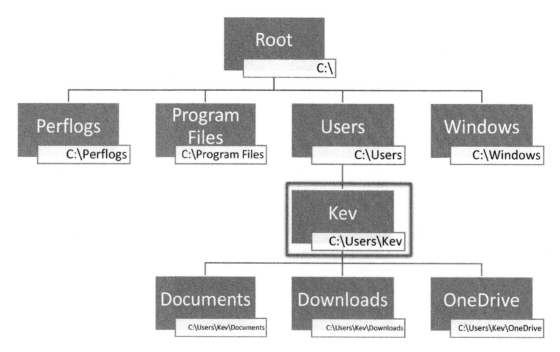

If you click the down arrow to the right of the address bar, you'll see a history of the folders or folder paths you've typed in.

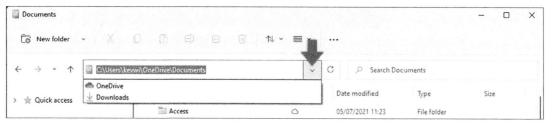

External Drives

You can attach storage devices such as USB sticks, external hard disk drives and memory cards to your computer.

External Hard Disks & USB Sticks

The most common ones are memory sticks - also called usb keys, usb sticks, flash drives or thumb drives. The other type is the portable hard drive.

Memory sticks are usually smaller in capacity ranging from 1GB all the way up to 256GB. Portable hard drives can be larger than 1TB.

To read the drive, plug the device into a USB port on your computer, then select file explorer from the task bar.

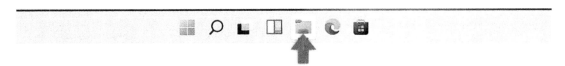

The drive will show up in File Explorer, under 'This PC' section.

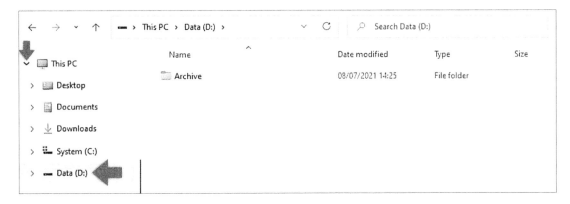

Click on the small arrow to the left of 'this PC'. Then click the drive icon to display the contents of the drive. The external drive will normally be any drive letter after C. In this case it's drive D.

Memory Cards

Many laptops and tablets now have memory card readers built in. The most common memory card being the SD Card. This can be a full sized SD card or a Micro SD card.

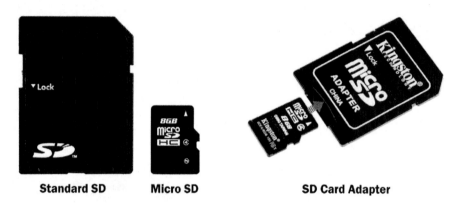

| Standard SD | Micro SD | SD Card Adapter |

Standard SD cards are commonly used in digital cameras, and many laptops have standard size SD card readers built in. Tablets, phones, and small cameras usually use micro SD cards.

You can get an SD Card adapter if your SD card reader does not read Micro SD cards.

There are various types of SD cards available, each are marked with a speed classification symbol indicating the data transfer speed. If you are merely storing files, the data transfer speed doesn't really matter as much, however, if you are using the card in a dash cam or digital camera, the faster data transfer speeds are necessary. To be safe, the higher the speed the better. You can see a summary in the table below.

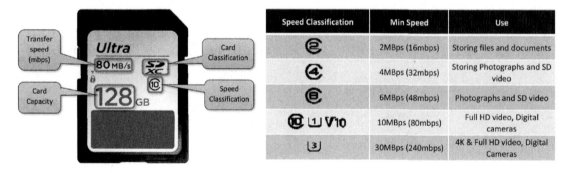

Speed Classification	Min Speed	Use
C2	2MBps (16mbps)	Storing files and documents
C4	4MBps (32mbps)	Storing Photographs and SD video
C6	6MBps (48mbps)	Photographs and SD video
C10 U1 V10	10MBps (80mbps)	Full HD video, Digital cameras
U3	30MBps (240mbps)	4K & Full HD video, Digital Cameras

SDHC stands for "Secure Digital High Capacity", and supports capacities up to 32 GB.

SDXC stands for "Secure Digital eXtended Capacity", and supports capacities up to 2 TB.

SDUC stands for "Secure Digital Ultra Capacity", and supports capacities up to 128 TB.

To read your SD Card, slide it into the card reader on your tablet or laptop. If your laptop or tablet has a built in reader, it is usually on either of the side panels or the front panel.

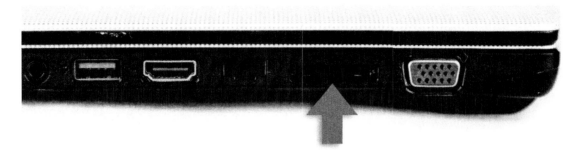

Select file explorer from the task bar.

The card will show up as another drive in file explorer, under 'This PC' section.

Click on the small arrow to the left of 'this PC'. Then click the drive icon to display the contents of the drive. The external drive will normally be any drive letter after C. In this case it's drive F.

To release the card, press the it inwards and it will pop out. Some other cards will just slide out, depending on your card reader.

Copying Files to an External Drive

You can copy files to and from the card as you would with a normal disk drive.

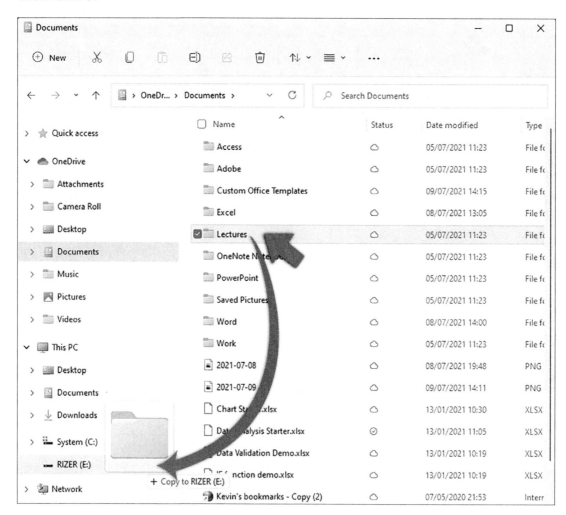

Just click and drag your files to the drive icon under the 'this pc' section in the left hand pane.

Formatting a Drive

Formatting a drive erases all the contents of that drive, so use with caution. To format a drive, open file explorer, right click on the drive in the 'this pc' section on the left hand side.

228

From the popup menu, select 'format'.

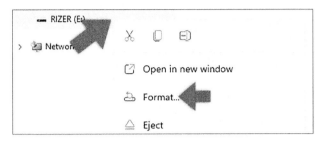

Here, you'll see the capacity of the drive and the file system. Select a file system from the drop down box.

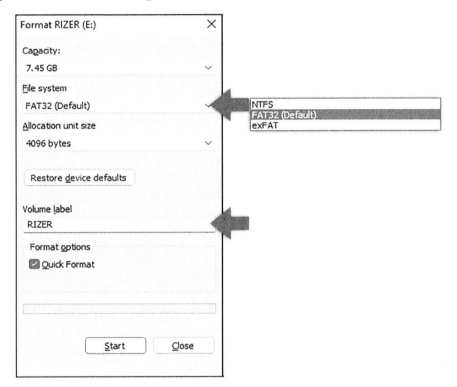

NTFS is the native file system for Microsoft Windows and is best suited for your system drive and other internal drives that will only be used with Windows. NTFS has no file-size or partition size limits.

FAT32 is an old file system that works with all versions of Windows, and Mac, as well as Linux and Game Consoles. This makes it ideal for use on memory sticks and external drives where you need compatibility. This file system has a 4 GB maximum file size limit and Windows will only format drives up to 32GB using the FAT32 file system.

exFAT is compatible with Windows and Mac, making it ideal for portability with no file-size or partition-size limits. This is the ideal file system to use for external drives and memory sticks larger than 32GB.

In the 'volume label' field, give your drive a meaningful name. Click 'start' to begin formatting.

6

Using Apps

There are thousands of Apps available for download from the Microsoft Store.

You can get an app for virtually anything, from games, entertainment to productivity apps for graphics, writing, drawing, typing and word processing.

In this chapter we'll take a look at

- Microsoft Store
- Downloading and installing apps
- Maps App
- Exploring and finding places
- Weather App
- News App
- Clock App
- Setting Alarms and timers
- Voice Recorder
- Calculator App
- To Do App
- Set reminders and to do lists
- PowerShell
- Use the command prompt

To help you better understand this section, take a look at the video resources. Open your web browser and navigate to the following site:

elluminetpress.com/win-11-using

Microsoft Store

Originally known as the Windows Store, Microsoft Store offers apps, games, music, films, and TV series.

You'll find the Microsoft Store on your start menu

In Windows 11, the store has been redesigned. Along the top of the app, you'll see a search field - here you can search for your favourite apps, TV programmes, movies and games.

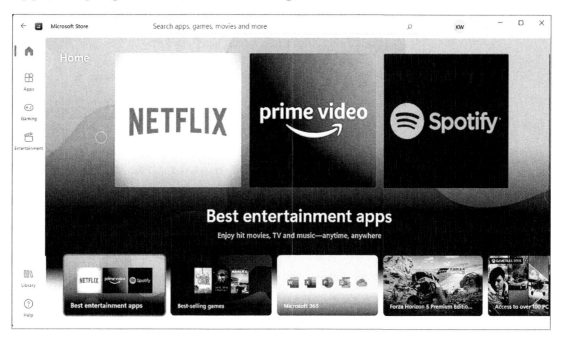

Down the left hand side, you'll see some icons. You'll automatically hand on 'home' where you'll see recommended apps, trending games, TV programmes, movies and so on. Click 'apps' to browse through various different apps from productivity, social media, to photography, as well as tablets and laptops for sale. Click 'gaming' to browse through the latest games, consoles, gaming PCs and accessories. Some apps and games you will need to pay for so you'll need to add payment details, and some are free. Click 'entertainment' to browse through the latest films, TV programmes and music albums.

On the bottom left, you'll see your 'library' and 'help'. The 'library' is where you'll find all the apps and games you've downloaded, as well as any TV Programmes or movies you've purchased.

Searching the Store & Downloading Apps

You can also search for specific types of apps by using the search field on the top right of the screen. Type what you're looking for into the search field, eg 'theory test'. Press 'enter' on your keyboard.

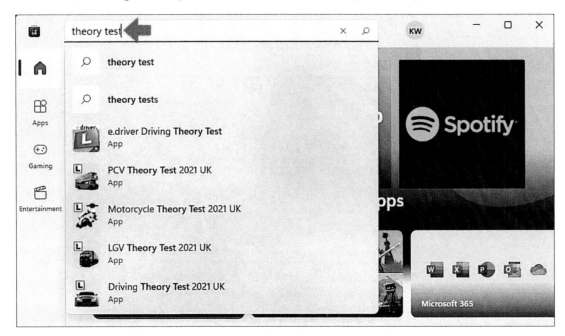

You can further narrow down the search using the options along the top of the window. You can search in all, in apps only, games, movies or tv shows.

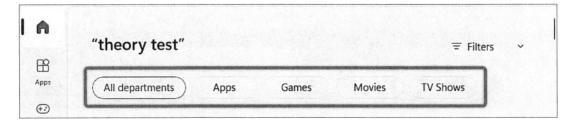

Click on the app's icon to show a summary of what the app is and what it does.

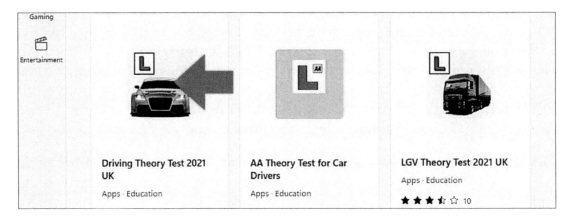

Here, you'll see screenshots of the app, reviews and information. Click the blue price tag or 'free' on the top right to purchase and download the app. You'll need to enter your Microsoft Account email address and password.

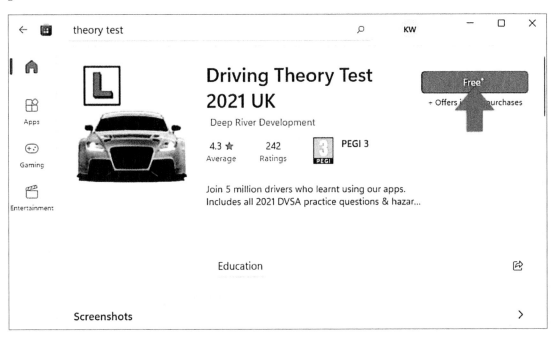

Once the app has downloaded and installed, you will be able to start your app using the start menu. If you downloaded a movie, or TV programme, you'll find it in your 'library' on the bottom left of the screen.

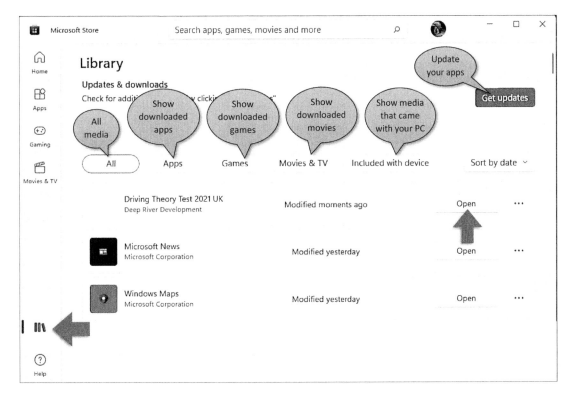

Payment Options

To enter or check your payment method, click your Microsoft Account icon on the top right of the screen and select 'payment methods'.

When your web browser opens, sign in with your Microsoft Account username and password.

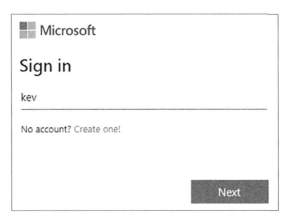

Select 'add a new payment method'.

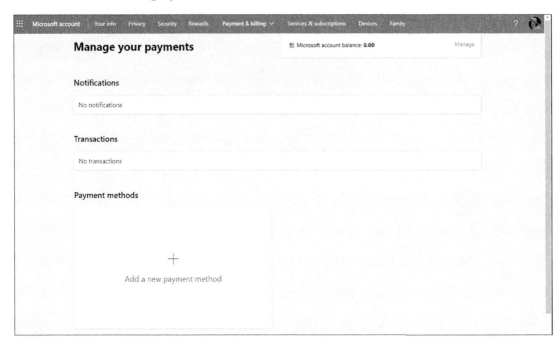

Select your country from the drop down menu at the top, then select the type of payment, eg credit card, mobile billing, or paypal. Scroll down the panel to view other payment methods.

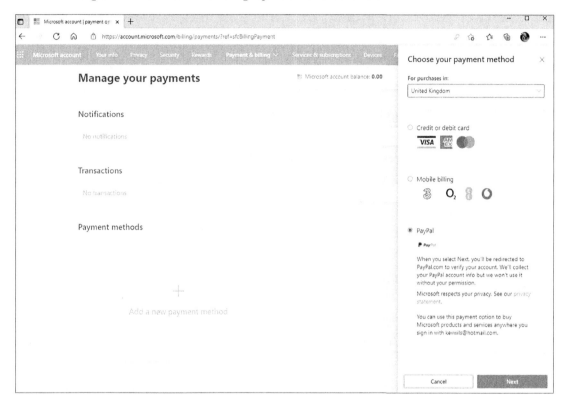

Enter your details in the panel on the right.

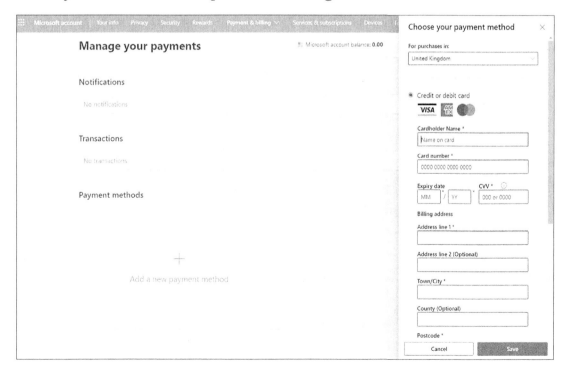

Click 'next' or 'save', then follow the instructions on the screen.

Maps App

The maps app is useful for exploring parts of the world, landmarks and famous places. It is also useful for finding driving directions to different locations. You can find the maps icon on your start menu - click 'all apps' if you don't see it.

You can search for pretty much any address, country, place or landmark. Just type it into the search field on the top left.

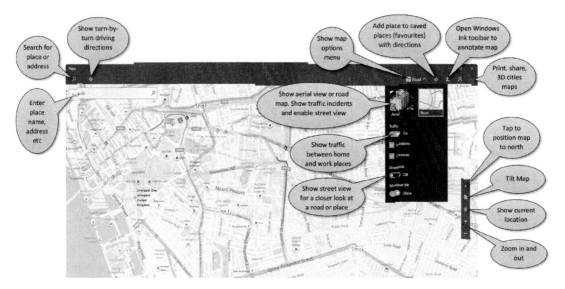

Maps App has an aerial map, and a road map. You can enable traffic flow, incident reporting, speed camera locations and street level view. To do this, select the 'map options' icon on the toolbar to reveal the popup menu.

Get Directions

You can get driving directions to any location or address you can think of. You can get directions from your current location or you can enter a start location and a destination.

As well as driving directions you can get local bus routes and in some places even walking directions.

To get your driving directions, click or tap the turn-by-turn driving directions icon on the top left of your screen, labelled below.

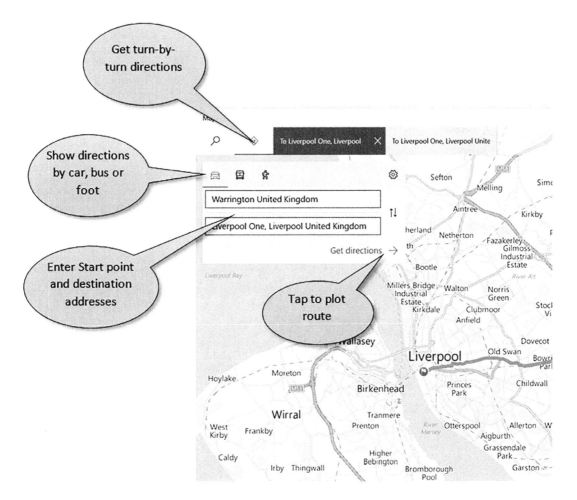

The first field will show your current location (Warrington in this example). You can also type in a location if you need to.

The second field is where you can enter your destination. Liverpool One Shopping Complex in this example. This can be a post code/zip code, residential address, town/city or place name.

Once you hit 'get directions' or tap the right arrow (next to your destination field), the maps app will calculate a route and display it on a map.

Chapter 6: Using Apps

You'll see a map on the right hand side with a list of driving directions listed down the left hand side. You might see a choice of different routes, the quickest one is usually at the top.

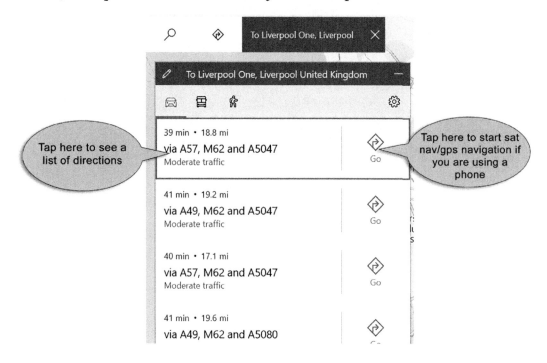

You can click on any of these directions and the map will zoom in and show you the road on the map.

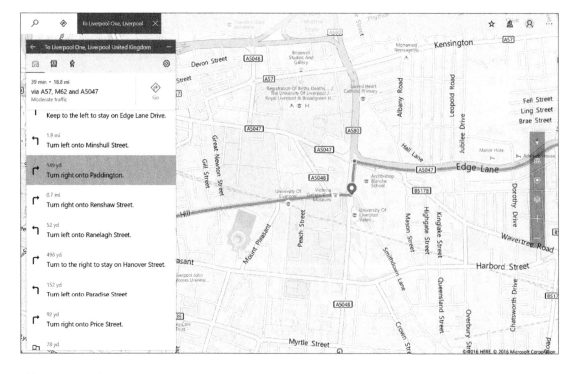

There is also an option to print the directions if needed but if you are using the maps app on your phone or tablet you can use it as a GPS or SatNav and the maps app will direct you as you drive.

Street View

Tap the map options icon on the tool bar on the top right hand side. From the popup menu turn on 'streetside'. You'll notice some of the roads will be highlighted. Main roads and highways are in blue, minor roads are in light green. To go into street view, tap on the part of the road you want to see.

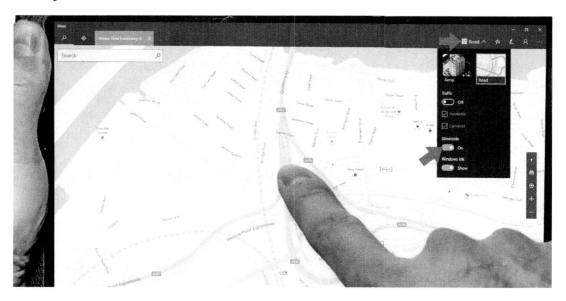

You'll see a street view of that section. To move forward, tap on a part of the road. To "look" left and right tap and drag your view to the left or right.

You can tap the part of the road you want to view on the map in the bottom pane.

Ink Directions

If I wanted to find some quick directions from my location or a specific location, to somewhere close by, I can draw directly onto the map and the Maps App will calculate a route. So in this example, I want to get from Westfield Primary School to Birch Road. Tap the Windows Ink icon, then select the directions icon from the drop down. Draw a line between your start and end points.

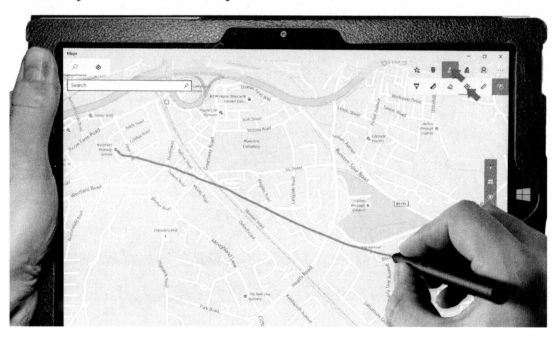

The Maps App will calculate the quickest route between your start and end points.

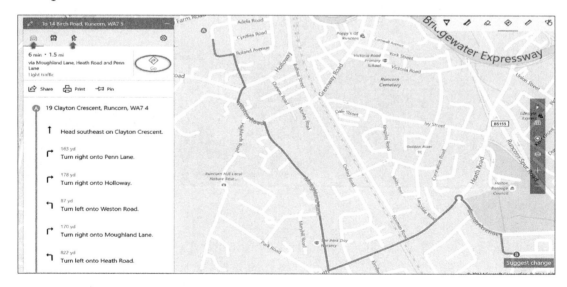

Down the left hand side, you'll see your turn-by-turn directions. Tap, the car icon for driving directions or tap, the little man icon for walking directions. Tap 'go' to start the navigation.

Measure Distances

Using the Windows Ink features, you can also measure distances between two points on the map.

Tap the Windows Ink icon, top right. Then from the drop down, select the measure tool.

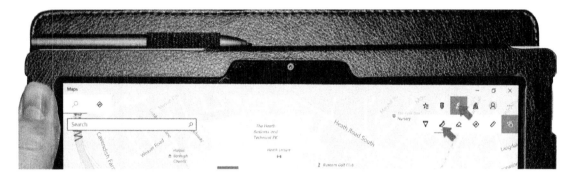

Now with your pen, draw a line between the two points on the map, you want to measure.

Remember this tool doesn't take into account roads or paths on your map, just the relative length of the line you have drawn in relation to the scale of the map.

Annotations

Using the Windows Ink features, you can draw directly onto the map with your finger or pen.

Tap the Windows Ink icon, top right. Then from the drop down, select the ball-point pen tool.

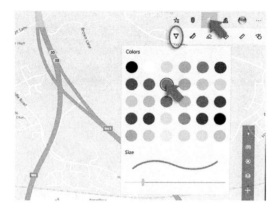

From the drop down menu, select a colour from the palette and adjust the size using the slider underneath. Drag the bar to the right to increase the thickness

Now with your pen, draw directly onto the map.

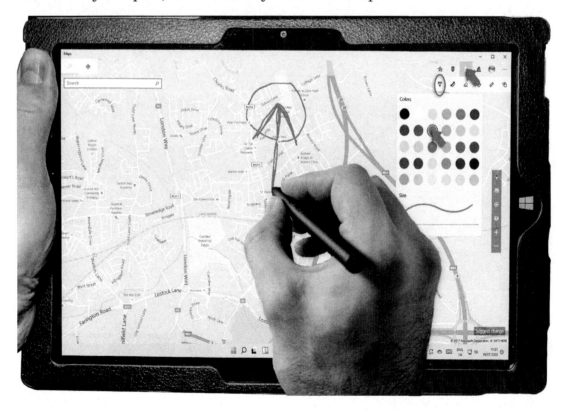

You can share these annotations with friends/colleagues or print them out.

Explore in 3D

This feature can come in handy if you want to explore landmarks or areas of interest. To start exploring 3D cities, click the 3 dots icon on the top right of the screen, then select '3D Cities'.

Down the left hand side you will see a number of famous landmarks cities, and areas you can explore in 3D. Not all cities will be in 3D yet but the ones that are will appear in this list.

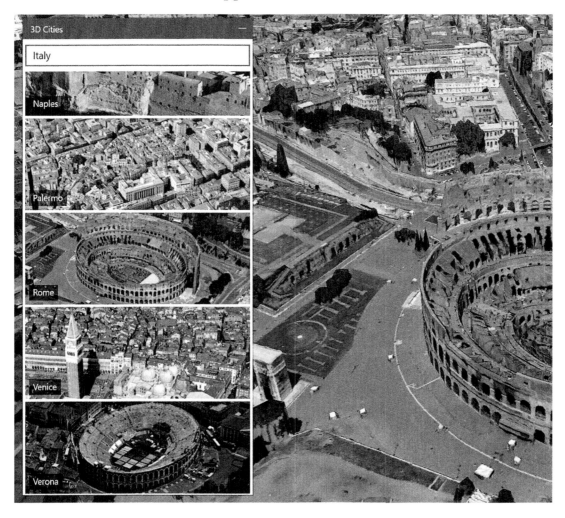

Perhaps you are going on holiday/vacation and you want to explore certain parts of the world you haven't been to - just remember the images you see aren't live and can be out of date.

Here you can see a fly-over view of a landmark. You can zoom in and out, rotate the map and move around as you explore.

Tap or click and drag the map around to explore, use the '+' and '-' icons on the right hand side to zoom in and out. Or use a pinch & spread gesture if you're using a touchscreen.

Try also searching for your favourite place by typing it into the search field.

Weather App

The weather app can give you a forecast for your current location or any location you choose to view. Click the weather icon on your start menu. If you don't see it, click 'all apps'.

When you first start weather app it will ask for your location, unless you have location services enabled, then it will automatically find your location. If not, type it into the field in the middle of the screen.

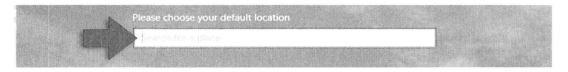

Once you have entered your location the weather app will show you a summary of the local weather conditions.

You can tap on each day to see more details, you may need to scroll down the page to see them.

Down the left hand side you have your navigation icons where you can see local weather, animated radar weather maps, historical weather and view your favourite locations list.

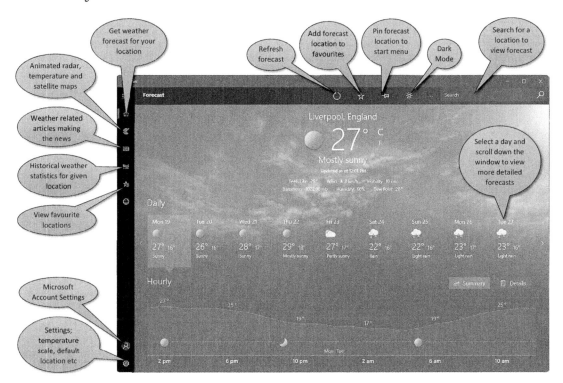

You can also find weather forecasts for other places. If for example you are going on holiday/vacation, you can enter the location's name into the search field and get a weather forecast.

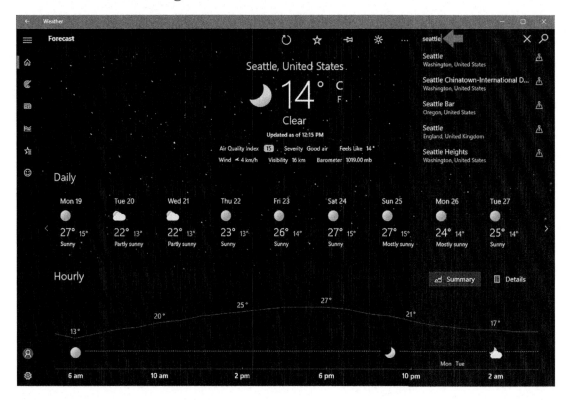

You can also add forecasts for locations to your favourites list so you don't have to keep searching for them.

To do this, just tap the 'add forecast location to favourites' icon along the top of your screen.

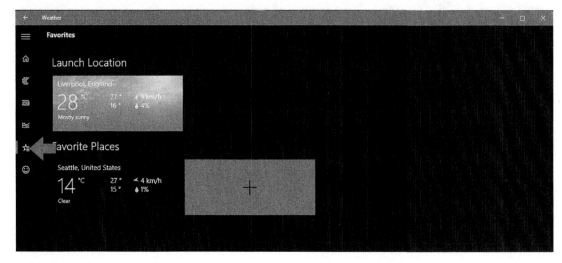

News App

The news app brings you local news headlines and stories from around the world. You can find the news app icon on your start menu.

Down the left hand side you have your navigation icons where you can browse different news sources such as news or sports channels.

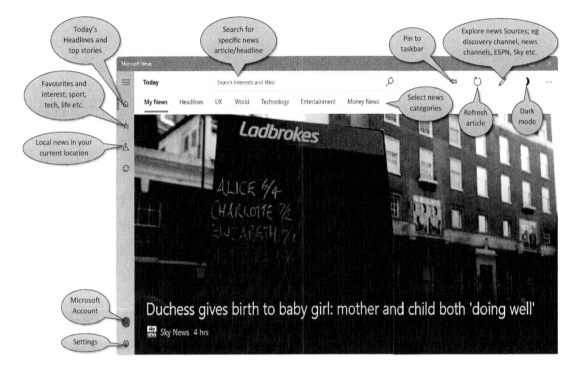

You can read the headlines, or local news, you can also watch video articles and reports.

You can find trending topics and news stories. Tap on the headlines to read the articles.

Clock App

With the clock app, you can set alarms to alert you, or set timers, world clocks and timers. You'll find the app on your start menu.

Timers

Along the left hand side, you can set a timer to time something.

Click 'add new timer' on the bottom right, then set the time duration. Give the timer a name. Click 'save'

To run the timer, click the play button on the timer screen.

248

Alarms

To set an alarm to sound at a particular time. For example, setting a time to get up in the morning. Select 'alarm' from the list on the left, then click 'add an alarm' on the bottom right.

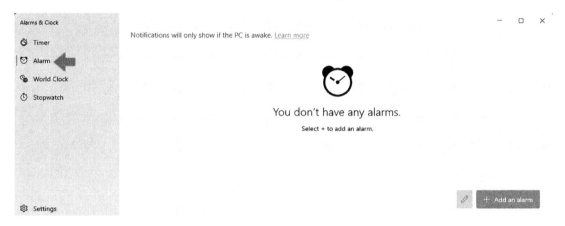

Enter the time you want the alarm to sound. Then click in the 'alarm name' field and enter a name.

Click in the 'repeats' field, select the days you want the alarm to sound, eg week days (monday - friday).

Choose a chime sound, and a how many minutes you want to 'snooze'. Click the 'save' on the bottom to save the alarm.

To set your alarm, click the switch on the top right of the alarm in the 'alarms' page.

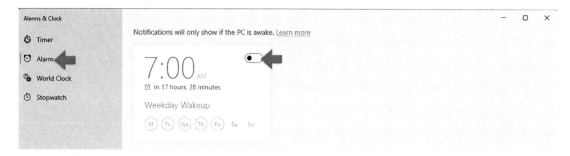

World Clock

This can be useful if you have colleagues or family in other countries, or just want to know what time it is there so when you skype them you aren't disturbing them in the middle of the night. To add a clock for another city in the world, click 'world clock', then click 'add new city' on the bottom right.

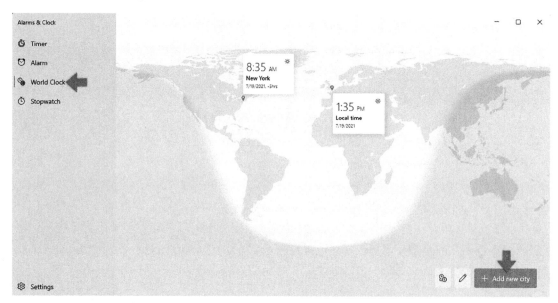

Enter the city/country name in the search field. Click the match in the search results.

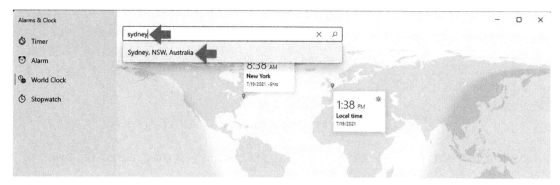

You'll see the city appear on the map

To remove a city, right click on the city, select 'delete'.

Stopwatch

Tap stopwatch to time something, for example, a race, lap times and so on.

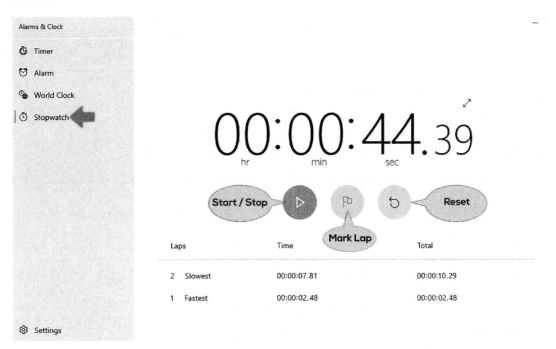

Hit the play button to start the clock. Hit the flag icon to mark a lap. Click the reset icon to reset the clock.

Voice Recorder

Voice recorder is your on-board dictation machine. You can make voice notes, record lectures, interviews and so on. To start recording just hit the microphone icon on the screen.

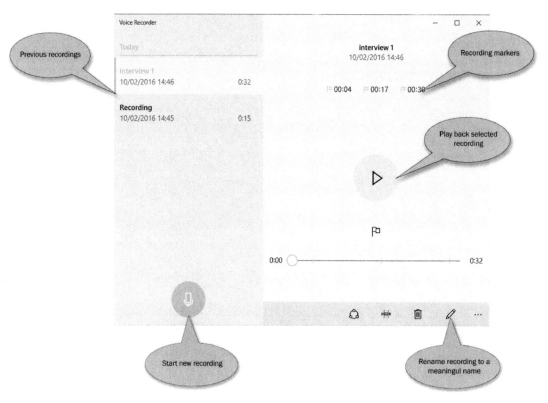

You can even add markers at important points during a recording.

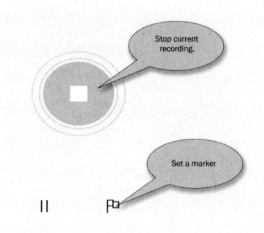

This way when you play back the recordings, you can go directly to the important points by clicking on these recording markers, illustrated in the top diagram.

Calculator App

The calculator app works like any calculator. You can choose the type of calculator you want; just a standard calculator for adding a few numbers together or a full scientific calculator for working out more complex equations.

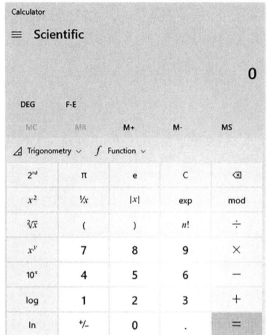

To change the calculator click the icon on the top left of your screen, and select 'scientific'.

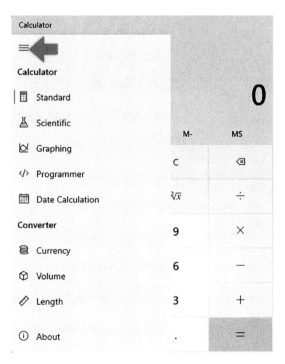

Unit Converter

You can also convert different units. You can convert between different currencies, weight, length, temperature, energy and so on. To open the converter, click the icon on the top left of your screen, shown below. Scroll down the list to the converters and select one, eg 'length'.

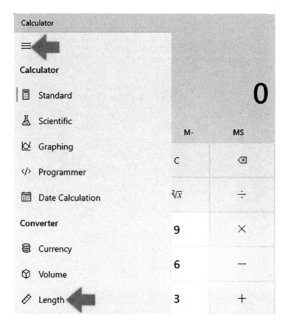

Useful if you want to convert metric measurements to ones you're familiar with. Eg: To convert from millimeters to inches, change the first one to millimeters and the second one to inches - indicated by the red arrows below.

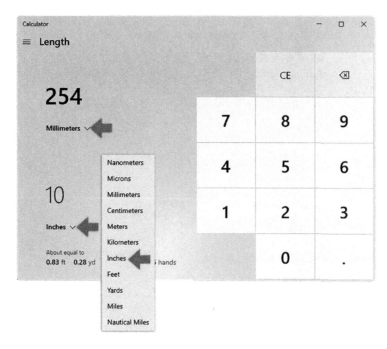

Click on the top number - it will turn to bold text. Now type in a value.

Currency Converter

Click the icon on the top left of your screen and select 'currency' from the drop down menu.

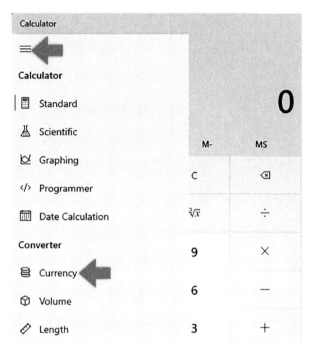

To change the currencies, click the currency name under the value, shown below. From the popup menu, select the currency you want.

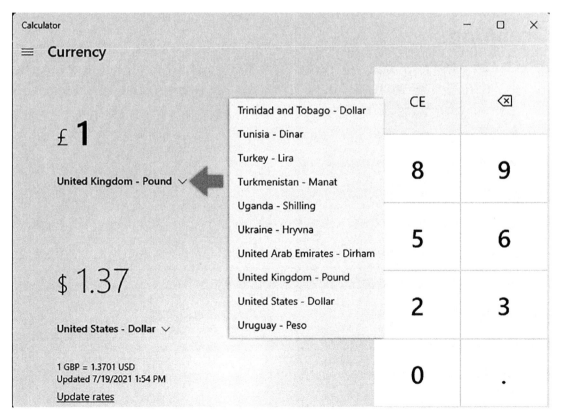

Click on the currency numbers and enter a value using the on screen keypad, as shown below. In the example below, I'm converting from British Pounds to US Dollars.

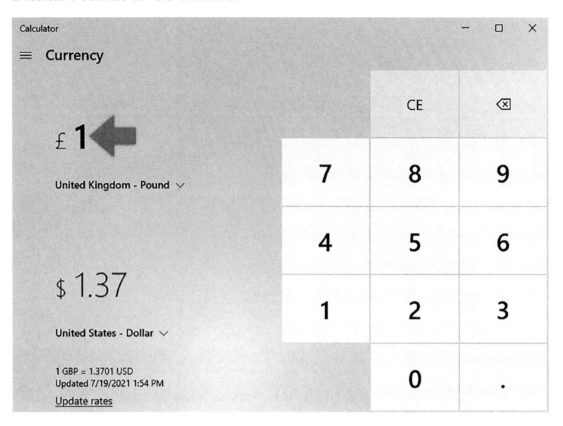

Graphing

With the graphing feature, you can plot various equations on the graph. To use the feature, click the icon on the top left of the screen and select 'graphing' from the menu.

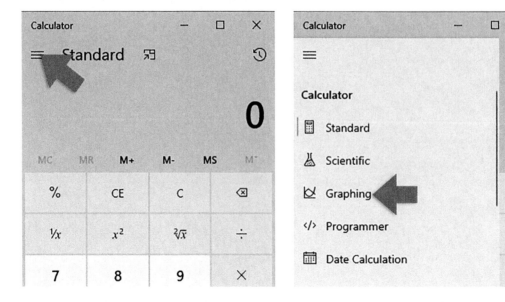

Make the window bigger, or go into full screen. As you do this, you'll see the graphing functions appear on the right.

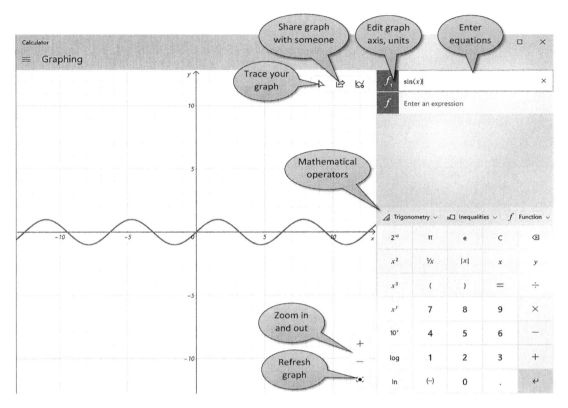

On the top right, enter your equations. Press enter to plot on the graph.

To Do App

The To Do App is a cloud based task management utility that allows you to set tasks and make to do lists. You'll find the icon on your start menu.

To Do

Once the app opens, you'll land on the main screen.

You'll see a menu down the left hand side. Here, you'll see options to view tasks for your day, tasks marked as important, planned tasks, tasks currently assigned to you, all tasks, and task lists.

To create a new list, click 'new list' on the left hand side. Give the list a name.

Click the share icon on the top right to invite other people in the team to join the task list. Select 'invite via email'. Enter the person's email address in the email app, then click send.

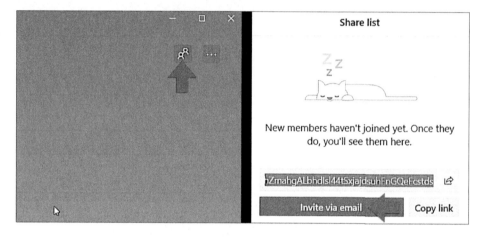

To add a task, type the activity into the 'add a task' field. Type @ then select the name to assign the task to someone.

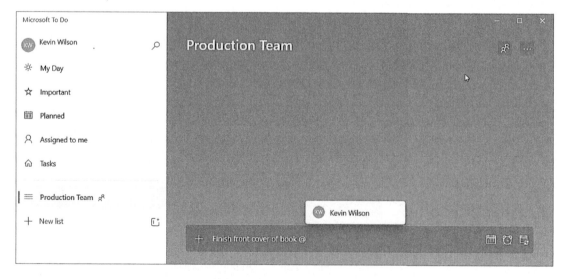

Click the calendar icon then select a due date. Click the alarm clock icon to add a reminder. Click the repeat icon to create a repeating task (daily, weekly, monthly etc).

PowerShell

The powershell is a command-line interface that allows you to execute commands by typing them in. Command line interfaces were the standard for computers in the early 1980s before the introduction of graphic user interfaces as seen in Windows or Mac.

To open the powershell, right click on the start button, select 'windows terminal' from the options. 'Windows Terminal' opens powershell as a standard user, 'Windows Terminal (admin)' opens the powershell as an administrator and is the option you choose if you want to run system utilities.

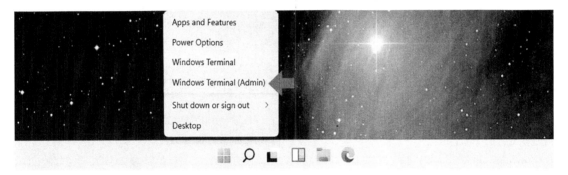

You'll see a window pop up, with a command prompt similar to the following.

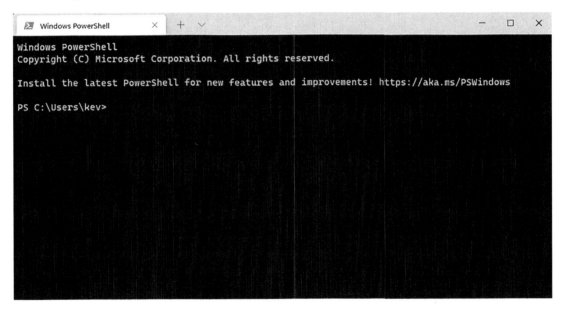

Here, the command prompt is made up of the letters 'PS' - meaning you're using PowerShell, followed by a drive letter, and the folder you're currently in with a greater than sign at the end.

```
PS C:\Users\kev>
```

This is where you type in your commands. For example, to list all files in the current directory (downloads), type `dir` then press enter.

```
PS C:\Users\kev> dir


    Directory: C:\Users\kev


Mode                 LastWriteTime         Length Name
----                 -------------         ------ ----
d-r---        05/07/2021     11:20                Contacts
d-----        05/07/2021     11:23                Documents
d-r---        11/07/2021     10:57                Downloads
d-r---        05/07/2021     11:20                Favorites
d-r---        05/07/2021     11:20                Links
d-r---        05/07/2021     11:20                Music
dar--l        19/07/2021     13:06                OneDrive
d-r---        05/07/2021     11:20                Saved Games
d-r---        05/07/2021     11:30                Searches
d-r---        05/07/2021     12:00                Videos


PS C:\Users\kev>
```

The powershell will return a list of files in the directory.

You can use sl or cd to move between folders. For example, from the folder listing we got in the previous step, if I wanted to move down to the OneDrive folder...

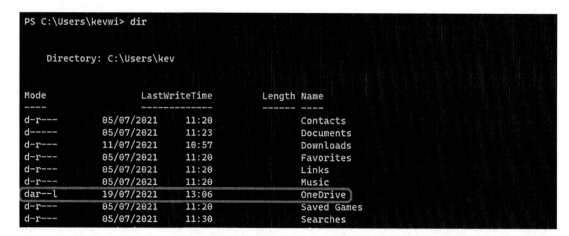

Use the sl or cd command followed by the folder name. So in this case to get to the OneDrive folder type `sl OneDrive`

```
PS C:\Users\kev> sl OneDrive
```

To create a new folder in the current folder use `mkdir` followed by the folder name.

```
PS C:\Users\kev\OneDrive> mkdir Work
```

To copy a file use the copy. To copy a file from the documents folder to my new work folder. First we need to go into the documents directory so we type `sl documents`.

```
PS C:\Users\kevwi\OneDrive> sl Documents
```

To copy a file use the `copy` command. The folder 'work' isn't in the documents folder so we need to tell the copy command where the folder is. Remember the folder tree. We need to go back a folder, then into the work folder

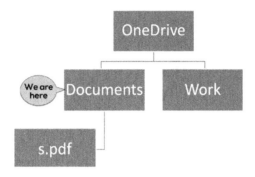

To do this use the double dot. So we type:

```
copy s.pdf ../work
```

The '..' means go back a folder. So the copy command will go back to OneDrive folder, then into the 'work' folder.

If we look in the 'work' folder, you'll see the file we copied.

You can open new powershell tabs, open the old command prompt, or an azure cloud shell. Click the arrow to the right of the tabs.

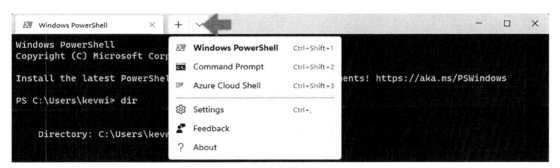

7

Internet and Comms

In this chapter, we'll take a look at the browser Microsoft Edge. We'll also take a brief look at Google Chrome as it is a good alternative to Microsoft Edge.

We'll also take a look at

- Mail App
- Calendar App
- Microsoft Teams
- Remote Desktop
- FTP
- SSH with PuTTY
- SSH from Windows Terminal
- Folder Sharing on a LAN
- Access a Shared Folder on a LAN
- Mobile Hotspot
- Your Phone App

We'll also take a look at how to get started using Microsoft Teams for making calls and collaboration.

Have a look at the video resources. Open your web browser and navigate to the following website

elluminetpress.com/win-comms

Microsoft Edge Browser

You'll find Edge on your start menu or taskbar. Click the icon to start the app.

When Edge starts, you'll see the main screen. Lets take a look at the different parts of Edge.

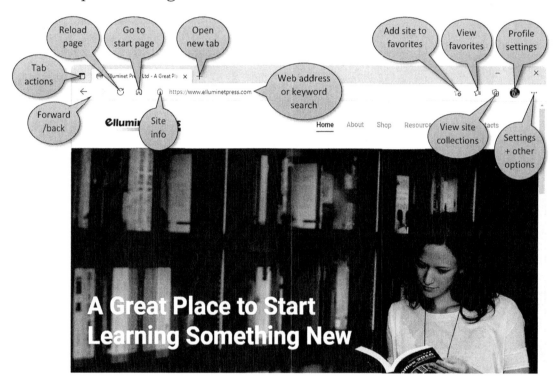

Along the top of the window you will find your address bar where you can enter search keywords, or website addresses (called URLs). You can add websites to favourites, make website collections, and annotate pages.

You can open websites in tabs instead of new windows. This helps to keep things organised when you have more than one website open at a time.

You can also access your Microsoft Account profile settings so you can sync your favourites, passwords etc across all your devices.

Set your Home Page

Setting a home page allows you to set a page to show when you first start Edge or when you click the home icon on the toolbar. Ideally you should set the home page to a website you use most often such as Google search.

To set your home page, click the 'three dots icon' on the top right of the screen, then from the menu select 'settings'.

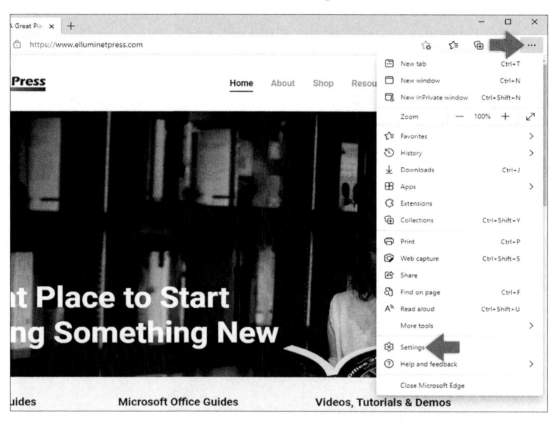

On the left hand panel click 'on startup'.

Select 'open a specific page or pages', then click 'add new page'

Enter the website address (URL) into the field (eg www.google.com).

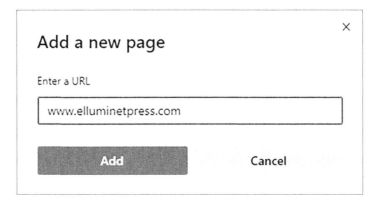

Click 'add'.

Favourites Bar

The favourites bar is where you can save websites. The bar shows up just below the address bar at the top of the screen. I'd advise you to only pin the websites you use most often to this bar, otherwise it can get a bit cluttered.

To enable the favourites bar, click the 'three dots icon' on the top right of the screen, and select 'favourites' from the menu.

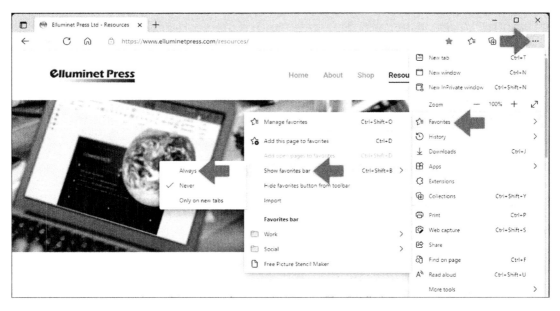

Go down to 'show the favourites bar'. From the slide-out menu select 'always' to turn it on.

Add Website to Favourites Bar

To add a website, first navigate to the page you want to add, then click the star icon on the top right of the address bar.

In the dialog box that appears, type in a meaningful name for the website.

Click on the drop down box next to 'folder'. Select 'favourites bar' to add the website to the favourites bar, or select the folder you want to save the website into.

Click 'done' at the bottom of the dialog box.

Organising the Favourites Bar

You can organise your favourites into folders. This helps keep sites of the same genre together. For example, you could have a folder called 'work' for all your business sites, a folder called 'social' for all your social media, or a folder for any interests you have eg gardening or photography. Create these on your favourites bar for easy access.

To create a folder, right click on the favourites bar, select 'add folder'.

Make sure you've selected 'favourites bar', then type in a meaningful name for the folder, eg: 'work'.

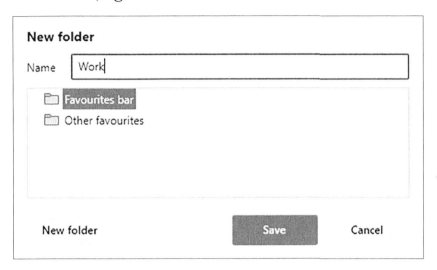

You'll see your folder appear on the favourites bar.

You can click & drag any favourite into the folder.

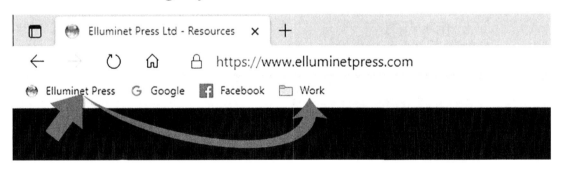

Click on the folder name to open it up

Revisit a Website on Favourites

To revisit your favourite sites just select them from the favourites bar.

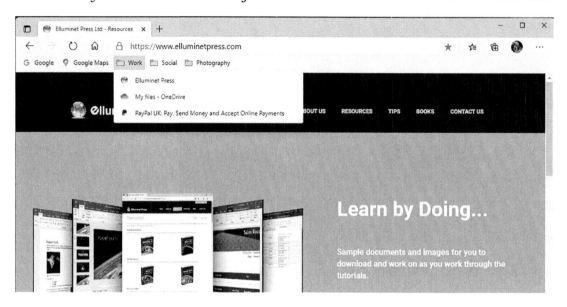

You'll also find your favourites using the 'favourites' icon on the top right of the screen.

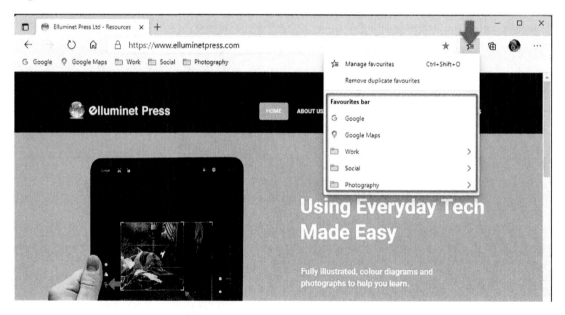

Managing Favourites

Click the 'favourites' icon on the top right of the screen. Select 'manage favourites'.

From here, you can drag sites into folders, change the order, create new folders, as well as delete favourited sites.

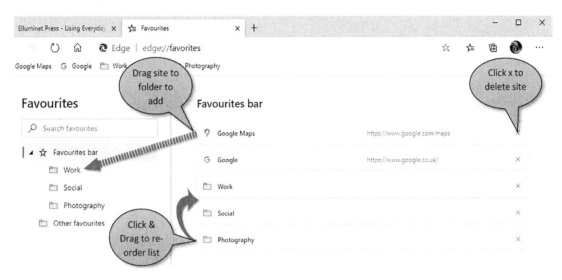

Import Favourites

You can import your favourites from other web browsers. To do this click the 'favourites' icon on the top right of the screen. Select 'manage favourites'.

On the favourites bar page, click the three dots icon on the top right, select 'import favourites' from the drop down menu.

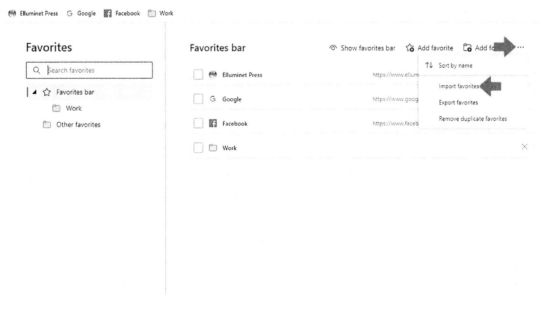

Chapter 7: Internet and Communication

Use the 'import from' field to select which browser to import your data from, eg Chrome. *(If you want to import from a file see bottom of page).*

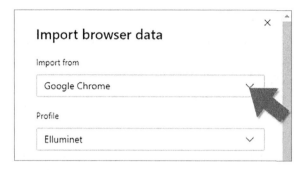

Select which data you want to import (favourites, passwords, etc).

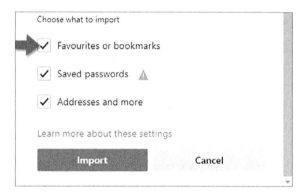

Click 'import'.

If you want to import from a file, click the 'import from' field then select 'favourites or bookmarks HTML file'.

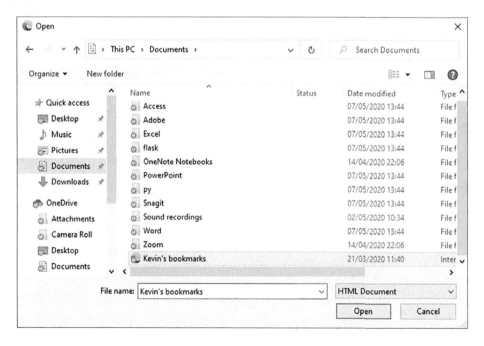

Browse to and select the HTML bookmarks file, then click ok.

Export Favourites

You can also export all your favourited websites to a file if you want to later import them on another machine or give them to someone else. To do this, click the 'favourites' icon on the top right of the screen. Select 'manage favourites'.

On the favourites bar page, click the three dots icon on the top right, select 'export favourites'.

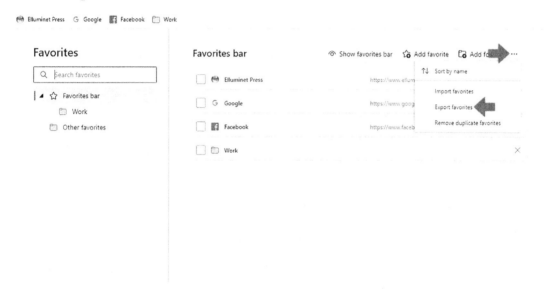

Browse to a folder to save the file, then click 'save.

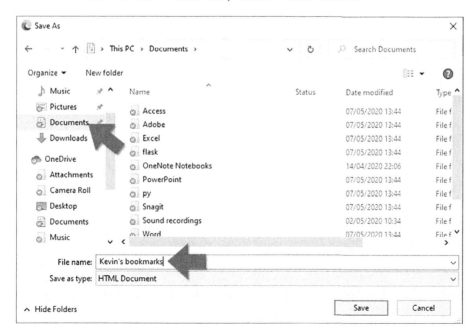

Collections

Collections allow you to organize content you browse on the web. You can gather text, images from the web and then place them inside a note page and share organized sets and export them to Office apps.

To create a collection, click the collections icon on the top right of the toolbar. Then click 'start new collection'.

Enter a meaningful name.

Highlight and drag content from webpages into the collection. You can drag paragraphs, images and videos.

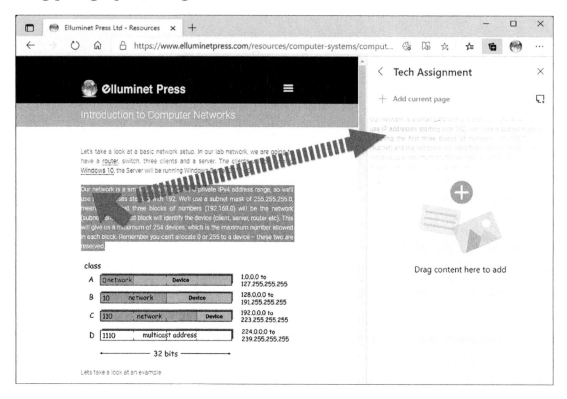

You can also add a whole page. To do this, navigate to the page you want to add, then in the collections panel, click 'add current page'.

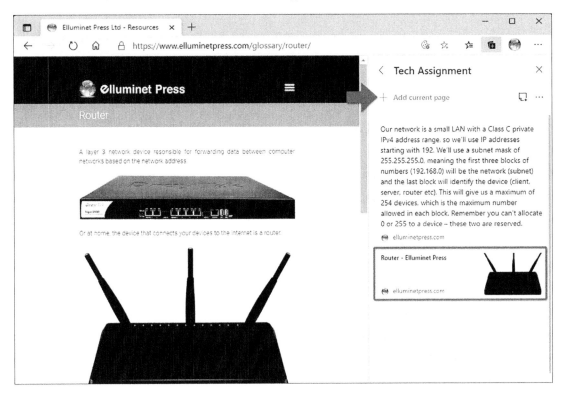

To add notes to your collection, click the notes icon on the top right of the collections panel.

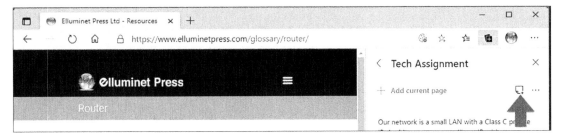

Type your note. You can format your note text as well as add bullet points and lists.

You can send your collections to Word or Excel. This will open your collection in a Word or Excel document using the online versions of these apps. Sign in with your Microsoft Account email address and password if prompted.

To share your collection, click the three dots icon on the top right of the collections panel. From the drop down menu, select the app you want to send your collection to. Eg 'word'.

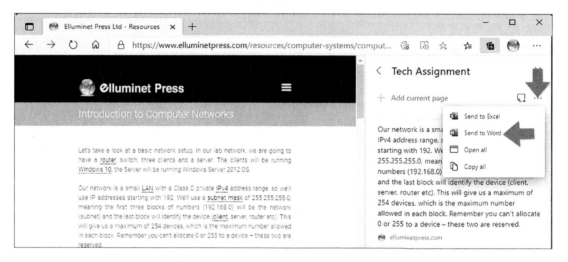

You'll see the collection open in the app within Edge.

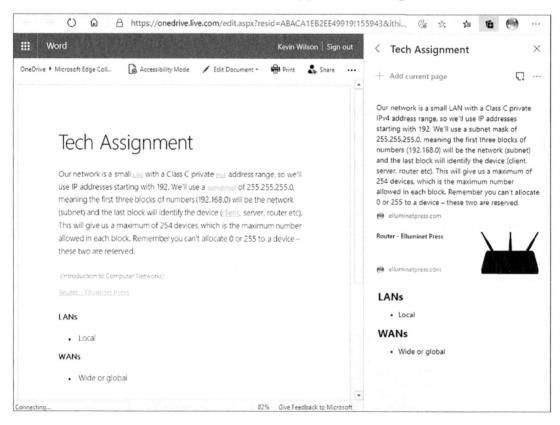

From here you can save the document, edit and share it.

Finding Files you've Downloaded

Whenever you download files from a website, you'll find the files in your downloads folder.

To open your downloads folder, click the 'three dots icon' on the top right of the screen, and select 'downloads'

Here, you'll see a history list of all the files you've downloaded. Down the left hand side, you can search for downloads, or you can use the categories in the list to find a specific type of tile such as an app, image or video.

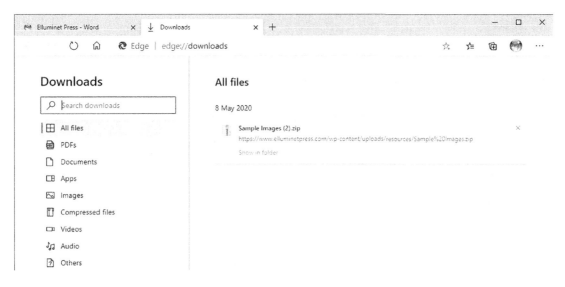

To open or run any of these downloads, double click on the link in the list.

To open your downloads folder in File Explorer, click 'show in folder'. From File Explorer, you can double click on the file to open it or run it.

Browsing History

Edge keeps a list of every website you visit. To find your browsing history, click the three dots icon on the top right. Select 'history'.

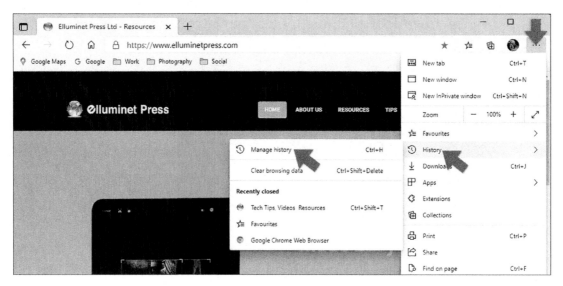

You'll see a list of the sites you've visited. Click on a site to revisit. To clear the history click 'clear browsing history on bottom left.

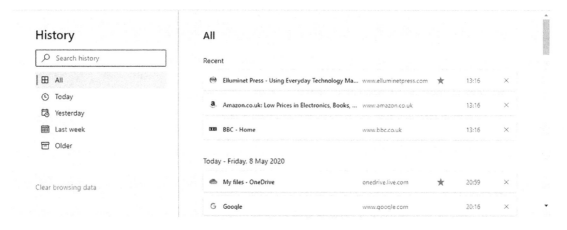

You can also see a list of sites you've visited while you've been browsing if you click and hold your mouse pointer on the back icon.

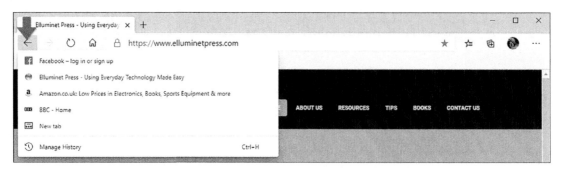

Click any of the links to return to the website.

Reading Mode

Some websites, especially those with a lot of text can be difficult to print or read on screen. You can use the immersive reader feature. To use this feature, click the reader icon to the right of the address bar. Or press F9.

From here, you can read the main text without adverts or any other distracting parts of a website.

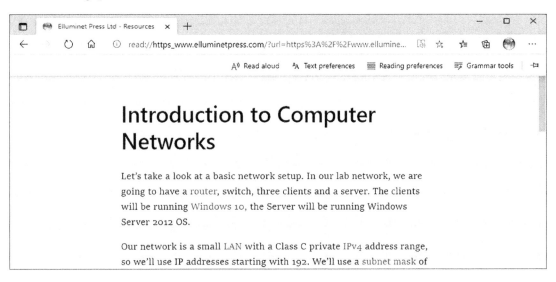

You can get Edge to read the document aloud - click 'read aloud'. You can change the size of the text or the background colour - click 'text preferences'. You can enable 'line focus' that allows you to concentrate on each line as you read - click 'reading preferences'. You can also highlight syllables, verbs, nouns and adjectives in the text using the grammar tools. Give it a try.

To exit reader mode, click the reader icon again or press F9

Page Translator

You can translate any page into another language. To do this, right click your mouse on the web page, then select 'translate to...'

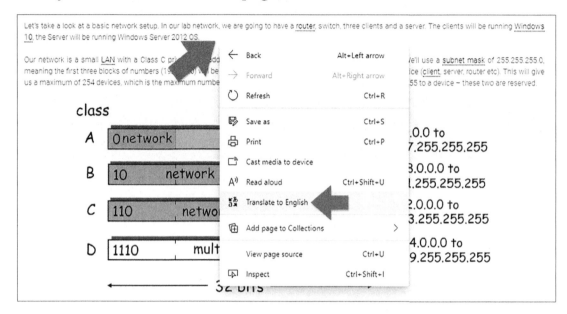

In the drop down box, select the language you want to translate the page into. Lets try Portuguese... Click 'translate', or 'try again'.

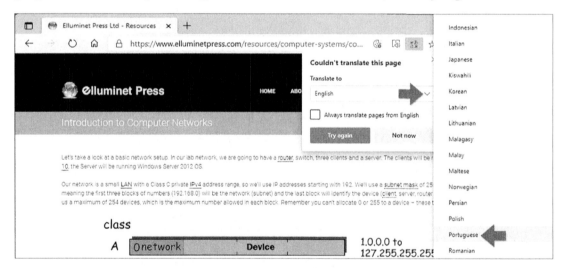

Here you can see Edge has attempted a translation. Translations aren't 100% accurate but will give you the general idea.

Print a Page

To print a web page, click the three dots icon on the top right of the screen, then select 'print' from the drop down menu.

From the panel on the left hand side, select the printer. Under 'copies', enter number of copies if needed.

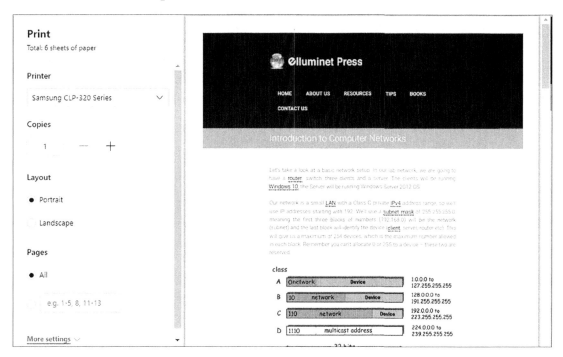

Under 'layout', select portrait or landscape. Under 'pages', enter the page numbers you want to print. You'll see the page numbers in the print preview on the right if you scroll down the page.

Click 'more settings' on the bottom left. From here you can print background graphics, add or remove headers and footers, or print more than one page to a sheet of paper, and change the paper size.

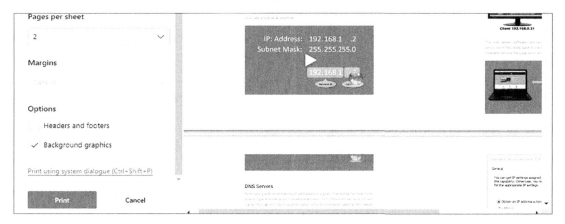

Share a Page

You can share a web page with anyone on your contact list using email, skype, teams, messages and so on.

To share a page, click the three dots icon on the top right of the screen. From the drop down menu, select 'share'.

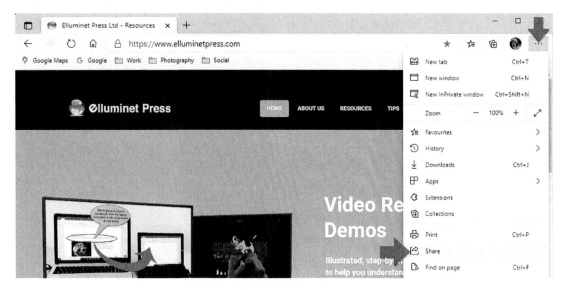

From the dialog box, select the person you want to share the page with, or select an app to share the page. Eg, email. Click 'find more people' or 'find more apps', if you can't see the person or app.

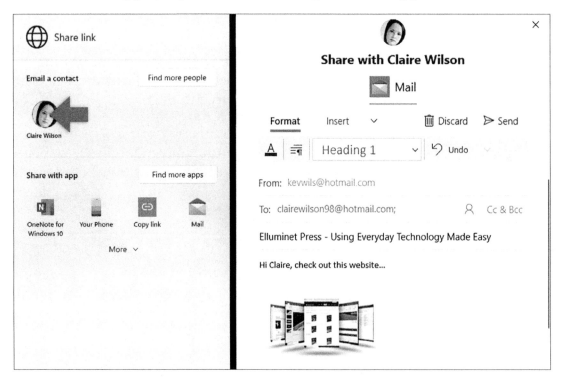

Type in a message, click 'send'.

Pin Website to TaskBar

A useful feature of Microsoft Edge is the ability to pin a website shortcut onto your taskbar. You should only really use this feature for websites you visit very often, as you can quite easily fill up your taskbar with clutter. Perhaps if you use a web based email or facebook - create a taskbar short cut.

To do this, open the website you want to pin in Microsoft Edge. Click the three dots icon on the top right, go down to 'more tools', select 'pin to taskbar' from the slide out menu.

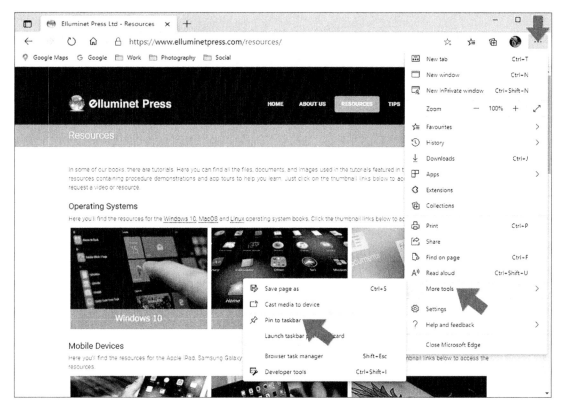

Give the site a name, then click 'pin'.

You'll see the website link appear on your task bar. The icon depends on the website's own icon.

Tabbed Browsing

Tabbed browsing allows you to have multiple websites open at the same time. Websites open up as tabs along the top of the browser window, this is known as horizontal tabbing. Here below, you can see there are three tabs open.

This makes it easier to switch between different websites you have open.

New Tabs

To open a new tab, click the 'plus' icon to the right of the browser tab.

A new tab will open up. You can navigate to any website from here. Use the address field at the top of the screen to do a web search or type in a website address.

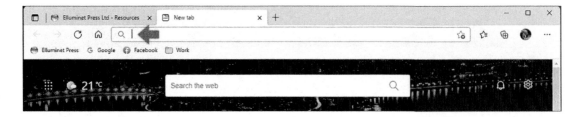

Switching Tabs

You can switch between tabs using the tab bar at the top of the screen. Just click on the tab you want to return to. You can also press Ctrl Tab on your keyboard.

Duplicate Tab

To duplicate a tab means to open a tab with the same website. To do this, right click on the tab, select 'duplicate tab' from the popup menu.

Pin Tab

You can pin tabs to your tab bar. This is useful for websites you visit frequently. Right click on the tab you want to pin. Select 'pin tab' from the popup menu.

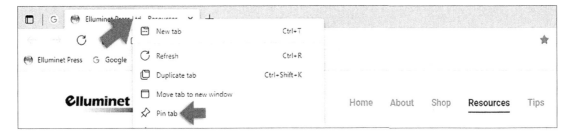

Pinned tabs appear on the top left.

Vertical Tabs

Vertical tabs are similar to the horizontal tabs we looked at in the previous section. The difference is, the tabbed websites are listed down the left hand side of the screen. To turn on vertical tabs, click the icon on the top left, then select

You'll see a sidebar open up on the left. Here, you can switch to other tabs in a similar fashion as before.

To go back to horizontal tabs, click the icon on the top left of the vertical tabs sidebar, select 'turn off vertical tabs'.

Edge Extensions

Extensions add functionality to the Edge Browser. To add extensions to Edge, click the three dots icon on the top right of your screen and select 'extensions'.

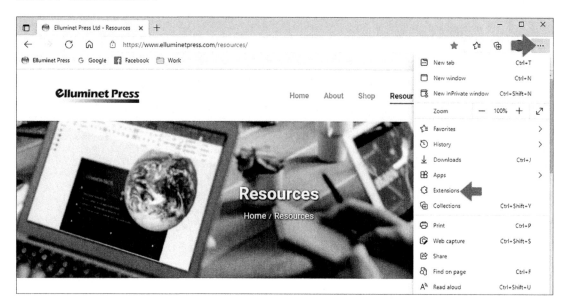

You'll see a list of any extensions that have been installed on the right. To install a new extension, click 'get extensions for Edge'.

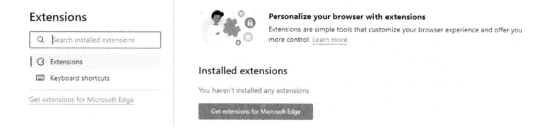

The Microsoft Store will open up showing the newest extensions available. In this example, I'm going to add the uBlock extension. So click 'uBlock Origin'.

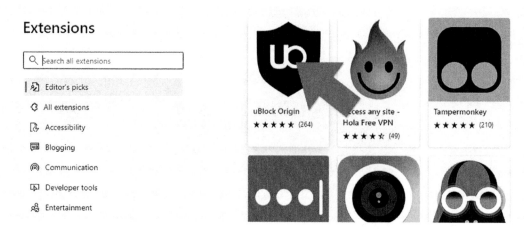

284

From the extension details page, click 'get'.

Click 'add extension' on the confirmation dialog box.

You can access your extensions anytime, just click the three dots icon on the top right of your screen and select 'extensions' from the menu.

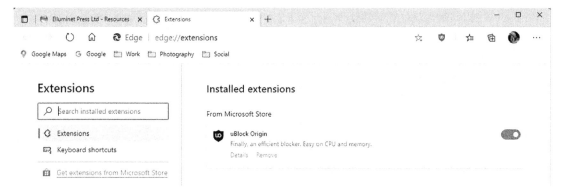

Any installed extensions will appear on the right. Click the icon to open the extensions settings.

You'll also see an icon appear on the toolbar.

Install Chrome Extensions in Edge

With the new Edge browser, you can install chrome extensions from the chrome web store. To do this, you first need to enable extensions from other stores.

Click the three dots icon on the top right, select 'extensions' from the drop down menu.

Enable 'allow extensions from other stores', on the bottom left.

Type `chrome.google.com/webstore` into the search bar in Edge.

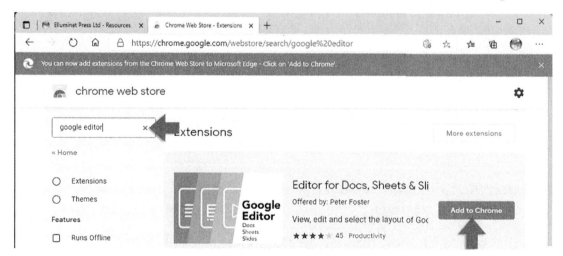

Use the search bar on the left hand side in the chrome web store to search for apps.

Click 'add to chrome' to install any app.

Google Chrome

Google Chrome is a fast and streamlined browser that is a good alternative to Microsoft Edge. To use Google Chrome in Windows 11, you'll first need to download it.

You can download Google Chrome from

        www.google.com/chrome

Hit the 'download chrome' button. Click 'accept and install'. Go to your downloads folder and double click 'chromesetup.exe'

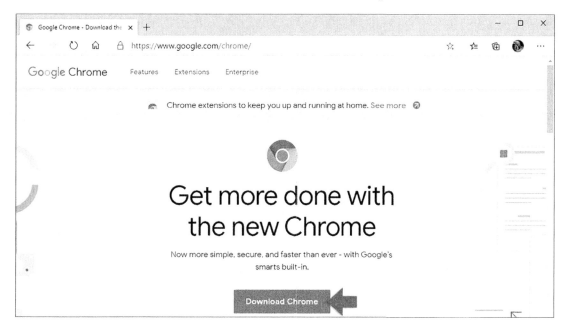

Follow the on screen instructions to install the browser. You'll find Chrome on your start menu and on your desktop.

Once Chrome has loaded, click the profile icon on the top right and enter your Google account username and password.

This is the same account that you use for Gmail if you have one.

You can use Chrome without a Google account, but you won't get any of the personalised features or be able to add apps to Chrome from the Chrome Store.

You can use Google Chrome in a similar way to Edge. This is Chrome's Start screen. You can type in your Google Search or type a URL if you know it into the search bar. Along the bottom you'll also see your most visited websites.

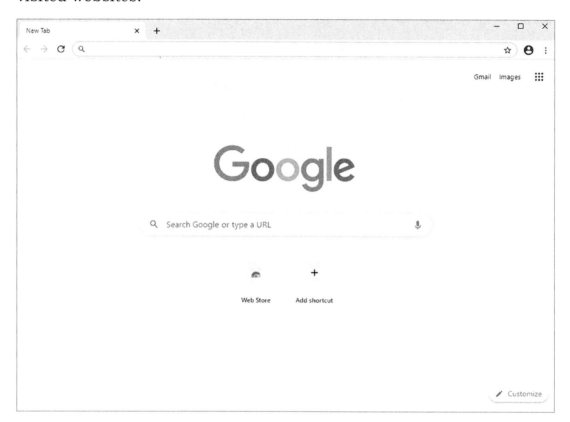

Let's take a closer look at Chrome's interface.

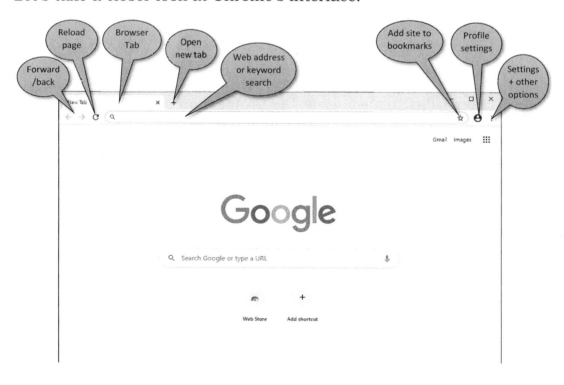

Bookmarks Bar

The bookmarks bar is where you can save websites. The bar shows up just below the address bar at the top of the screen. I'd advise you to only pin the websites you use most often to this bar, otherwise it can get a bit cluttered.

To enable the bookmarks bar, click the 'three dots icon' on the top right of the screen, and select 'bookmarks' from the menu.

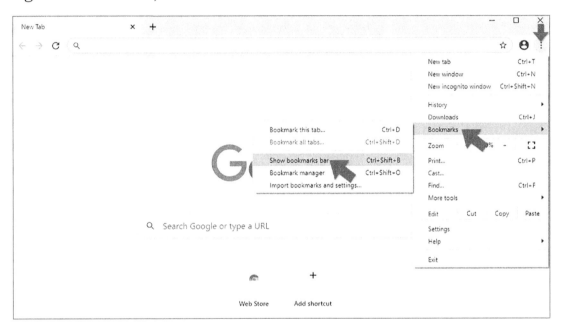

Click 'show bookmarks bar' to enable it.

Add Website to Bookmarks Bar

To add a website, first navigate to the page you want to add, then click the star icon on the top right of the address bar.

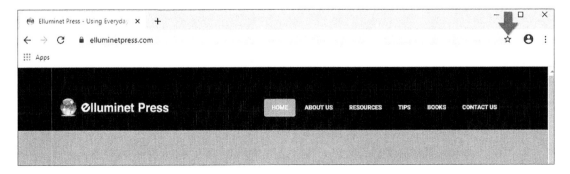

In the dialog box that appears, type in a meaningful name for the website.

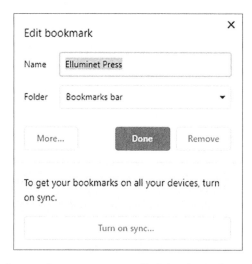

Click on the drop down box next to 'folder'. Select 'bookmarks bar' to add the website to the bookmarks bar, or select the folder you want to save the website into.

Click 'done' at the bottom of the dialog box.

Organising the Bookmarks Bar

You can organise your bookmarks into folders. This helps keep sites of the same genre together. For example, you could have a folder called 'work' for all your business sites, a folder called 'social' for all your social media, or a folder for any interests you have eg gardening or photography. Create these on your bookmarks bar for easy access.

To create a folder, right click on the bookmarks bar, select 'add folder'.

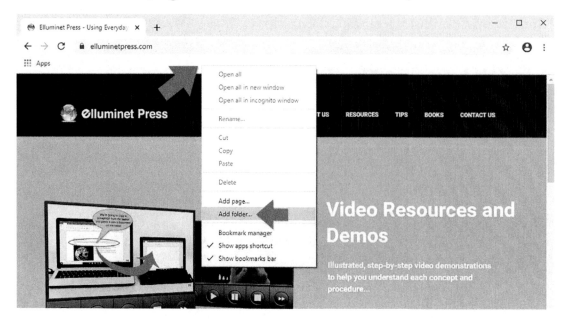

Type in a meaningful name for the folder, eg: 'work'.

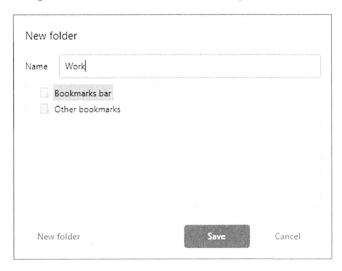

You'll see your folder appear on the bookmarks bar.

You can click & drag any bookmarks into the folder.

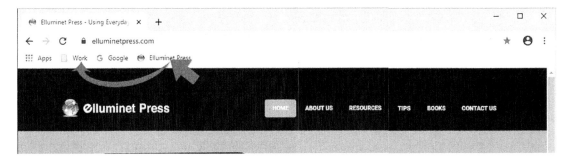

Click on the folder name to open it up

Chapter 7: Internet and Communication

Browsing History

Chrome keeps a list of every website you visit. To find your browsing history, click the three dots icon on the top right. Select 'history', then click 'history' on the slide out menu.

You'll see a list of the sites you've visited. Click on a site to revisit.

You can also see a list of sites you've visited while you've been browsing if you click and hold your mouse pointer on the back icon.

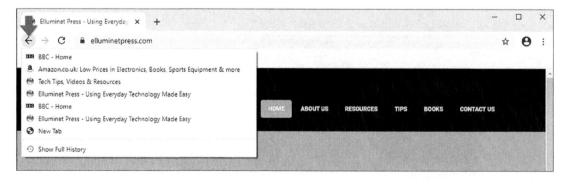

Click any of the links to return to the website.

Finding Files you've Downloaded

Whenever you download files from a website, you'll find the files in your downloads folder.

To open your downloads folder, click the 'three dots icon' on the top right of the screen, and select 'downloads'

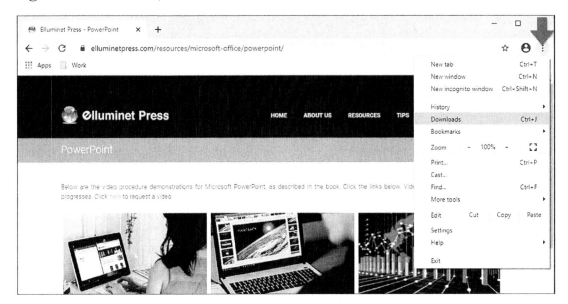

Here, you'll see a history list of all the files you've downloaded. To open or run any of these downloads, double click on the link in the list.

To open your downloads folder in File Explorer, click 'show in folder'. From File Explorer, you can double click on the file to open it or run it.

To delete the download from your list, click the x on the right hand side of the download item in the list.

Printing Pages

To print a web page, click the three dots icon on the top right of the screen, then select 'print' from the drop down menu.

From the panel on the right hand side, select the printer. Under 'copies', enter number of copies if needed.

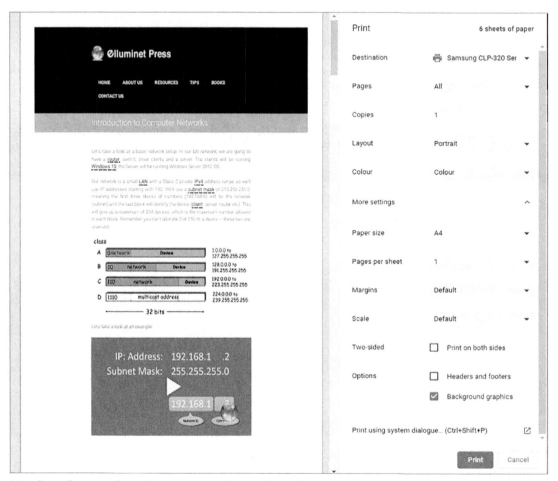

Under 'layout', select portrait or landscape. Under 'pages', enter the page numbers you want to print. You'll see the page numbers in the print preview on the left if you scroll down the page.

Click 'more settings' on the bottom left. From here you can print background graphics, add or remove headers and footers, or print more than one page to a sheet of paper, and change the paper size.

Extending Chrome

Extensions are small apps that add functionality to the chrome browser. To see what extensions are installed on your chrome browser, click the three dots icon on the top right. Select 'more tools', then click 'extensions' from the slide out menu.

You'll see a list of any extensions that are installed. To add new extensions, click the hamburger icon on the top right.

Select 'open chrome web store' on the bottom left.

In the web store, you can search for an app.

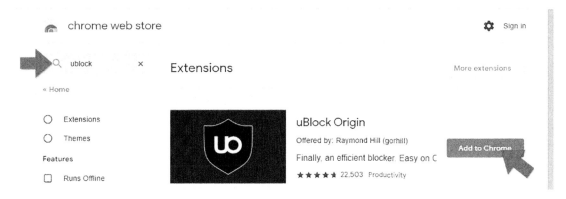

Click 'add to chrome' to install the extension.

295

Mail App

With the mail app you can check your Microsoft Account email, as well as other email accounts from Yahoo or Google you might have.

You'll find the mail app on your start menu.

If this is the first time you are using this app, you may be asked to add your email account.

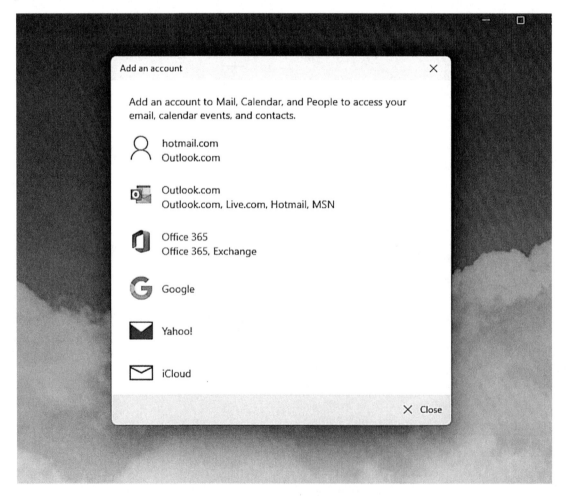

If you are using your Microsoft Account, select your Microsoft Account email address at the top.

If you use Gmail, click 'Google'. If you use Yahoo, click 'yahoo'. If you use iCloud click 'icloud'.

Reading Mail

When you open mail app it will check for email, any new messages will appear in your inbox.

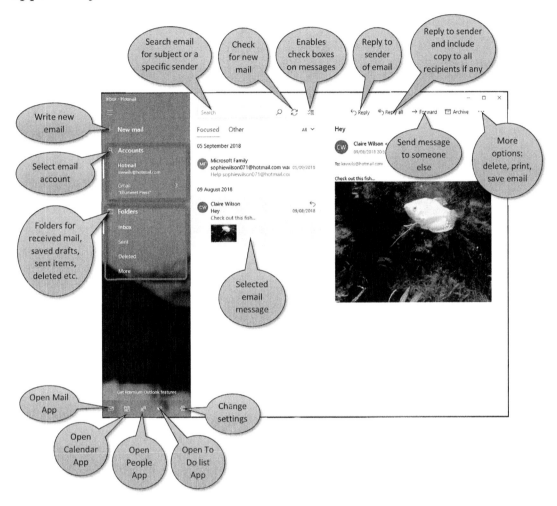

Click on the message in your inbox. The contents will be displayed in the reading pane on the right hand side.

Writing a New Message

To start a new message, click 'new mail' on the top left hand side of the main screen.

First you need to enter the person's email address in the 'To' field. Click the people icon on the far right to open up your contacts. Scroll down and select the person you want to send the email to.

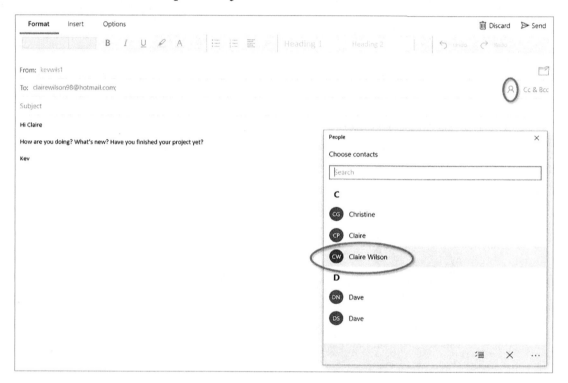

Add a subject, then type your email in the body section. In the body section, you can use the normal text formatting tools such as bold, change the font colour or size and so on, using the format tool bar as you can see below.

For example, select the text, click bold icon. Change text size, select text, click font size. Change font, select text, click on font name in toolbar.

Hit 'send' on the top right to send your email message.

Reply to a Message

To reply to the message, click the reply icon at the top of the screen.

You'll see a screen that looks a bit like a word processor. Here you can type in your message. Your message will appear at the top. The original message will be appended to the end of the email.

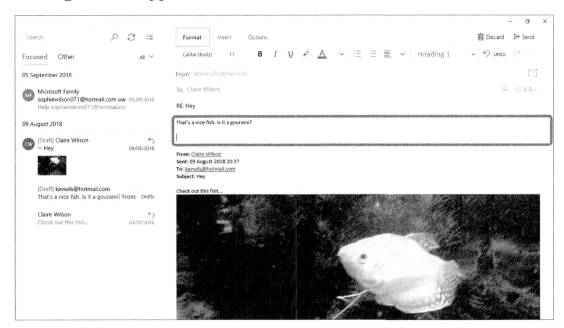

You can use the basic formatting tools. You can make text bold - select the text and click the 'B' icon on the toolbar. Or you can make text into a list. Select the text and click the list icon, then select a number style.

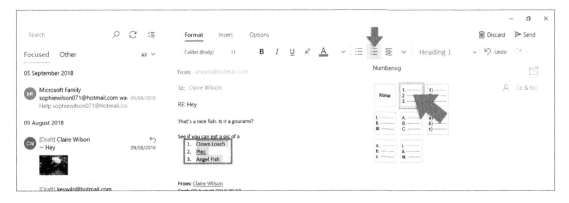

Adding Attachments

To attach a file, click 'insert' then select 'files'. Select the file you want to attach. Use this option to attach files such as documents, videos, music or photos.

Select your file from the dialog box. Hold down the control key to select multiple files. Click 'open' when you're done.

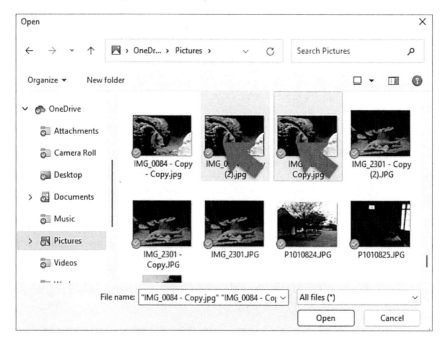

These attachments will be added to the end of the email.

Once you are done, click 'send' on the top right.

Inserting Images

Inserting images is a little different from adding an attachment. When you insert an image, you insert it into the body of the email message so it appears inline with the text.

In your email message, click 'insert'. From the options, select 'pictures'.

Select your picture from the dialog box. Hold down the control key if you're selecting more than one picture. Click 'insert'.

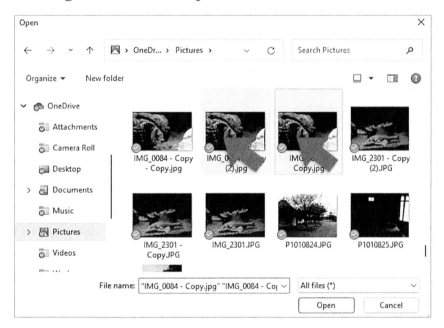

Click the 'send' icon on the top right when you're done.

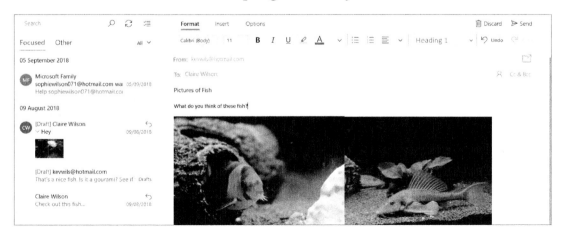

Images are inserted in the body of the email message.

Adding Other Email Accounts

If you have another email account such as Gmail or Yahoo you can add these too.

To do this click the settings icon on the bottom left of the screen.

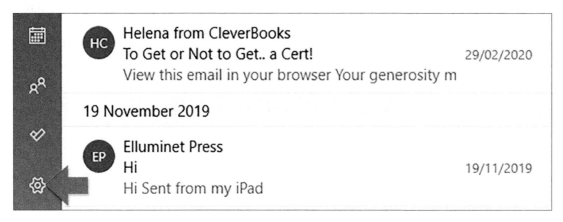

Click 'manage accounts' on the side panel on the right hand side of the screen.

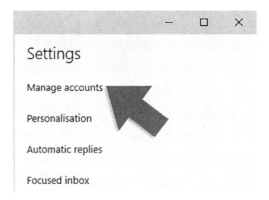

Click 'add account'.

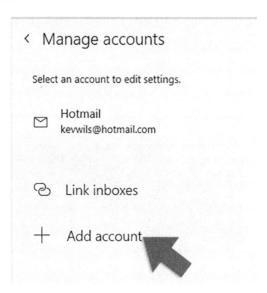

Select the account provider. Eg if you are adding a GMail or Google account, click 'Google', if it's Yahoo, click 'Yahoo', or Apple, click 'iCloud'.... If your provider isn't in the list above click 'other account'.

In this example, I want to add my Gmail account. So I'd select Google.

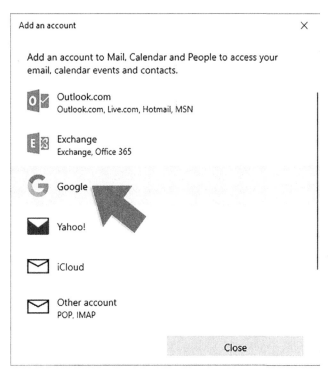

In the 'connecting to a service' dialog box, type in your email address for the email account you're adding. Click 'next'.

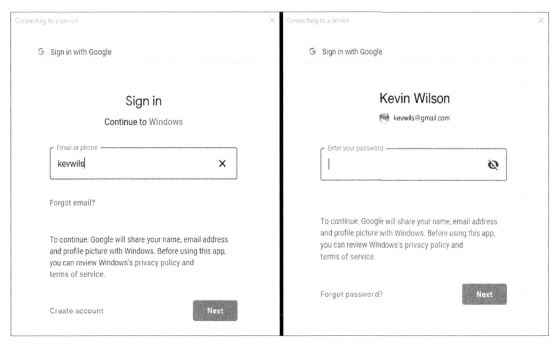

Enter your password on the next screen, click 'next'.

In the next window, scroll down and select 'allow' to give Windows permission to access your account. Then click 'done'.

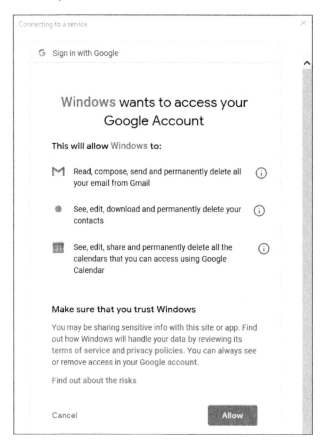

All your email accounts will appear under the accounts section on the left hand side of the screen. Click the hamburger icon on the top left of the screen to reveal the full sidebar.

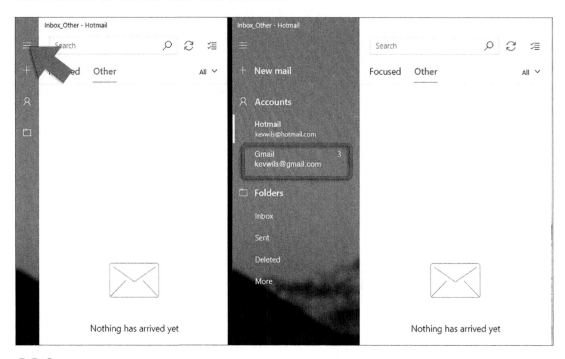

Contacts List (People App)

The People App is your contacts list or address book and is used to access your contacts in Microsoft Teams, Chat, Mail App, and Calendar. You can find the People App on the bottom left of the Mail App.

When the People App opens up, you'll see a list of your contacts on the left hand side. Any contact you click on, their contact details will appear in the right hand pane.

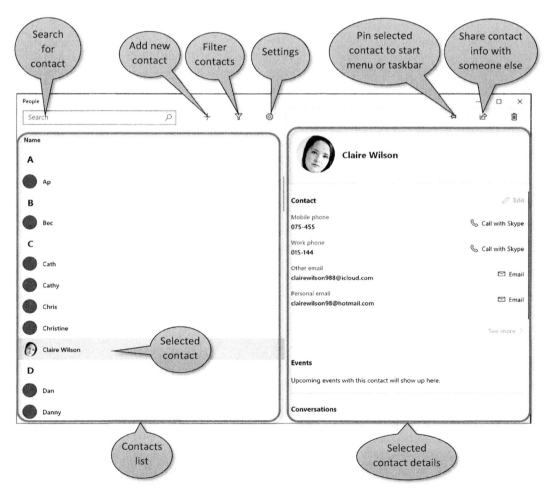

Edit Contact

You can click on any of the contacts in your list to view or edit their contact information.

Here I've clicked on Claire in the contacts list. In the right hand pane, you'll see her contact details, plus upcoming calendar events she's been invited to or involved in and recent messages. Click 'see more' to see all of these.

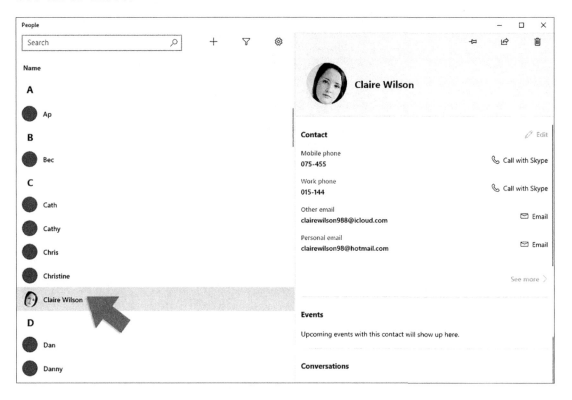

To edit her contact details, click 'edit'. In the new window you can edit her name, add phone, email addresses and physical address.

Click the plus sign next to the one you want to add. For example 'address'.

Select whether the address is 'home' or 'work'.

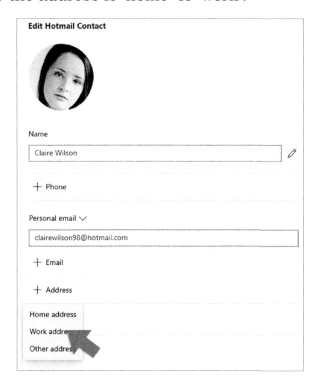

Enter the details into the fields that appear.

Click 'save' when you're done.

Calendar App

The calendar app is useful for keeping appointments, events and so on. You can find it on your start menu.

If this is the first time you are using this app, you may be asked to add your email account. Click 'add account'. Add your email address.

If you use another email account click 'add account' then enter your username/email and password details given to you by the account provider.

Once you have done that, you will see your main screen.

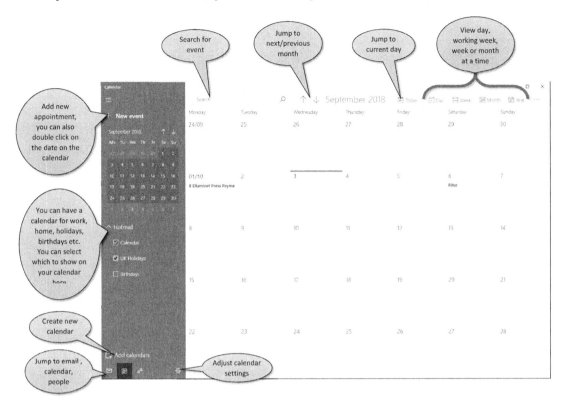

Add an Event

You can add events and appointments by clicking on the 'new event' button or click on the date in the calendar.

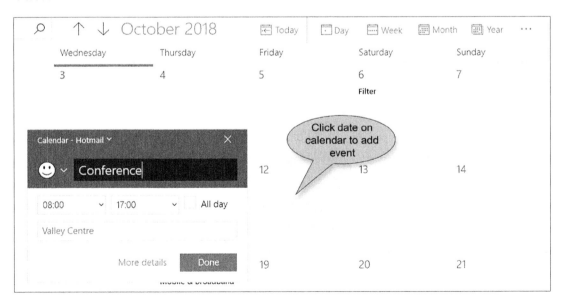

Type the location where you are meeting. Un-tick 'all day' and enter start and estimated finishing times. Unless it's an all day event.

Hit 'more details'.

You can add notes and any details about the event in the large text box at the bottom of the screen.

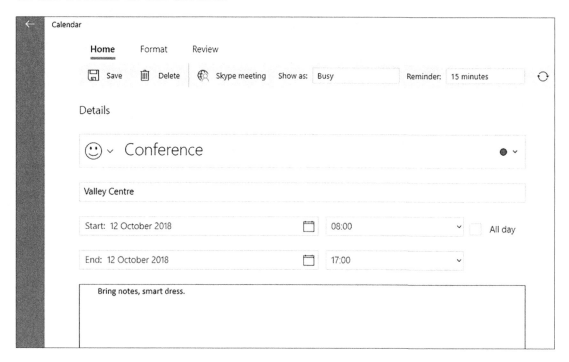

You can add a reminder too, by changing the reminder field. You can set it from none, 5 mins before, 15 mins before, a day before and so on. Reminders will pop up in your action centre as they occur.

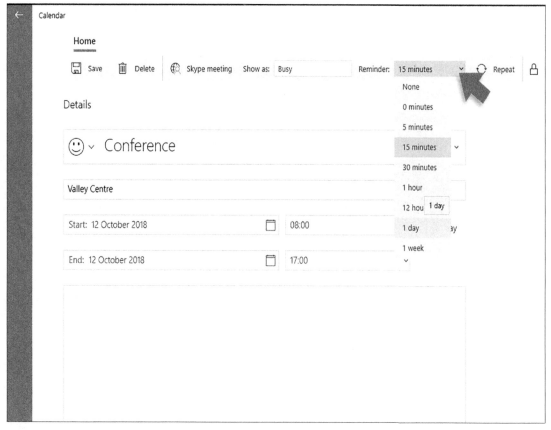

If the event is recurring, eg happens once a week or once a month, you can set this by clicking 'repeat'.

Under the 'repeat' section, you can set the event to occur on a daily, weekly, monthly and yearly basis. This saves you having to enter it for every occurrence.

Next, change any specifics such as what day a week/month the event occurs. In this example, the event occurs every week on a Tuesday.

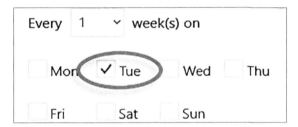

If the event ran every two weeks on Tuesday, we would change the top line to every 2 weeks.

In the next bit, you can set the date your recurring event ends. Eg if it is a course it might be weekly for 6 months or a year.

Hit 'save and close' on the top left of the screen when you're done.

Chat

Using the Chat App you can video chat with friends, family, or colleagues, as well as send messages. You'll find the chat icon on your taskbar.

Once you start the app, a panel will open up. From here, you can start a video chat/meeting (click meet), or you can start a text chat where you can type messages, and share files with your group (click chat).

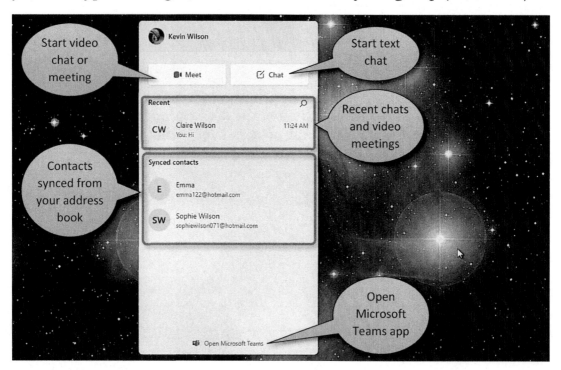

Underneath, you'll see any recent chats or meetings you have had, as well as any contacts that have synced with your address book (or people app).

Start a Chat

You can have 1:1 or group chats with people. To do this, click the 'chat' icon on the top right of the chat window.

In the 'to' field at the top of the window, type the name, email or number of the person or people you want to contact.

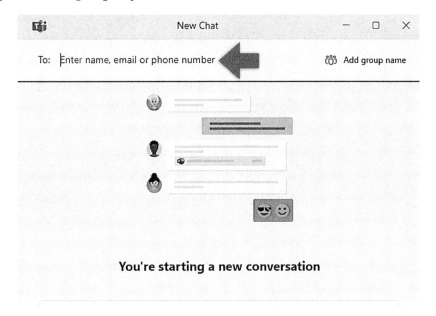

If you've added more than one person, add a group name.

Send a Message

Type in a message at the bottom, then click the send icon.

Chapter 7: Internet and Communication

You'll land on the chat page. Let's take a look around the screen.

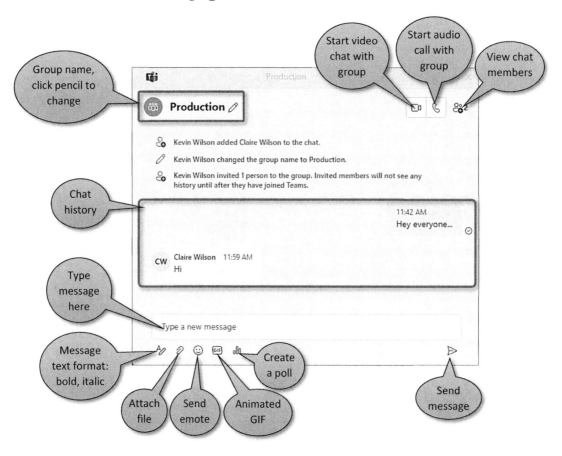

To format your message, click the format icon. Here you can change the font, size, typeface, as well as bold, italic and underlined text.

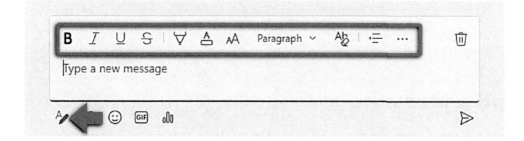

Send a File

To send a file, click the attach file icon. Then select 'upload from computer'.

Select your file then click 'open'.

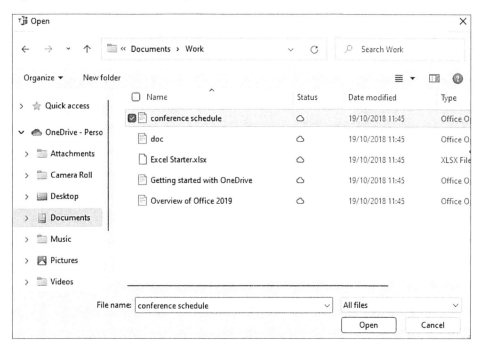

The file will attach to a message. Click the send icon to send.

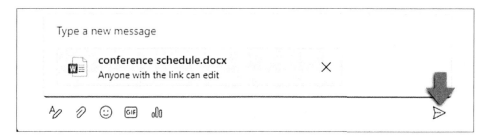

Video Calls

To make a new video call, open the chat window, click 'meet' on the top left.

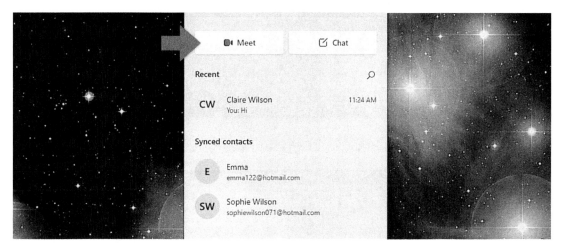

Chapter 7: Internet and Communication

Set up your camera and mic. Click the two switches on the bottom left to enable your microphone and camera.

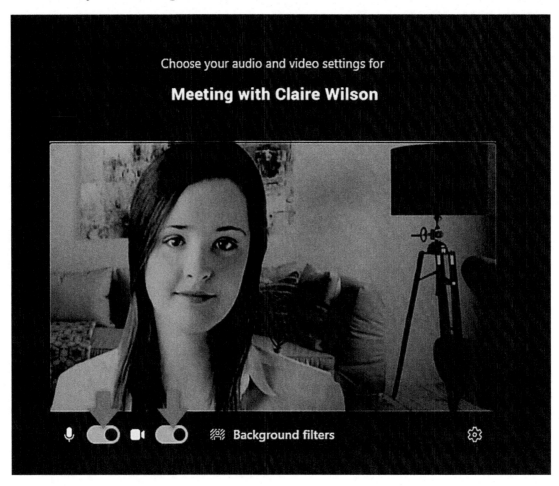

If you want to blur out the background, click 'background filters', then select 'blur'.

Click 'join now' at the bottom of the window.

Share the link via email, enter the email addresses of the people you want to invite. Click 'send'.

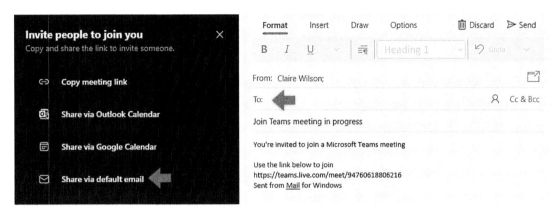

Once everyone else joins. Click 'admit' to allow the person in.

You'll see the people you're talking to appear in the meeting window. You'll see your own camera on the bottom right of the screen.

Along the top right of the screen, you'll see some controls.

Lets take a closer look at these controls.

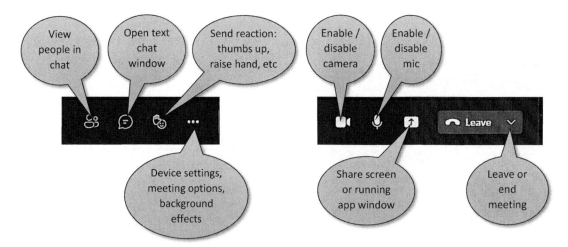

Share Screen

To share your screen, from the meeting window, click the 'share screen' icon.

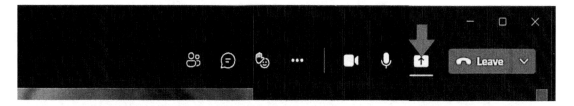

Here, you can share your entire screen, or just a certain app.

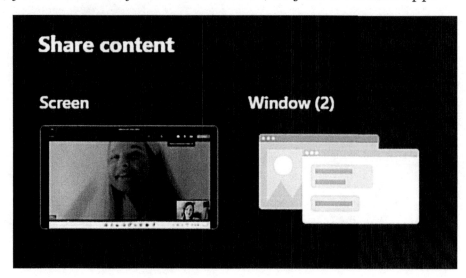

It is probably safer to share an app, as if you share your entire screen, the other people in the meeting can see everything. This includes the desktop background and all apps running or files open, so make sure there is no sensitive information visible.

To share an app, open the app using the start menu, eg I'm opening Microsoft Edge to show a website.

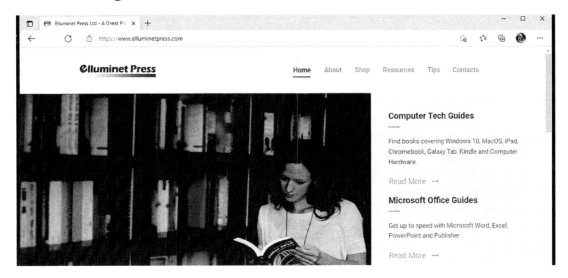

Click the teams icon on the taskbar to switch back to the teams app.

Select 'window', then select the app you want to share with the team.

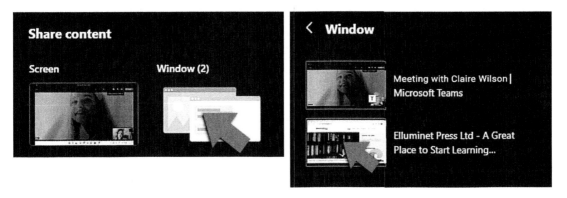

The shared app window will show up with a red border. This means this app is being shared with the team.

To stop sharing the app window, click back onto the teams app icon on the taskbar.

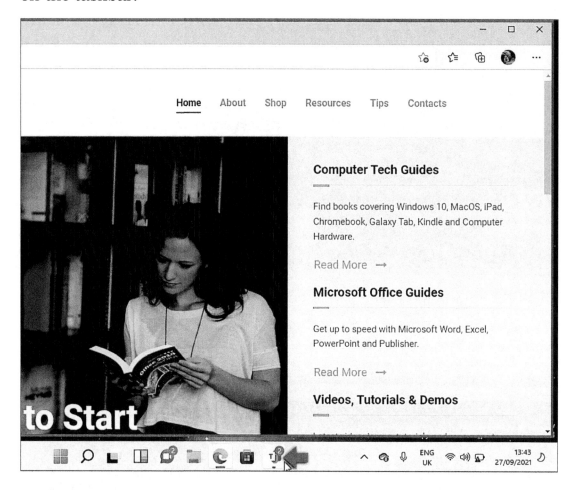

Click the 'stop sharing' icon on the toolbar on the top right.

Microsoft Teams

Teams is a video chat and collaboration platform designed for group work, keeping in touch with friends and colleagues, as well as hosting various online meetings and sharing files. With Teams you can:

- Use text based chat
- Make voice over IP (VoIP) calls between Teams clients
- Host or join video meetings
- Share your screen
- Share files

Before we begin, let's take a look at some of the terminology you'll come across when using Microsoft Teams. The first one is a team. Teams are groups of people who connect to chat and collaborate on a project.

You can use channels to organize your communications by topic. Within a channel you can chat, have meetings and work on files together with your team. A channel can either be public or private, and can include a couple of users or hundreds.

At the top of each channel you'll see some tabs, these link to files, apps and services. Some common tab names include posts for the messages people have sent and files for the documents people have shared within the channel.

Users can use mentions to message and alert other users. To do this you add the @ symbol before the person's name, team or channel

The activity feed provides a summary of messages, replies, mentions and other activity happening within team channels. The activity feed can be filtered by unread messages, mentions and other categories, as well as the user's own activity.

A series of messages between users is called a thread.

A stripped down version of Microsoft Teams is included with Windows 11. To start Teams, open you start menu, click 'all apps' on the top right.

Scroll down the list, select 'Microsoft Teams'.

Initial Setup

The first time you launch Teams, you'll need to select your Microsoft Account. Enter select it from the list, or click 'use another account' then enter your details.

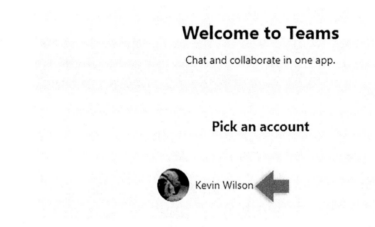

Enter your cell/mobile phone number.

Verify your account. Check the SMS messages on your phone and find the code sent from Microsoft. Click 'next'.

Confirm your details, click 'lets go'.

Chapter 7: Internet and Communication

Once you've signed in, you'll land on the main screen. Down the left hand side, you'll see three icons. Here, you can view all mentions, other participant's reactions to messages, and any notifications. Using the chat icon, you'll see a list of all your recent chats and meetings, along with contacts. At the top, you can filter out chats by participants name, as well as start a new video meeting or text chat.

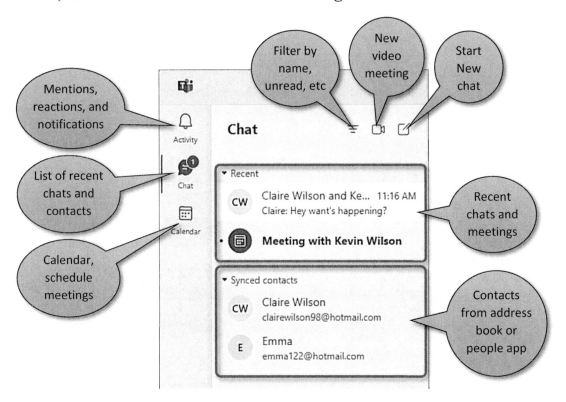

If you select a recent chat, the chat history will appear in the main window. Along the top, you'll can view the chat history, files shared during the chat.

On the far right hand side, you can start a new video meeting or voice call with the participants.

New Meeting

To start a new video meeting, select 'chat' from the three icons on the top left, then click the new video meeting icon

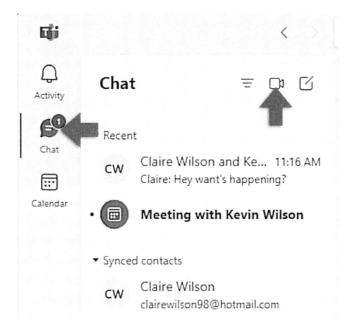

See page 315 for more info.

New Chat

To start a new chat, select 'chat' from the three icons on the top left, then click the new chat icon

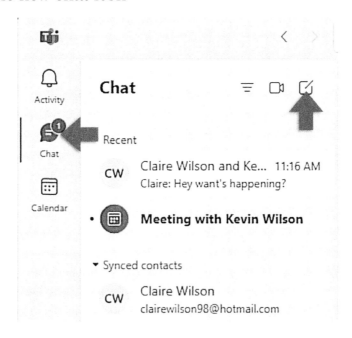

See page 313 for more info.

Remote Desktop

Remote Desktop, also known as terminal services allows you to connect to another machine remotely over a network connection. The user interface is displayed from remote machine onto the local machine and input from the local machine is transmitted to the remote machine – where software execution takes place. Only Windows 10 or 11 Professional allows remote access and isn't available in the home edition. To enable remote connections, open the settings app, select 'system' from the list on the left. Scroll down the list on the right, select 'remote desktop'.

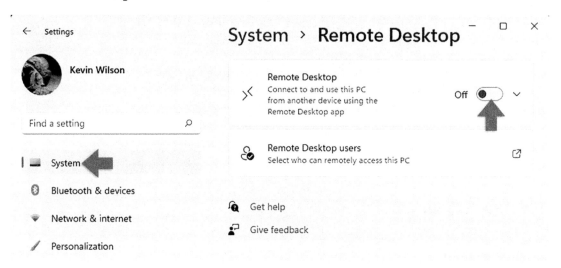

Set the 'enable remote desktop' switch to on. This allows other machines to connect to this PC. Click 'confirm' on the blue dialog box.

Now you need to find out the IP address of the machine. To do this open the Windows terminal. Right click on the desktop, select 'windows terminal' from the popup menu.

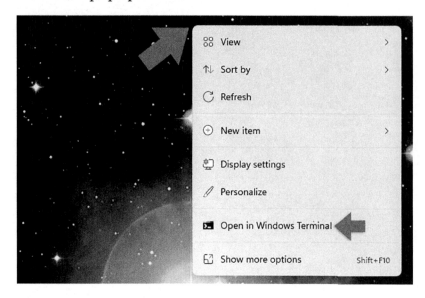

Now, type ipconfig and find the IPv4 address. In this case 192.168.1.13. Note down this IP address, you'll need it later.

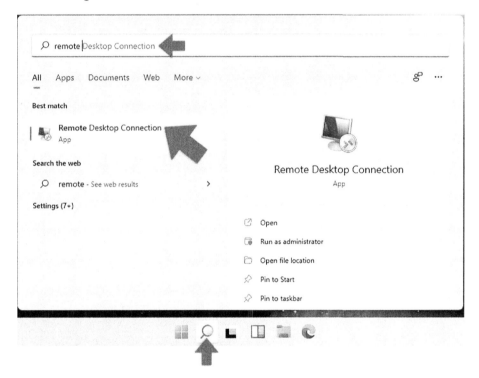

Now you can connect from another machine on the LAN. To do this, on another machine, open the remote desktop connection app. Type 'remote desktop connection' into the search field on the bottom left.

Type the IP address you noted earlier into the app. Click 'connect'.

Enter your windows username and password when prompted. You'll see your desktop appear in the remote desktop window.

FTP

FTP (File Transfer Protocol) is a protocol for transferring files to and from a remote machine. You can connect using a program called FileZilla.

```
filezilla-project.org
```

First you need to download and install the program. You can download FileZilla here. Double click on `FileZilla_3.47.2.1_win64-setup.exe` to begin the setup. Follow the instructions on screen to install.

To connect to an FTP server click the 'site manager' icon on the top left.

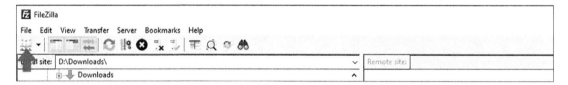

Click 'new site' on the bottom left, in the 'general' tab on the right, select a protocol from the 'protocol' drop down list - usually SFTP or FTP.

In the 'host' field, enter the server name or IP address of the server you're connecting to.

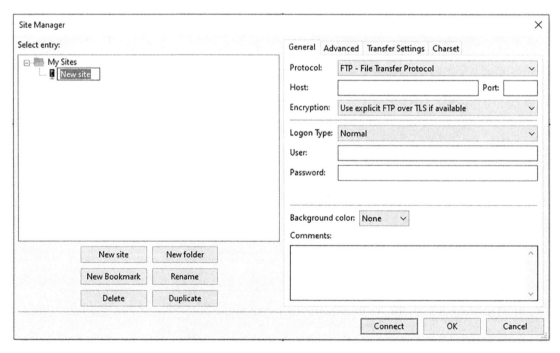

In the 'user' and 'password' field, enter the username and password for the server you're connecting to. Click 'connect' when you're done.

Now you can transfer files.

SSH with PuTTY

SSH (or Secure Shell) is a protocol for secure remote login to another machine. This provides a command prompt where you can issue commands to execute programs or perform tasks on the remote machine. You can connect using a program called PuTTY or using the command prompt.

First you need to download and install the program.

```
www.putty.org
```

Go to your downloads folder then double click `putty-64bit-0.73-installer.msi` to install PuTTY. Follow the instructions on screen.

Once installed, launch the app from your start menu, then in the configuration window, enter the IP address or hostname of the machine you're connecting to.

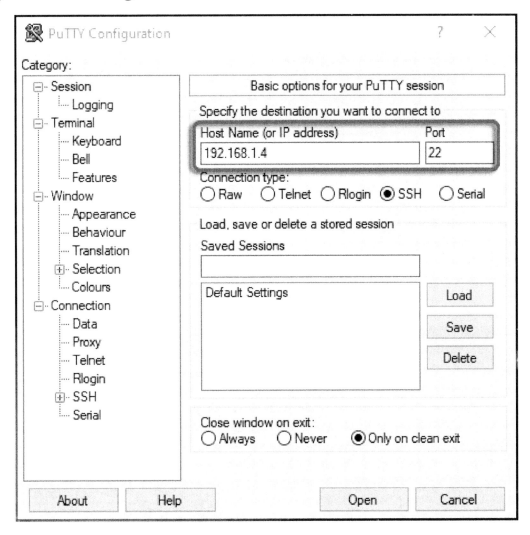

Enter the port number – usually 22. Click 'open'.

When a connection is established, enter your username and password for the machine you're connecting to.

Once authenticated you can issue various commands from the command prompt.

SSH from Windows Terminal

First, open windows terminal. Right click on the desktop, select 'windows terminal' from the popup menu.

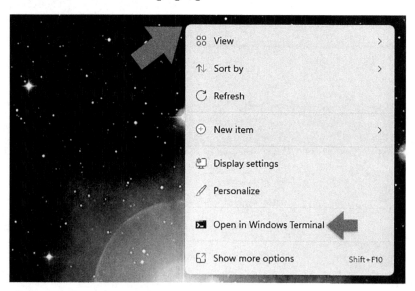

You'll land on the PowerShell windows terminal.

To connect to the server type:

```
ssh username@hostname
```

So for example, with 'pi' as the username:

```
ssh pi@192.168.1.3
```

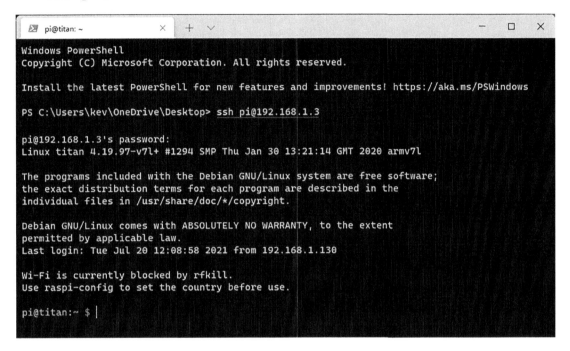

Enter the password for the username when prompted.

Folder Sharing on a LAN

File sharing over a network (or LAN) allows you to share files and folders on your computer with other users in your workgroup or domain. Here in the example, we have two computers connected to a wireless LAN. Were are going to share a folder on PC 1, then connect to it from PC 2.

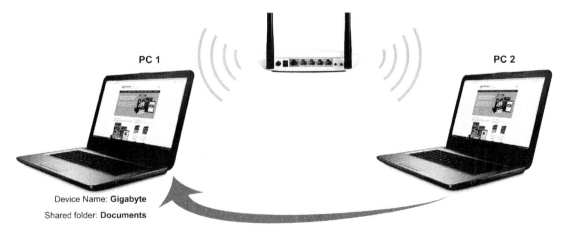

331

First, on the PC you're sharing the folder from (PC 1), you need to create usernames for the people you want to share the folder with.

To do this, see page 95 for information on creating local user accounts on your machine.

Sharing a Folder

Now on PC 1 ie the PC you're sharing the folder from, open file explorer then navigate to the folder you want to share. To share a folder, right click on it, then select "properties" from the popup menu.

Select the "sharing" tab, then click "advanced sharing".

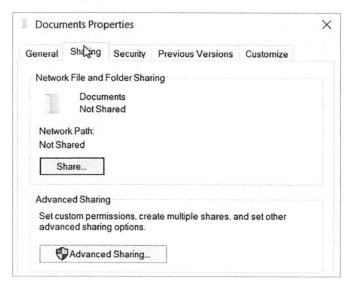

Click "share this folder", then select "permissions".

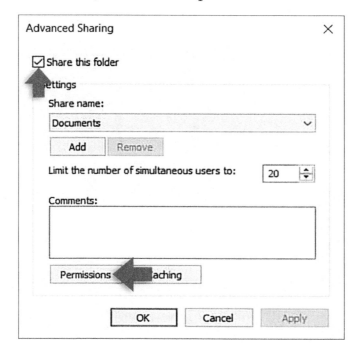

Set the permissions for this folder. In other words choose the people you want to have access to this folder. Note that you will need the account you created earlier. To add a user, click "add".

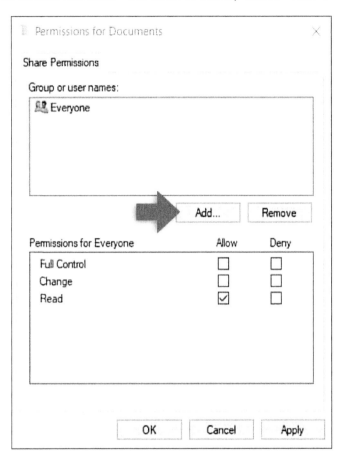

Type the person's username in the field below, then click "check names". Click "ok".

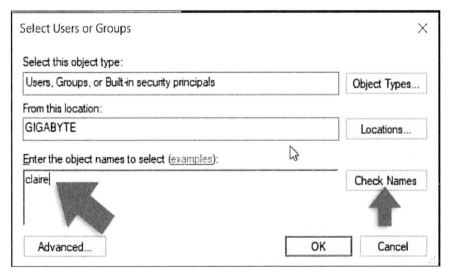

If it doesn't work, click 'advanced', then click 'find now'. Select the username from the list.

Now set the permissions. If you select "everyone", this means anyone connecting to your PC can view the folder. This might be ok on a small private network, but on larger networks, you should only allow the people you want to grant access to.

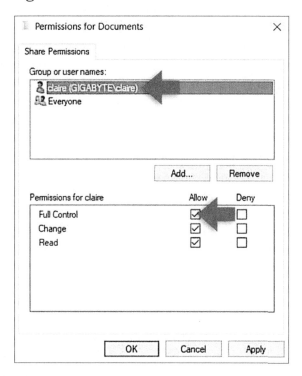

To grant access, in the top panel of the dialog box, click on the user you just added. In the panel underneath, click "full control" to allow the user to add files, as well as read and write to existing files. If you just want them to view files, select read only. Click 'ok'.

Access a Shared Folder on a LAN

If we wanted to connect to the shared folder we created in the previous section (the folder on PC 1), we need to know the PC's name and the name of the shared folder.

On the PC sharing the folder (ie PC 1), you can find the PC's name in the settings app. Click on "system". Select "about" from the list on the right.

You'll see the PC's name under "device name".

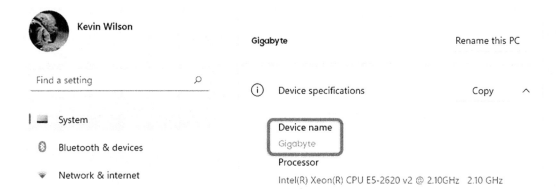

If it's too difficult to remember, click "rename this PC" then enter a name". Click "next".

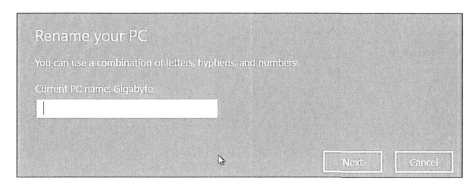

Restart your PC for the change to take effect.

To connect to a shared folder, you'll need to enter the UNC path to that folder. The UNC path is the name of the PC sharing the folder, followed by the folder name.

```
\\PC-Name\Shared-Folder-Name
```

On another machine on the network (PC 2 in our example), open File Explorer.

Device Name: **Gigabyte**

Shared folder: **Documents**

Type the UNC path to the shared folder into the address bar along the top of the window. In this case:

```
\\gigabyte\documents
```

Press enter when you're done.

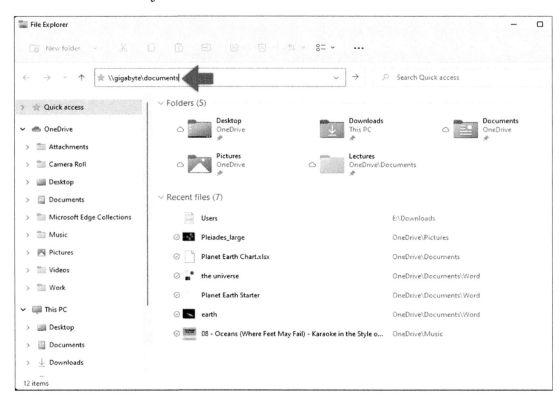

Enter the username and password you created for this user (the username and password you created on page 332)

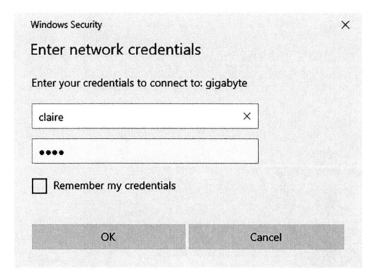

If you connect to this folder often, click 'remember my credentials'.

Click 'ok' when you're done.

Your PC will connect to the shared folder. Here, you can see we're now connected to the documents folder on PC 1.

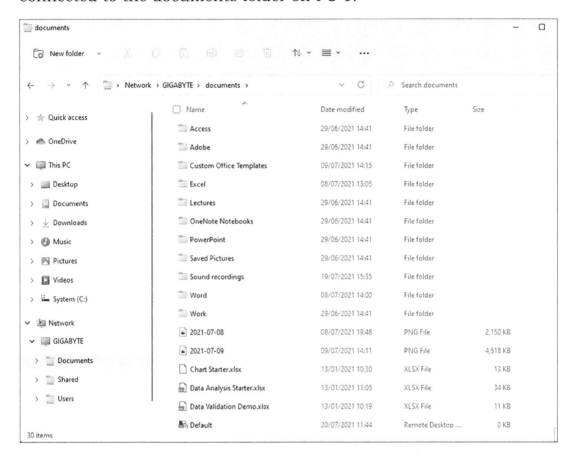

Mobile Hotspot

Also known as tethering, this feature allows you to share your internet connection with your other devices and does this by creating a temporary WiFi hotspot. This can be useful if you have a 4G data connection on your phone but no WiFi available and need to access the internet on a tablet or laptop.

Enable the mobile hotspot on your phone. On Android phones go to settings, select 'connections', then 'mobile hotspot and tethering'. Turn on 'bluetooth tethering'. To view hotspot settings, tap on 'mobile hotspot'.

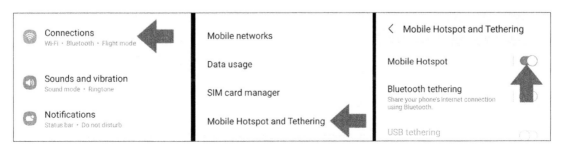

On your laptop or tablet, tap on the WiFi icon on the right hand side of your taskbar to reveal the available networks.

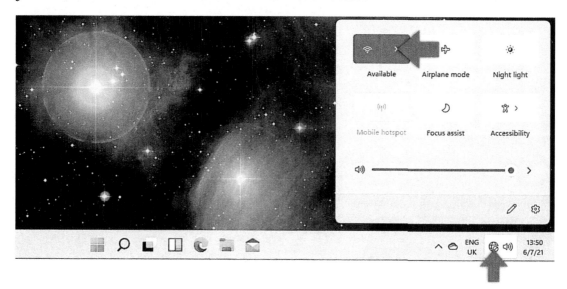

The network name is usually the name of your phone. Look at the mobile hotspot settings. You'll find the network name and password.

On your laptop or tablet, select the network name from the list and enter the password. Click 'next'.

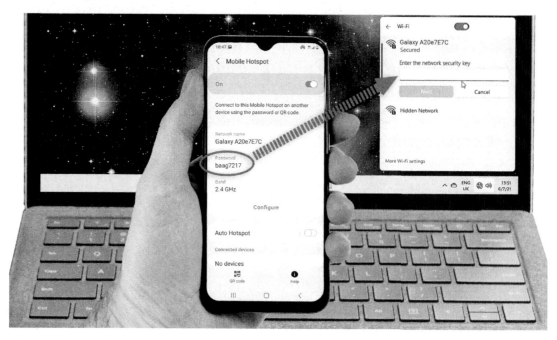

Your Phone App

This app works best with an smartphone running Android 7 or later. You'll find the app on the taskbar.

If not, open your start menu, select 'all apps', scroll down to 'your phone'. See "Linking your Phone" on page 112 for details on how to link your phone and set up the app.

When the app starts, you'll land on the home screen.

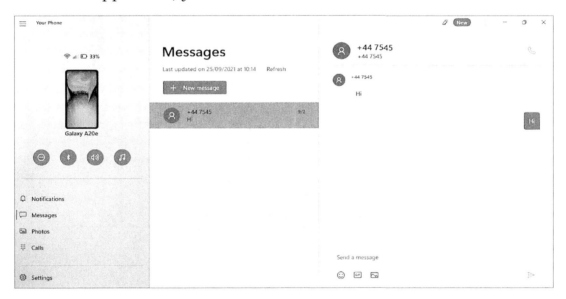

On the left hand panel, you'll see an image of your phone. Lets take a look.

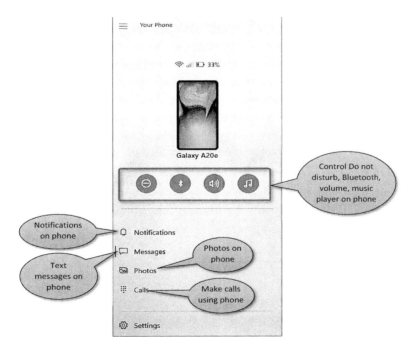

Notifications

In the notifications section, you'll see notifications from your phone. Any notifications that popup on the notifications screen on your phone will appear in the notifications section of the 'your phone' app.

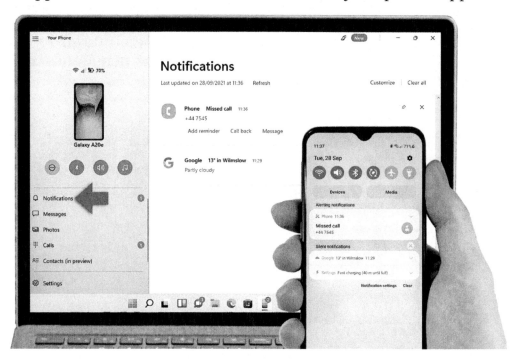

Messages

In the messages section, you'll see a list of all the text/sms messages you've sent or received on your phone.

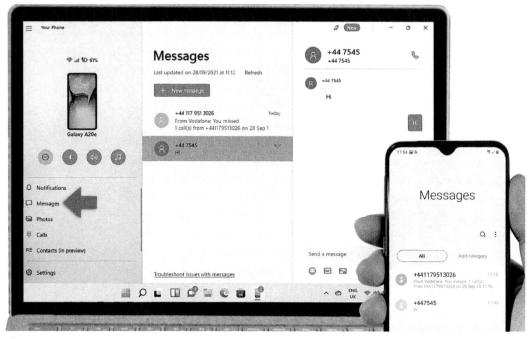

If you want to view a message, just click on it in the 'messages' section of the 'your phone' app. To reply, type your message into the 'send a message' field at the bottom of the message.

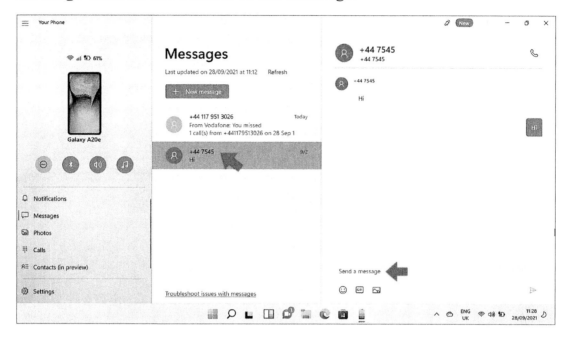

To send a new message, click 'new message'. Enter the person's phone number in the 'to' field, type your message in the 'send a message' field.

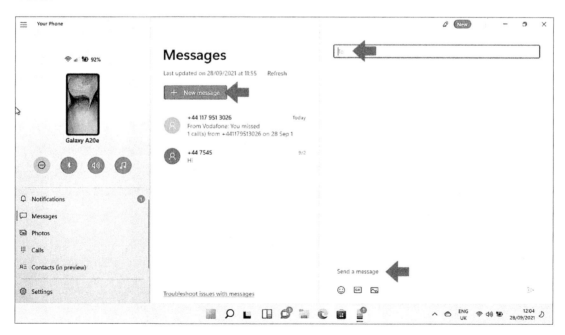

If you want to send a picture, click the image icon at the bottom, select the photo, click the 'send' icon.

Photos

You can view photos you've taken on your phone. Click 'photos' on the left hand panel. Here, you can see the photos from the phone.

You can save the photos to your PC, drag & drop them into another app.

In the demo below, I took a photo with my phone. Here, you can drag and drop the photo into another app, such as a word processor.

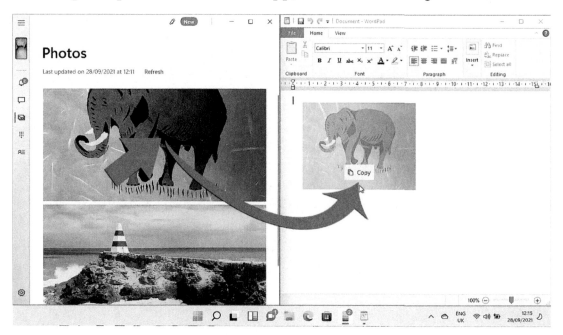

Calls

You can make calls from your PC. Select 'calls' from the panel on the left hand side. Here, you'll see a list of calls you're made, received or missed on your phone.

To return the call, click on a call in the calls list, then click the 'call icon'.

To make a call, key in the phone number using the keypad on the right hand side of the screen. Hit the green call button when you're done.

Multimedia Apps

Windows 11 has several multimedia applications available. There is an app to organise and enhance your digital photos whether it be from your phone or digital camera. There is also an app to take photographs using a windows tablet.

We'll also take a look at

- Movies & TV App
- Playing DVDs & Blu-Rays
- Spotify
- Microsoft Paint

Windows 11 doesn't come with the ability to play DVDs but you can download some software that will allow you to still enjoy your DVD collection.

Let's begin by taking a look at the Photos app.

Have a look at the video resources. Open your web browser and navigate to the following website

elluminetpress.com/win-mm

Photos App

With Windows 11, Microsoft has updated the Photos app with a few user interface improvements. The app still looks very similar to previous version, however there are a few differences. You'll see a new photo editing toolbar appear along the top of your photo, as well as a film-strip along the bottom showing photos from the same album or folder.

You'll also see a new multi-view feature that allows you to compare photos, or see multiple photos in the same window.

To open the photos app, click on the photos icon on your start menu.

When you start the app, you'll land on the home screen. Let's take a look.

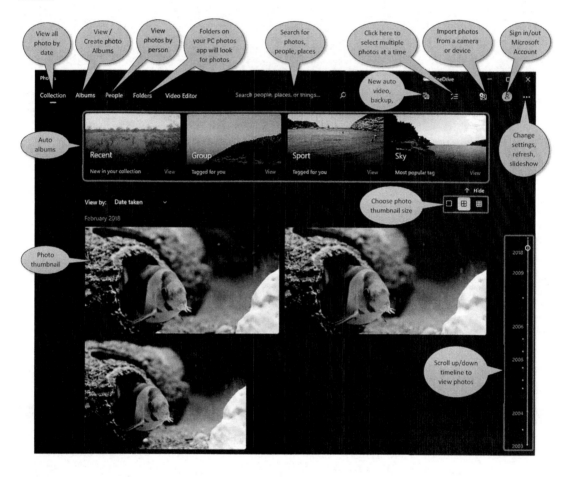

View a Photo

To view a photo, tap or click on the image thumbnail, this will open the image in view mode.

In view mode, you'll see the photo you selected appear full screen. Along the top of the photo you'll see a toolbar with some options

Along the bottom you'll see a film strip with photos from the same album or location.

Crop & Straighten a Photo

Open your photo in 'view mode' as shown on page 346, then select the edit icon from the toolbar.

Select the crop icon.

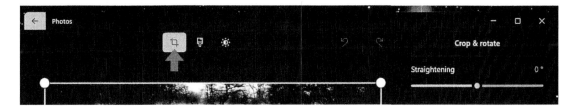

Chapter 8: Multimedia Apps

If I wanted to crop my zebra photo, you'll see a box around the photo with four white dots on each corner. These are called crop handles.. Click and drag the white dots to resize the box so it surrounds the part of the photo you want to keep, as shown below.

To straighten the photo, click and drag the slider.

Click 'save a copy' when you're done.

Adjusting Brightness & Colour

Open your photo in 'view mode' as shown on page 346, then select the edit icon from the toolbar.

Select adjustments icon at the top of the screen.

A panel will open up on the right hand side. Click 'light' to reveal the brightness, exposure and contrast settings.

You'll see four sliders appear. Drag the sliders left or right to adjust the contrast, the overall brightness (or exposure), highlights (ie the bright parts of the image such as the sky), and the shadows (ie the dark parts of the image).

349

Now click 'color'. This will allow you to correct the white balance of the photograph (the warmth). Drag the slider to the left to make the image cooler (more blue), or to the right to make the image warmer (more orange).

Click 'save a copy', when you're done.

Spot Fix

The spot fix brush allows you to correct small blemishes on your photograph. To use the spot fix brush, open your photo in 'view mode' as shown on page 346, then select the edit icon from the toolbar.

Select adjustments icon at the top of the screen.

Scroll down the panel on the right hand side, select 'spot fix'.

With the brush, click on the area of the image you want to fix.

Click 'save a copy' when you're done

Adding Filters

Open your photo in 'view mode' as shown on page 346, then select the edit icon from the toolbar.

Select filters icon at the top of the screen.

From the panel on the select a filter. Use the 'filter intensity' slider to increase or decrease how much the filter affects the photo.

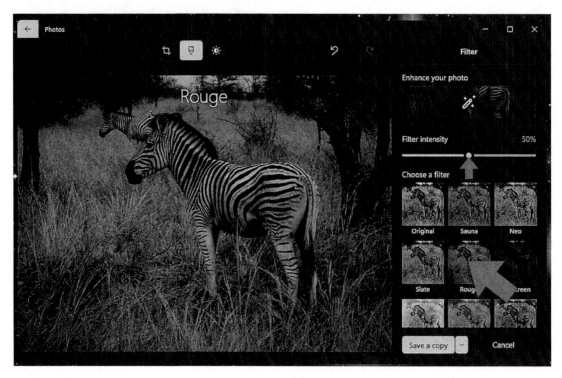

Click 'save a copy' when you're done.

Annotating Photos

If you have a device with a touch screen, you can use your pen or finger to draw on the photo. To do this open your photo in 'view mode' as shown on page 346, then select the annotate icon from the toolbar.

Draw with your pen or finger to annotate your photograph.

Along the top of your screen you'll see a tool bar. You can select from three different writing tools: a pen, a pencil, and a calligraphy pen.

The next icon along is an eraser. This allows you to use your pen or finger to rub out parts of your drawing.

You can also save photos with your annotations using save icon.

Video Editor

The Video Editor, part of the photos app, allows you to quickly blend 3D effects, photos, and videos together into a video clip that you can share on social media, send to a friend, or use to promote an idea.

To start video editor, open your start menu, click on the photos app. From within the photos app, select 'video editor' at the top of the screen..

The photos app will open in 'video editor' mode.

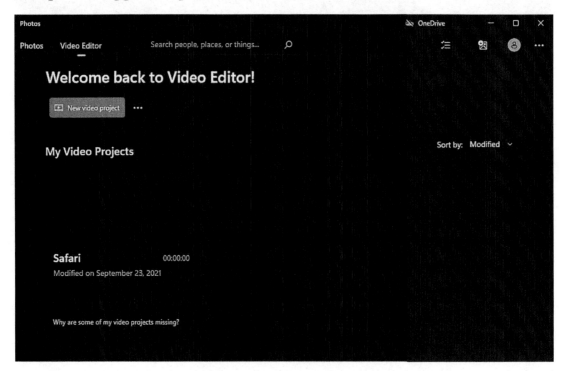

You'll see a list of video projects you've previously created.

To start a new project, click 'new video project' at the top of the screen.

Creating Videos Automatically

Click the photos/videos you want to include in your video. Hover your mouse over the top right corner of the image and click the tick box. Do this on all the images/videos you want to include.

Click 'new video' on the toolbar at the top of the screen, then select 'automatic video' from the drop down menu.

Type in a name for your video.

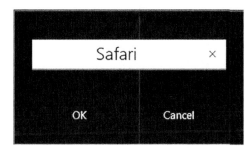

Click 'ok'

Chapter 8: Multimedia Apps

When it's finished, you'll be able to see a preview of the video remix has created..

If you don't like the style, you can click the 'remix it for me' button and Photos App will generate a new video.

If you have any people in your video, an image of them will appear for you to select. Click 'choose a star' and select the main people in the video. This highlights them in the video.

To make any custom changes just click 'edit video' on the bottom right. This will take you to the custom edit screen where you can make changes to your video.

If you're happy with the results, click 'export or share'.

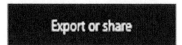

Creating Videos

To create a video, click the photos/videos you want to include in your video.

Click 'new video' on the toolbar at the top of the screen, then select 'new video project' from the drop down menu that appears.

Type in a name for your video.

Click 'ok'

Chapter 8: Multimedia Apps

You'll see the main editing screen. Lets take a look at the different parts.

Top left, you'll see all the photos and videos you selected in the previous step. On the top right you'll see some icons to add themes, music, audio files, narrations, as well as an export feature so you can share your creations.

Underneath that on the right hand side you'll see a large preview screen. This is a preview of your video. You can scrub through it using the progress bar underneath.

Along the bottom is your storyboard or timeline. This is the sequence of photos and videos that will make up your video.

Along the top of the storyboard are some icons that allow you to add a title screen, photo filters, add text overlay titles, motion effects and some 3D effects. These help to make your video more interesting for viewers to watch.

Add and Arrange your Media

On the top left, you'll see all the photographs and videos you added at the beginning. You can drag and drop these onto the storyboard along the bottom of the screen.

Along the bottom, you'll see the order of photos/videos you have added. To reorder these, drag them across to the position in the sequence you want them.

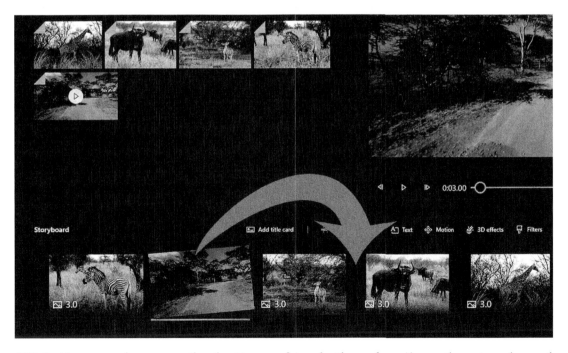

Click the numbers on the bottom of each thumbnail on the storyboard to change the duration of each photo/video

359

Add Text Titles

You can add text to your video. First, select the photo or video you want the text to appear. Then select 'text' from the bar along the top of the storyboard.

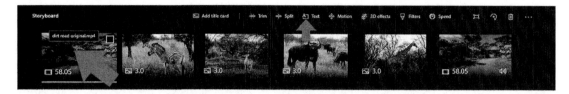

Select a template from the bottom right (I'm going to choose 'adventure'). Type your title into the text field on the top right.

Under layout on the bottom right, select where you want the text to appear: centre, top, left...

Move the two blue markers to indicate where you want the effect to start and finish, and how long you want the effect to stay on the screen for.

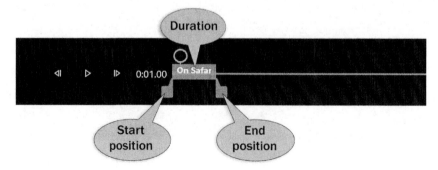

Click 'done' on the bottom right when you're finished.

360

Add Music

Now, how about some music. Select the 'background music' option on the top right of the screen.

I'm going to use the 'explorer' music - seems appropriate. From the popup window select 'explorer'. *To hear a preview of the music, click the small triangle icon next to the name.*

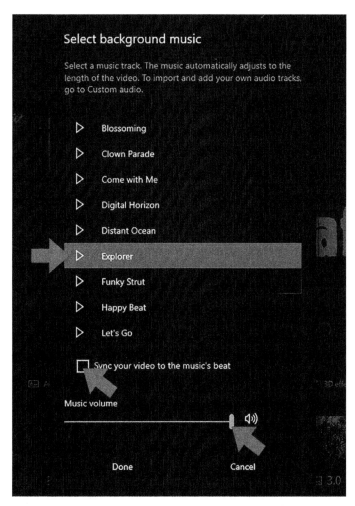

Select 'sync your video to the music beat'. This will cut your video in time with the music.

Set the music volume using the slider.

Click 'done'.

Add Audio File

You can also add your own music, narration, or audio file. Click on 'custom audio'.

Click 'add audio file' on the top right.

Navigate to your music folder on your computer - this is usually called 'music' and select a track.

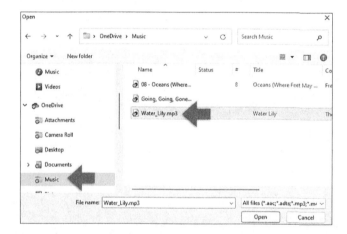

Move the blue markers to mark the beginning and end of the audio

If you want to add another file, click 'add audio file' again, and select the file.

Click 'done' when your happy.

Slideshow Motion

To change the motion of your photographs in your slideshow, select the photo slide you want to change.

Now select a motion style from the options on the right hand side of the screen

Here you can select 'zoom in right', which will slow zoom into the right hand side of the image; or 'zoom in left' zooms into the left hand side of the image. These are useful if the subject in the photograph is on the left or right hand side of the image - helps draw attention to your subject. You can also pan across the image or zoom into the centre.

3D Effects

3D effects can only be added to video clips not still photographs. If you select a still photograph, the 3D effects button will be greyed out.

Click '3D Effects'.

Scrub to the part of the footage you want the effect to appear, using the progress bar underneath your video preview.

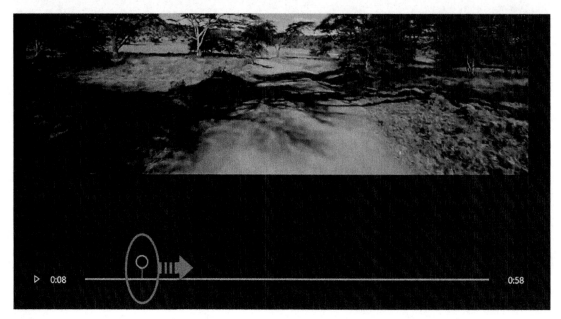

Select the 'effects' icon on the top right to reveal the effects panel, if they are not visible.

Browse through the effects listed down the right hand side of the screen.

Drag and drop the effect onto the position you want the effect to appear in the video.

In this example, I want the "impact on sand" effect to appear to the right of the dirt road.

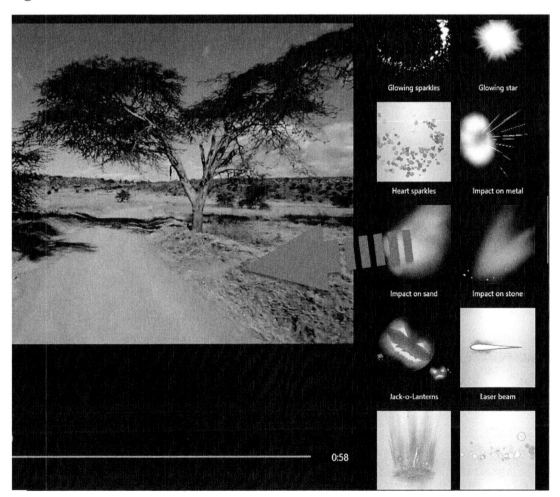

You can rotate the effect around the frame using the tree axis handles indicated with the arrows below. You can move the effect by moving the surrounding grey box and you can resize the effect using the square resize handles on the corners of the resize box.

Now to make the 3D effect more realistic, you can anchor it to a position in the video clip. Turn 'anchor to a point' to the on position.

Make sure the blue anchor on the effect is in the position you want the effect anchored to. When you play the video, the effect will stay in that position even if the camera moves.

Some of the effects have sound. You can adjust this using the volume control in the panel on the right hand side

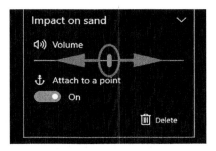

Add more effects if you want to using the drag and drop method described earlier.

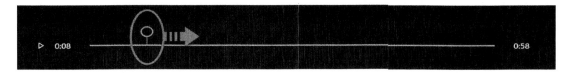

You can also add effects to other parts of the clip. Scrub across your clip using the progress bar, as before. Lets add a portal.

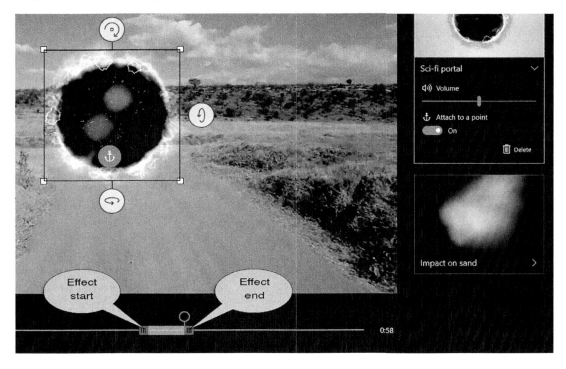

Notice below on the progress bar, you'll see a range bar appear. This will allow to adjust the duration of the effect. To adjust the range, click and drag the start and end handles, and drag them along the progress bar.

When you have added all the effects you want, click 'done' at the top right hand side of the screen.

Adding 3D Models

You can add 3D models to your videos. To do this, click '3D Effects'. You can add 3D models from Microsoft's Remix library or even your own models from Paint 3D.

Scrub to the part of the footage you want the effect to appear, using the progress bar underneath your video preview.

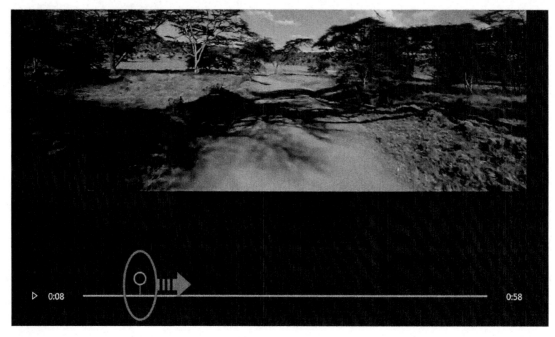

Select the '3D Models' icon on the top right to reveal the models panel, if they are not visible.

Browse through the models listed down the right hand side of the screen.

Drag and drop the model you want, onto the position you want it to appear in the video.

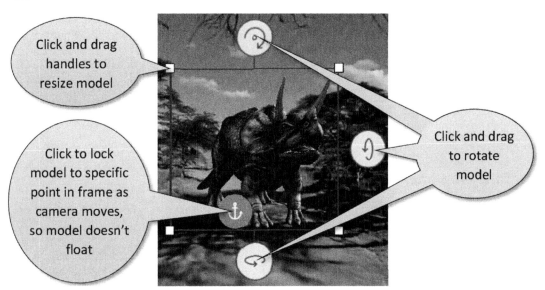

Use the handles to rotate, resize and position the model in the frame, as you would do for the effects we added earlier. Under the video preview window, adjust the length of time you want the model to remain on-screen. Use the beginning and end sliders as shown below. The black dot is where you are in the video, eg 58 seconds into the video clip.

Export your Video

To export your finished video project, click 'finish video' on the top right of the screen.

This will allow you to save the video project as an mp4 video file. Select 'high 1080p' from the 'video quality' dialog box, then click 'export'.

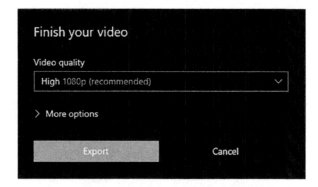

Select your 'videos' folder on your computer. Give your video a meaningful name.

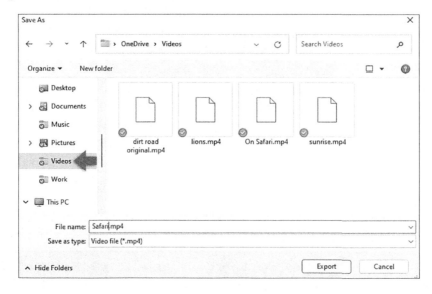

Click 'export'.

Camera App

The camera app makes use of the on board camera on your windows tablet to take photographs. To start the camera app, open the start menu, select 'all apps' on the top right, click on 'camera'.

Camera

Your tablet usually has two cameras: a front facing camera, and a rear camera. The rear camera is usually higher quality and for taking photos/videos of things, while the front facing camera is usually for video calls and selfies.

When you start up the camera app, you'll see an image from your camera on screen.

371

Chapter 8: Multimedia Apps

Tap on the small camera icon to take a photo.

Once you have taken your photo, you can view them by tapping/clicking the icon on the bottom right to view in photo app.

You can also take movies by tapping on the 'switch to video' icon, on the right hand side. This works just like a video camcorder.

You can also take panoramic photos. To do this, tap the panoramic photo icon, on the right hand side. You'll see a square box appear along the centre of the screen. Point the camera at the position in the scene you want the panoramic photo to start. Tap the large white button, on the right hand side of your screen. Now, pan the camera to your right, rotating around your hips/shoulders, until you have covered the scene. You'll see the box in the centre of the screen start to build your image.

Tap the large white button again, to finish.

You can also adjust your exposure settings such as ISO, White Balance, Shutter Speed and Brightness on your camera, as well as set a timer delay. To access these settings, tap the 'pro' icon on the top of your screen.

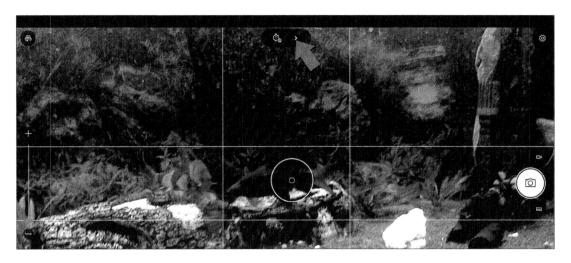

This will reveal the exposure settings.

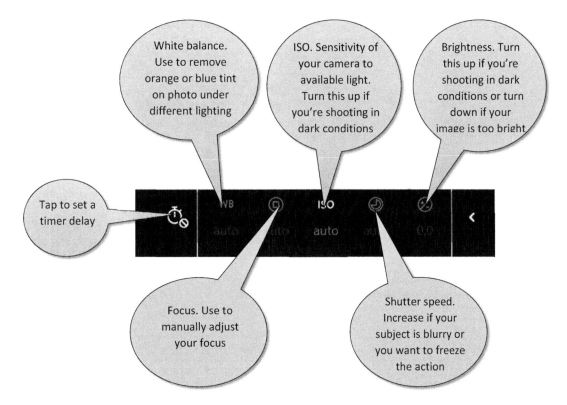

To adjust the settings, tap on one of the icons.

In this example, I am going to adjust the ISO. So tap on the ISO icon.

When you do this, you'll notice a semi-circle control appear around the 'take photo' icon, on the right hand side of your screen.

To make the adjustment, tap on 'ISO', on the right of the screen, then drag this upwards to increase the ISO, drag it downwards to decrease the ISO, as illustrated below.

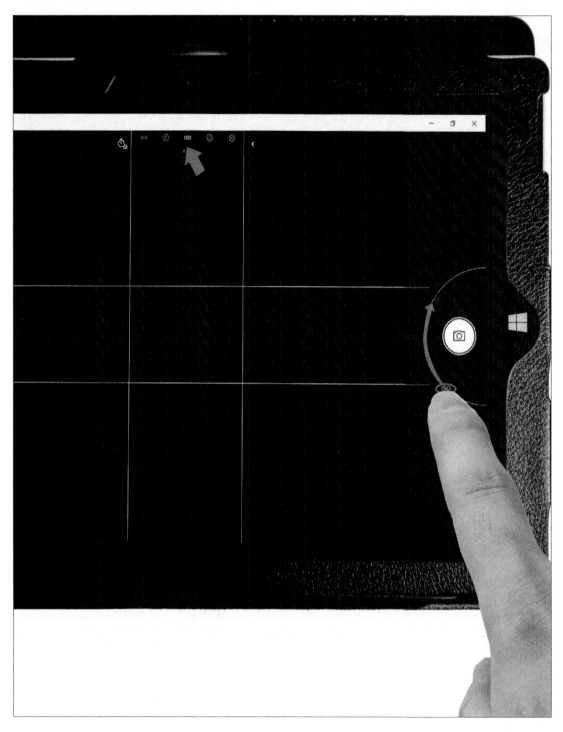

You'll see the value in the centre increase or decrease as you make your adjustment. In this example, I've set the ISO to 1600.

You can use this technique for the other settings too (white balance, focus, shutter speed and brightness).

Movies & TV App

With the Movies & TV app you can watch the latest TV shows and movies, as well as your own video content you've taken with your phone or a digital camera. You can find the Movies & TV app on your start menu.

Along the top of your screen you'll see three categories: Explore, Purchased and Personal.

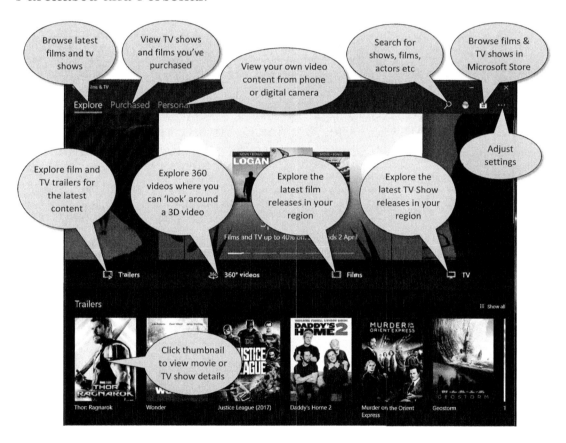

In the 'explore' category you'll be able to browse through the latest TV shows and movies that have been released in your region/country. You can scroll down the page and select the ones you're interested in.

In the 'purchased' category, you'll see a list of all the movies and TV shows you have purchased. This is where you can select them to watch.

The 'personal' category will show you video content you have taken with your camera

Purchasing Content

Once you have found the movie or TV show you want to watch, select the thumbnail cover to view the show's details.

You'll be redirected to the Microsoft Store. On the store page you'll see some details about the series or movie. To buy the movie, or buy a whole season if it's a TV show, click the 'starts at' or 'buy' button.

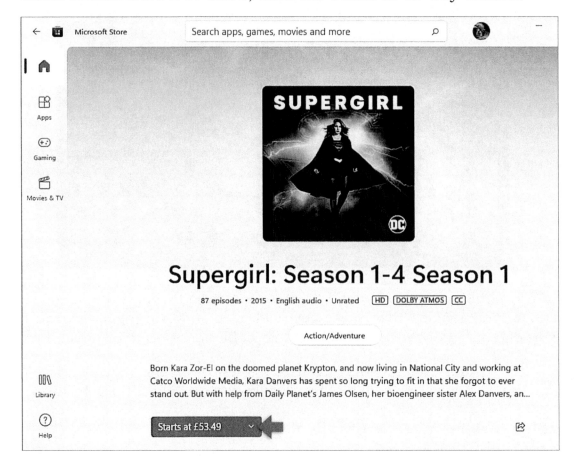

Scroll down further and you'll see a list of each episode. Here you can purchase individual episodes. To do this just click the price button next to the episode you want

Select 'High Definition' if prompted, then enter your microsoft account email and password, along with payment details. Follow the instructions on screen.

Viewing Purchased Content

You'll find all the movies and TV shows you have purchased in the 'purchased' section on the main screen.

Click thumbnail to play, then select an episode if you're watching a TV show.

Make sure you click the little play button next to the episode title.

Search for New Content

To search for TV shows and movies, click the magnifying glass icon on the top right of your screen.

In the search field, type in the show's name or the film's title. Press enter

By default, the search algorithm searches your purchased collection. To search for new content, you'll need to select 'search in microsoft store'

Here you'll be able to click on the thumbnails to view details and purchase the content.

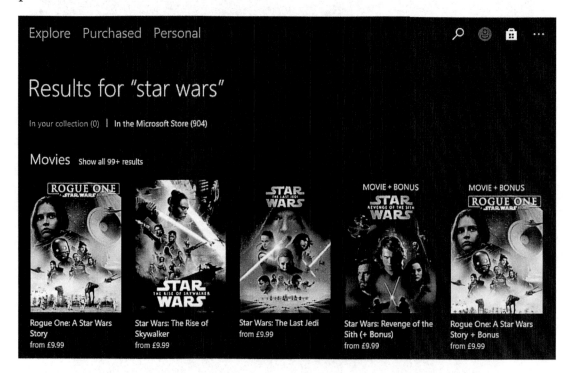

Just click on the cover of the movie you want to watch.

You'll find all the movies and TV shows you have purchased in the 'purchased' section on the main screen.

Personal Content

This is where you can see the video content you have taken with your camera. Select the 'personal' category from the top of the main screen.

Along the top of the personal content window you'll see: 'video folders', 'removable storage' and 'media servers'.

Select 'video folders' to see video clips stored on your device or PC. You can also add other folders - to do this click 'add folder'.

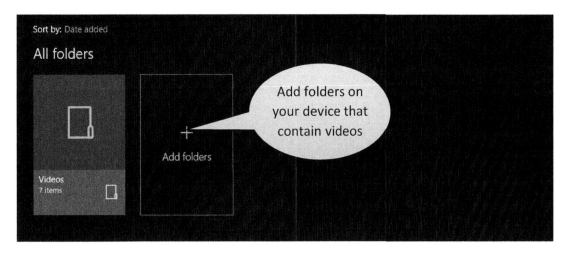

Scroll down a bit further to see all the clips in the folder.

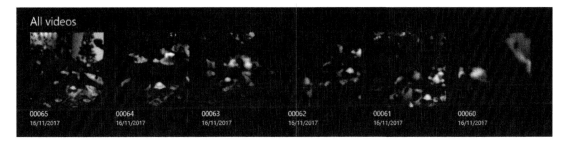

Click on one of the clips to view.

Playing DVDs & Blu-Rays

If you like watching DVDs or Blu-rays on your PC, Windows 11 can't play them out of the box, nor do the latest devices have DVD drives, so you'll need an external DVD drive and a free media player.

The best one I found is VLC Media Player, which can play DVDs, Blu-ray, CDs and a range of other file types.

Just go to the following website and download the software.

```
www.videolan.org
```

Click the 'Download VLC' on the homepage.

Click 'Run' when prompted by your browser and follow the instructions on screen.

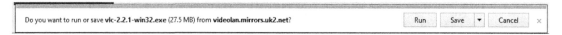

DVDs & Blu-rays are becoming obsolete, thanks to high speed internet services available to most homes, video/film streaming services that allow you to access on demand films, and television programs you can access from the comfort of your favourite arm chair.

Many computers, particularly laptops and mobile devices no longer include a Blu-ray/DVD drive. You can still buy external USB DVD / Blu-ray drives if you need them.

Once you've installed VLC player, you'll find it on your start menu. Click 'all apps', then scroll down to 'VideoLAN', then click 'VLC Media Player'

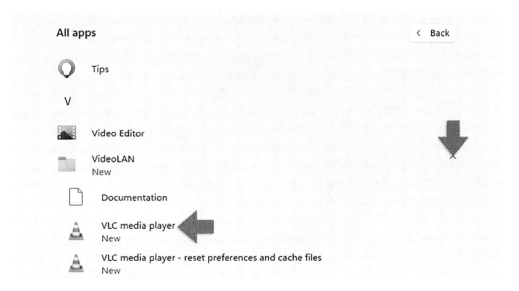

Insert the disc into the DVD/Blu-ray drive either on your computer or an external USB drive.

Chapter 8: Multimedia Apps

Click the play button on the bottom left of the VLC Media Player window.

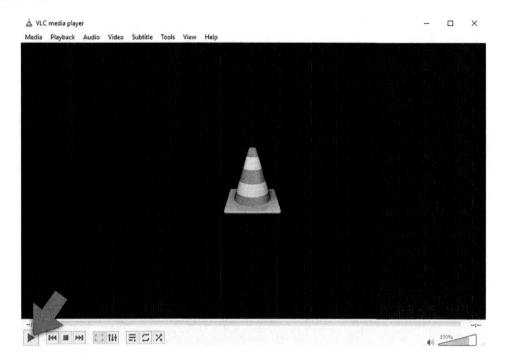

From the pop up dialog box, select the 'disc' tab along the top.

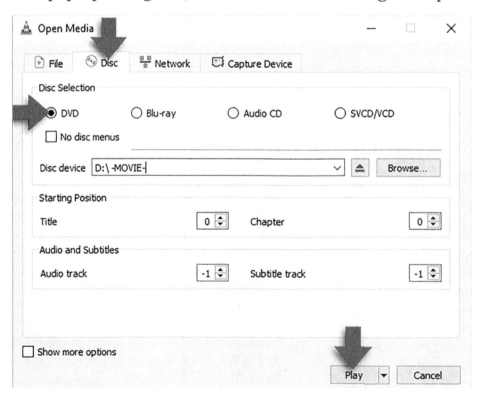

Make sure 'DVD' is selected from the 'disc selection' options for DVD movies, and 'blu-ray' for blu-ray movies. Click 'play' to start playing the movie.

Spotify

Spotify is a music streaming app where you can stream all your favourite music for free. The free service is supported by adverts, although you can subscribe to the service for £9.99 a month ad free.

You'll find the spotify music app on your start menu.

If you don't see it, go to the Microsoft store, then search for and download spotify.

Once downloaded and installed, you can start the spotify app from your start menu. You'll need to sign up for a free account. Click 'sign up for free' and fill in your details. If you already use spotify, click 'log in'.

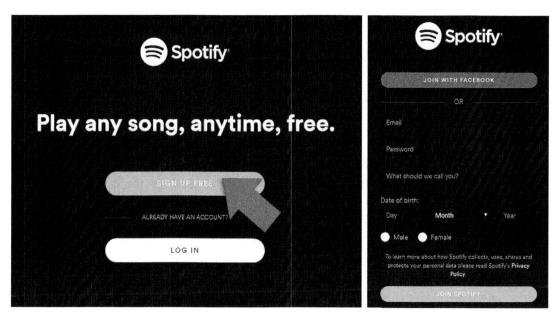

Click 'join spotify' when you're finished.

Chapter 8: Multimedia Apps

With spotify, you can search for any song, album or artist you like. Just type it into the search field at the top of the screen.

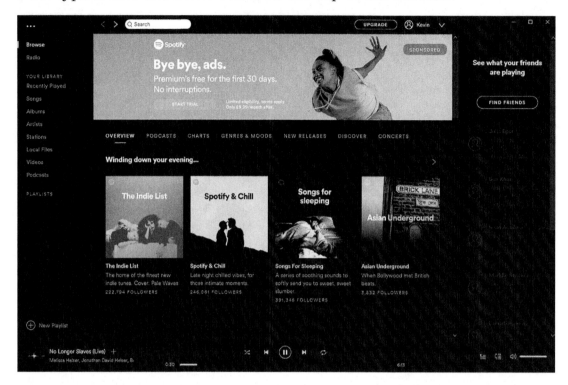

You can scroll down the main page and browse through the genres. Once you've found a song, either by searching or browsing through your favourite genres, you can add them to your library. To do this, click the '+' sign to the left of the track name.

You'll find the tracks in your library on the top left of the main screen

Click on the track to play.

Microsoft Paint

Paint is a simplified graphics editor able to edit Windows bitmap, JPEG, GIF, PNG, WEBP, HEIC, ICO and single-page TIFF formats.

You'll find the paint icon on your start menu.

Paint

Once paint opens, you'll land on the main screen. Along the top of the window you'll find your tools. Select a brush, a size, then a colour.

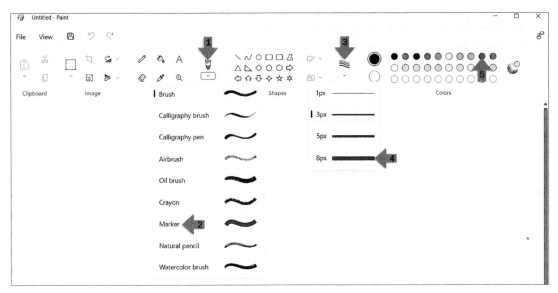

Now you can draw on the canvas.

9

Tablets & Touchscreens

Windows 11 is designed to run on a tablets and touchscreen devices. There is no more tablet mode like there was in Windows 10. In Windows 11, you get a much more consistent experience across devices.

In this chapter, we'll take a look at

- Touchscreens
- Touchscreen gestures
- How to Tap, Drag, and Zoom In & Out
- The Widgets Panel
- The Notifications Panel
- On-screen Keyboard
- Changing Keyboards
- Snipping Tool
- Sticky Notes
- Microsoft Whiteboard
- Using Pens
- Cases
- External Keyboards
- Hybrid Devices

Have a look at the video resources. Open your web browser and navigate to the following website

elluminetpress.com/win-11-nav

Touchscreens

Windows 11 supports touch screens. Here in the image below is Windows 11 running with a keyboard attached. You'll notice the interface is geared towards point and click navigation using a mouse pointer.

When you remove a keyboard from a device, such as a Surface Tablet, the icons on the taskbar appear more spaced out, making it easier for you to tap on the icon with your finger. Scroll bars and window edges are also a bit bigger making them easier to drag or resize. Here in the image below is Windows 11 running without a keyboard. Windows 11 automatically adjusts to touch oriented navigation.

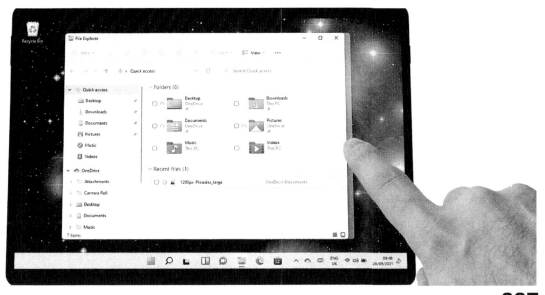

Touchscreen Gestures

On your tablet's touch screen, you can use various gestures using your forefinger and thumb.

Tap (Left Click)

Tap with one finger to select icons, links, files, or open apps on the start menu- equivalent to a click with a mouse. Tap twice with your finger to 'double click' - eg use this to open a file in file explorer.

Two Finger Tap (Right Click)

Tap two fingers on your screen. This is equivalent to the right click on a mouse, and is used to invoke a context menu.

Drag

Use this to move objects such as windows and icons around the screen. Tap on an object, then without lifting your finger, slide your finger across the screen. This is the same as click and drag with the mouse.

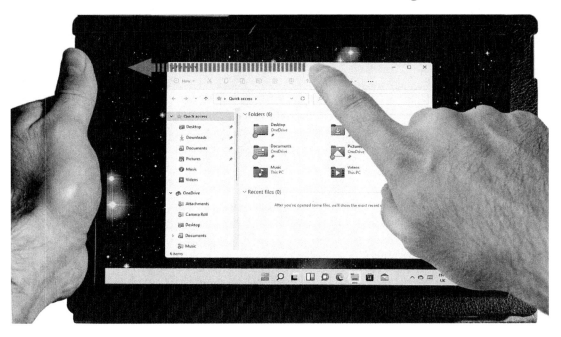

Zoom In & Out

Use your forefinger and thumb to zoom in and out. Spread your finger and thumb apart to zoom in, pinch your thumb and finger closer together to zoom out. Use this gesture on maps or when viewing photos.

Open Widgets Panel

Swipe from the left edge of the screen opens the widgets panel on the left hand side.

Open Notifications Panel

Swipe from the right edge of the screen opens your notifications.

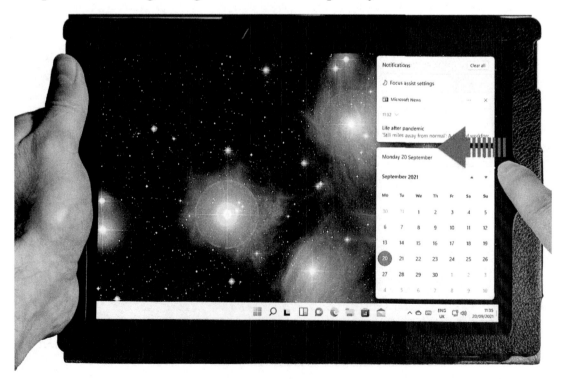

On-screen Keyboard

Your on-screen keyboard will appear whenever you tap inside a text field. To bring up the keyboard at any other time, tap the icon on the right hand side of the task bar. Note this icon wont appear if you have a keyboard plugged into your tablet.

Your keyboard will open up on the bottom third of the screen.

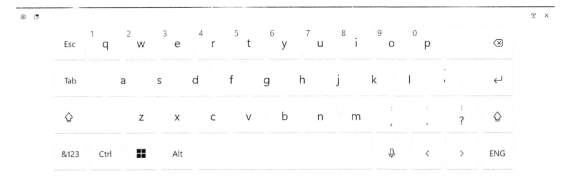

You can type normally using the keys. To quickly type in a number, use the keys on the top row, you'll notice a small number in the top left hand side of the key. To do this, tap and hold your finger on the key with the number you want to type, eg press and hold 'r' for the number 4. Tap the number in the popup.

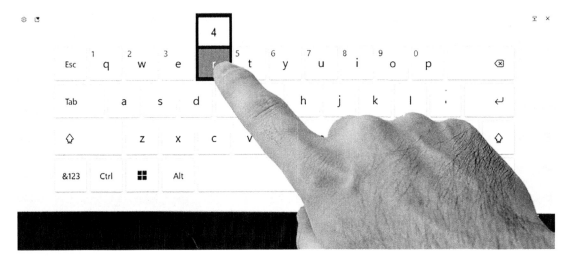

If you're typing in more than one number, tap the '&123' icon on the bottom left of the screen and use the keypad. Tap 'abc" to get back to the standard keyboard.

Changing Keyboards

You can also select different keyboards: default which is a standard keyboard, small - which is a small floating keyboard, split keyboard is one where the keyboard is split in half - one half on each side of the screen, and a traditional keyboard which is similar to a hardware keyboard.

To change the keyboard, tap the settings icon on the top left of the keyboard. Tap 'keyboard layout', then select a keyboard from the list.

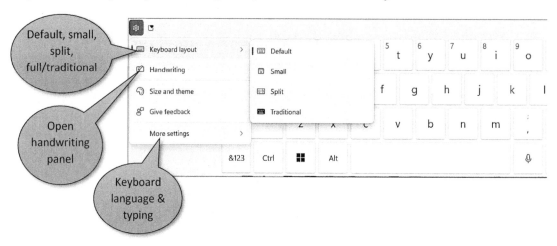

On a split keyboard, half appears on the left and the other half appears on the right. This can be more comfortable to type.

A small floating keyboard is useful if the default keyboard gets in the way.

You can drag a floating keyboard anywhere on the screen.

The on-screen keyboard also has a hand writing recognition feature that instead of typing, you can actually write words and sentences using your pen or finger.

To do this, tap the settings icon on the top left of the keyboard, then select handwriting from the drop down menu.

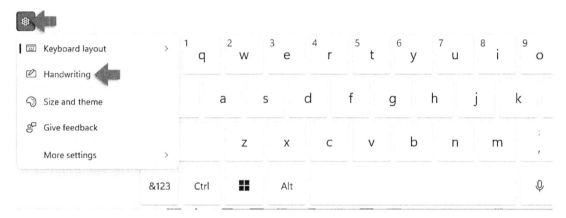

You'll see a panel open up. Tap in the field you want to enter text into. Write the text you want to 'type' in on the line. For example, when saving a file, you can write the file name instead of typing it, and the text appears in the text field.

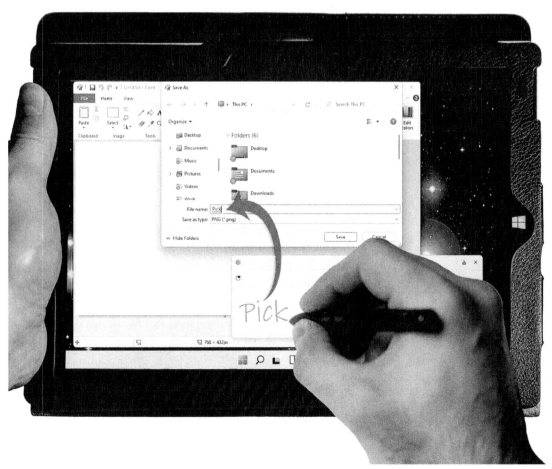

Snipping Tool

With the snipping tool, you can take a screenshot of whatever app you have open and handwrite annotations onto it with your pen. You can 'snip' the whole screen or just a section of it. To open the snipping tool, click on the start button, select 'all apps' on the top right, scroll down the list, click on 'snipping tool'.

When you start the app, you'll see a toolbar at the top of your screen. Here, you can create a new screen snip, set what you want to capture - rectangle, a window, whole screen or draw a shape.

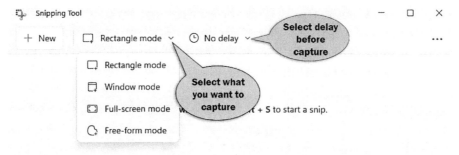

Open up the app you want to capture. In this case, I'm taking a rectangular screen ship of a page in Edge.

Click and drag the marker around the part of the page you want.

This is where you'll find pens and highlighters for you to annotate the screenshot.

If you want to choose the pen, tap on its icon, on the tool bar. To change the colour and size, tap and hold your pen on the pen icon until a drop down menu appears. Tap on the colour and sizes you want.

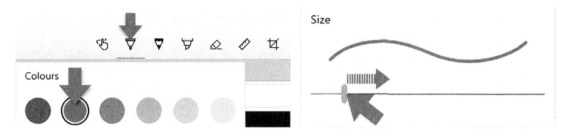

Draw directly onto the screen with your pen. If you want to change colour or size, select the pen icon again then choose a colour. You can also use a highlighter, to do this click the highlighter icon on the toolbar, select a colour and size from the drop down.

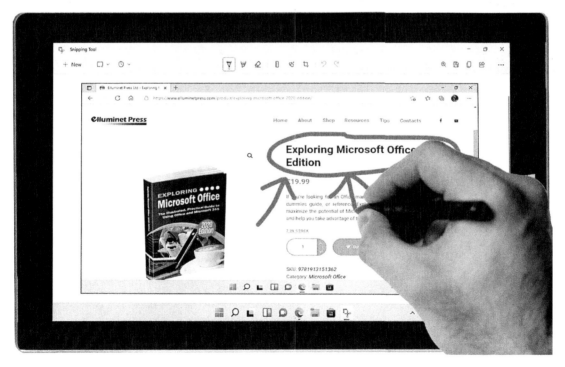

You can **save** your annotation as an image. To save, tap the 'save' icon on the top right of the screen. Enter a filename, then tap 'save'.

To **share**, tap the 'share' icon on the top right of the screen.

Tap the app you want to use to share, eg mail.

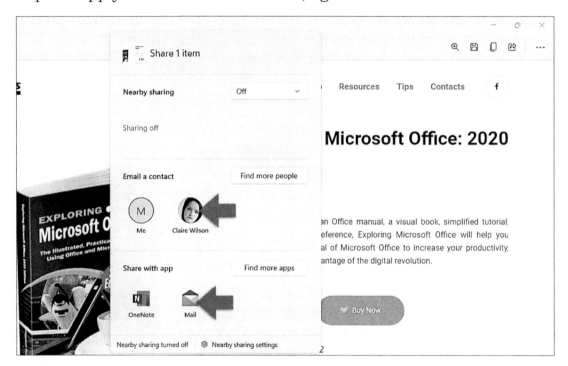

Fill in the email address and write a message, then tap the send icon.

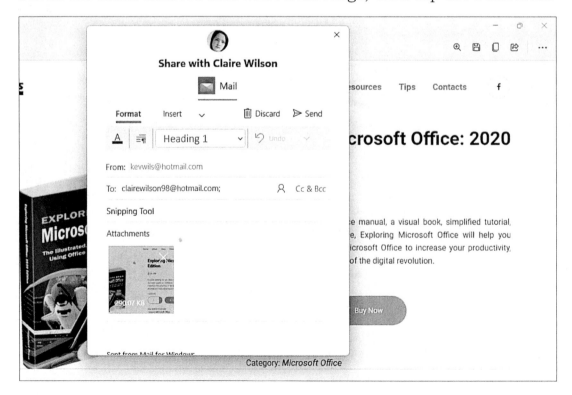

Sticky Notes

Sticky Notes allow you to hand write or type notes that you can pin to your desktop. You'll find sticky notes on your start menu, select 'all apps', scroll down, click on 'sticky notes'.

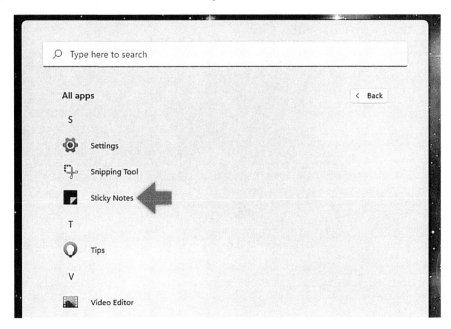

You can write notes, delete notes, and add new notes using the icons indicated below.

Microsoft Whiteboard

Microsoft Whiteboard is useful when giving presentations, teaching, online collaboration, or drawing. You can also save and share your illustrations created while using Whiteboard. You'll find the whiteboard app on your start menu, or on the Windows Ink pen menu on the bottom right of your screen.

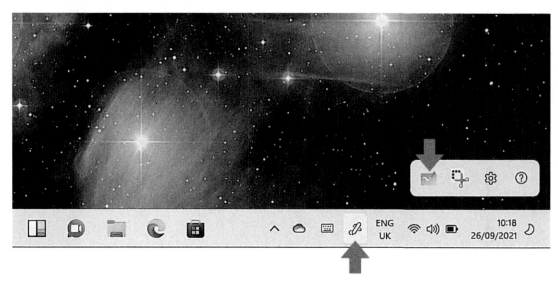

On the start screen, you'll see a thumbnail list of all the whiteboards you have created. Click on one to revisit. To create a new whiteboard, click 'create new whiteboard'.

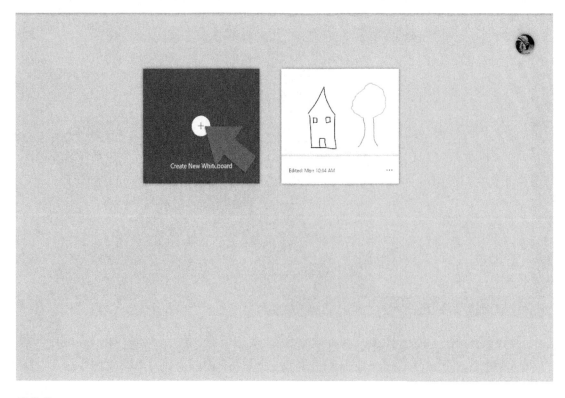

Getting Started

Select a template from the panel on the left hand side, or tap on the blank screen to start from scratch.

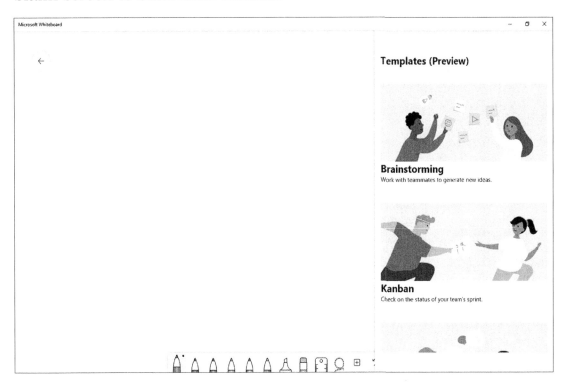

In the screen that opens, you'll see a tool bar appear along the bottom of your screen. Here, you'll find your pencils, pens, and highlighters you can use to draw onto the screen. Let's take a look:

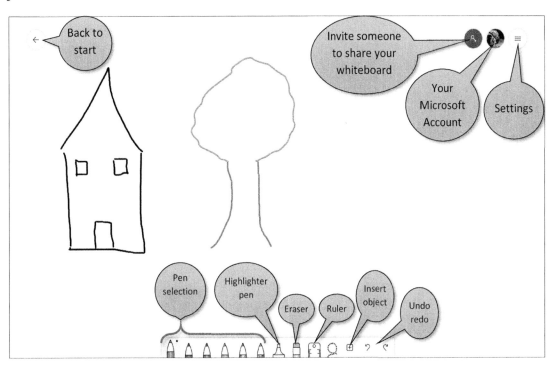

If you want to choose the pen, tap on its icon, on the tool bar.

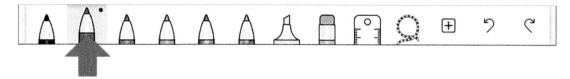

To change the colour and size, tap on the pen icon until the popup menu appears. Use the four circles on the left to select the thickness of the pen, then tap on a colour.

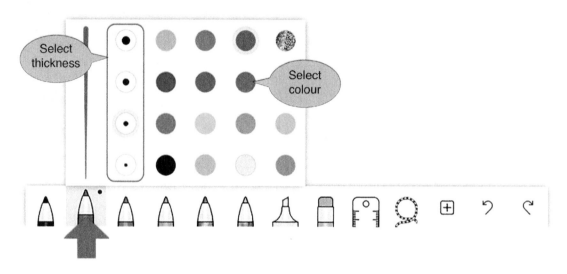

Now you can draw directly onto the screen with your pen.

Inserting Objects

You can insert objects such as photographs, diagrams, tables, notes, as well as insert office documents and PDFs. To do this, tap the insert icon on the toolbar along the bottom of your screen. Select the object type you want to insert (eg an image)

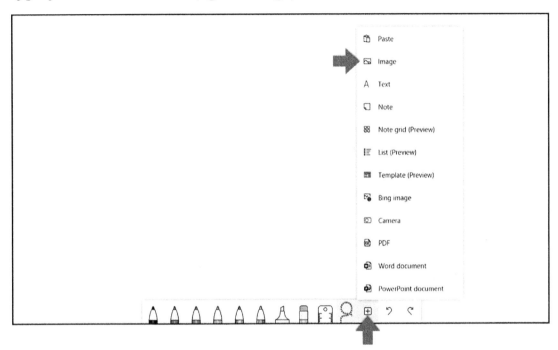

From the dialog box, select the image you want to insert.

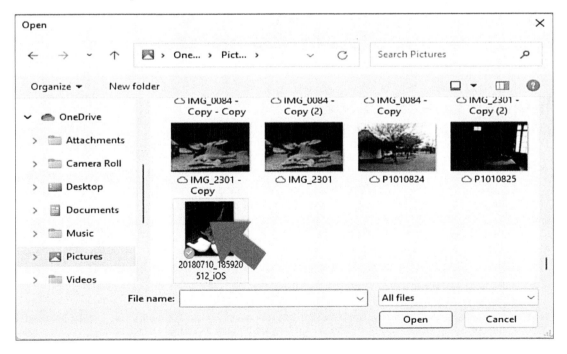

Click 'open'

Place the image on your whiteboard. Click and drag the image into position. You'll see a toolbar appear above the image.

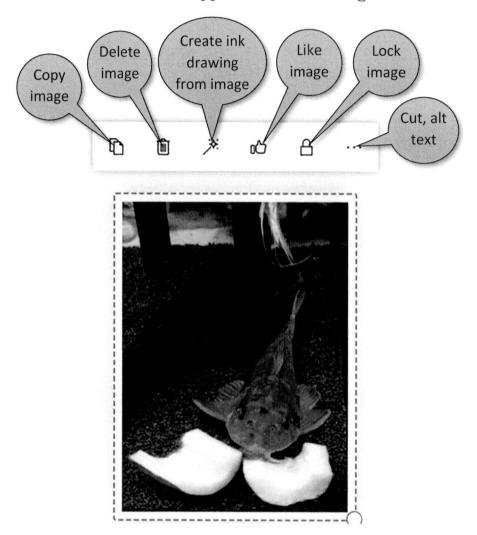

Inviting Collaborators

To invite other people to your whiteboard, click the sharing link on the top right of the screen.

Turn on 'web sharing link'. Whiteboard will generate a link you can send to other people.

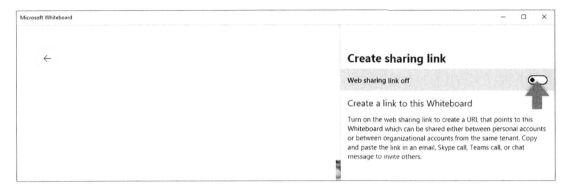

Now, once the link has been generated, click 'copy link' and paste it into an email or message to send to other people.

Once other people join, you'll see their contributions marked with their badge.

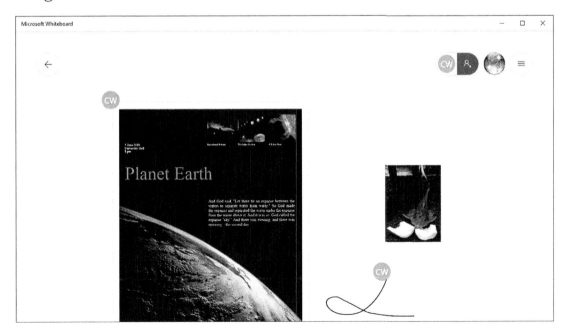

Ink to Shape

This feature creates clean geometric shapes from your drawings, such as squares, circles, etc. To enable ink to shape, click the hamburger icon on the top right.

Select 'ink to shape'.

Draw your shape on the canvas.

Ink to Table

This feature allows you to create clean tables by drawing them on your screen. To enable ink to table, click the hamburger icon on the top right.

Select 'ink to table'.

To draw your table, first draw a square. Then divide the square in half.

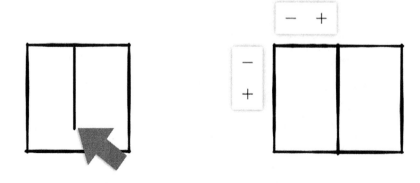

Pens

You can buy pens and styluses to use with your tablet. These come in useful for Windows Ink & OneNote, as well as any art apps out there that you can find in the Microsoft Store.

Here is the Microsoft Surface Pen that is used with many surface tablets and laptops.

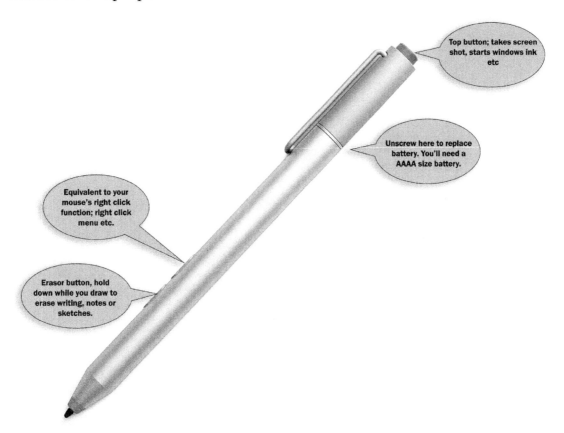

These come in various types but the ones that work best have bluetooth capability, meaning you can pair the pen with your tablet giving you extra features such as shortcut buttons, mouse button equivalents and so on.

Third party pens also work well. You can pick these up quite cheaply in any electronics store.

Cases

A case is a must for any tablet. A case helps to protect your tablet from scratches. Some cases double as a stand to allow you to prop your tablet up which is useful if you want to watch a movie. Some also come with pockets and a place to keep your pen.

External Keyboards

Some cases come with built in keyboards. Most of these types connect to your tablet using bluetooth. You can pair them in the usual way - see pairing bluetooth devices on page 79.

Hybrid Devices

Hybrid devices are a combination of a tablet and a laptop. They often have detachable keyboards such as the surface tablet...

...or keyboards that flip back behind the screen such as the lenovo yoga.

When you attach your keyboard, the display is optimised for point and click desktop use. When you detach the keyboard, the icons become larger and further apart making it easier to use on a touch screen.

10

System Maintenance

Computer maintenance keeps your computer in a good working order.

In this chapter, we'll take a look at

- Backing Up your Files
- PIN Recovery
- Password Recovery
- Changing Passwords
- Windows Update
- Activating Windows
- System File Check
- Managing Drives
- Add/Remove Windows Features
- Maintaining Apps
- System Recovery
- Media Creation Tool
- Windows Security
- Windows Firewall
- Anti Virus Software

Let's begin by taking a look at some backup strategies.

Have a look at the video resources. Open your web browser and navigate to the following website

`elluminetpress.com/win-sys`

Backing Up your Files

If you have ever lost data because of a computer glitch or crash you know how frustrating it can be. So we all need a good backup strategy. I'm going to go through the strategy I have found that has worked well over the years.

Windows 11 has a built in backup utility called File History that allows you to select files and back them up to an external hard drive.

Creating a Backup

First of all go buy yourself a good external hard disk - go for at least 1TB. This is a small device that plugs into a USB port on your computer.

Plug in your external drive into a free USB port.

To open File History, click the search icon on your taskbar, type

```
File History
```

Click on 'File History' in the search results.

On the screen that appears, click 'Turn On' to enable File History.

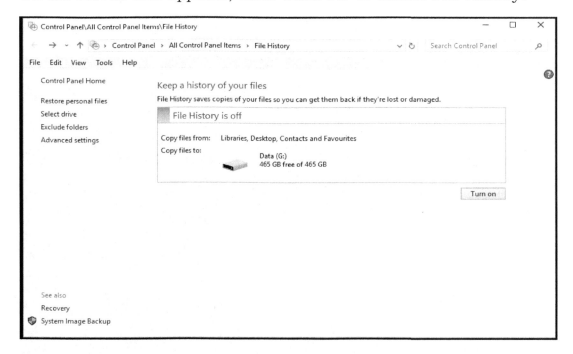

Once you have turned on File History, it will start to copy files from your libraries (documents, pictures, music etc) onto your external hard drive.

Adding Folders

If you want to add folders to your backup, just add them to your libraries. Remember your desktop, documents, photos, music & videos folders and their contents are already included.

For example, if I wanted to include my downloads folder which is on another hard drive, open file explorer, right click on the folder you want to backup, then go down to 'show more options'.

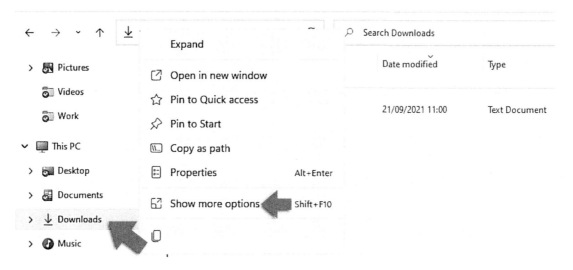

Then from the legacy menu, click 'include in library'. From the slide-out menu, select 'create new library'.

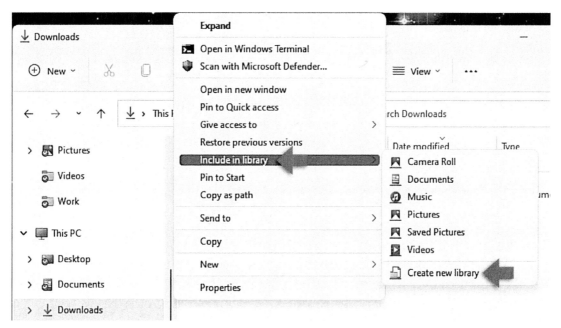

This folder will now be backed up with the rest of your libraries.

Setting Backup Schedules

By default, File History saves files every hour, but you can change this by clicking on "Advanced Settings" listed down the left hand side of the screen.

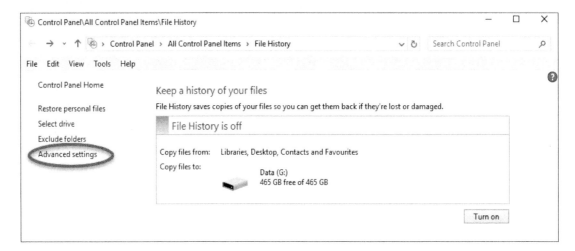

A good guide is to set how often File History saves files to "Daily". This will tell File History to save copies of your files once a day. For most users this is sufficient.

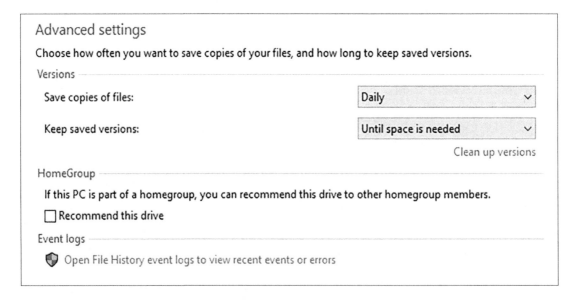

Set 'keep saved versions' to 'until space is needed'. This means that File History will keep creating backups while there is sufficient space on the hard drive, then once the drive fills up, File History will start to delete the oldest backups to make space for new backups.

Good practice would be to plug in your external drive at the end of each day to back up what you have done throughout the day.

Backups can take a while depending on how much you have done.

412

Restoring Files

Plug in your external Hard drive. Open up File History and click 'Restore Personal Files'

Use the left and right arrows at the bottom to navigate to the date backed up when you know your file still existed or was working.

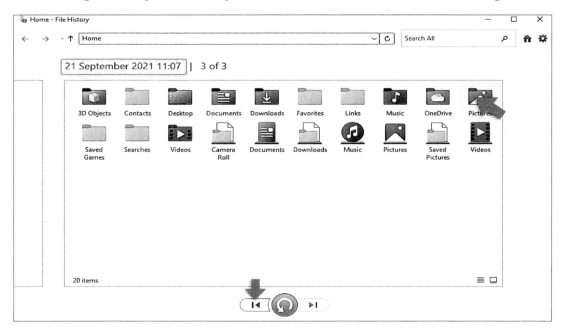

Then in the library section double click in the folder the file was in eg pictures if you lost a photo.

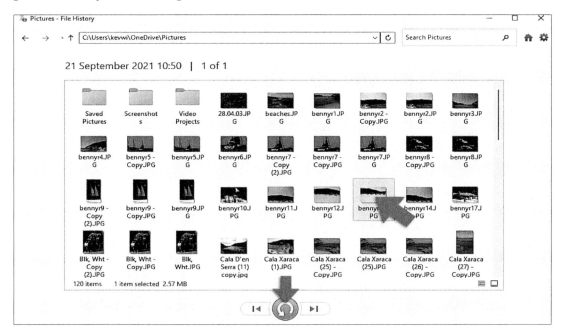

Select the photo and to restore it click the green button at the bottom of the window.

PIN Recovery

You can recover a forgotten Microsoft Account password from the login screen. Click 'I forgot my PIN' underneath the password field. If you don't see this field, it usually appears after you've entered an incorrect PIN.

Enter your Microsoft Account Password.

Click 'sign in'.

Select your recovery email address. This is the email address you entered when you signed up for a Microsoft Account. Select the email address, then type in your email address to confirm. Click 'send code'.

Now, go and check that email address - the account for the email address you just entered above. You'll see an email from 'microsoft account team' with a code. Enter the code in the field below and click 'verify'.

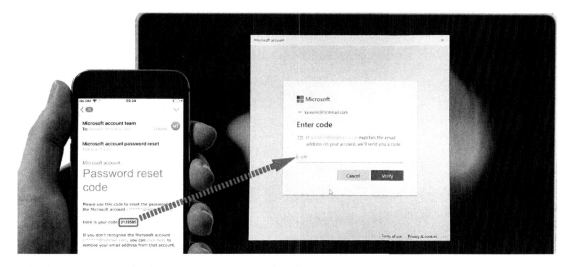

Click 'verify'. Click 'continue' on the 'are you sure' confirmation screen.

Now enter your new PIN, then click 'ok'.

Password Recovery

You should make every effort to remember passwords and keep them safe, as recovering them can be tricky.

Microsoft Account

You can reset your password for a Microsoft Account from a web browser on another device or phone.

Open a web browser and navigate to the following website.

```
account.live.com/password/reset
```

or

```
account.live.com/acsr
```

Follow the instructions on the screen.

Local Account

Select the Reset password link on the sign-in screen. The reset link only appears after you enter an incorrect password.

Answer the security questions you setup when you created the account.

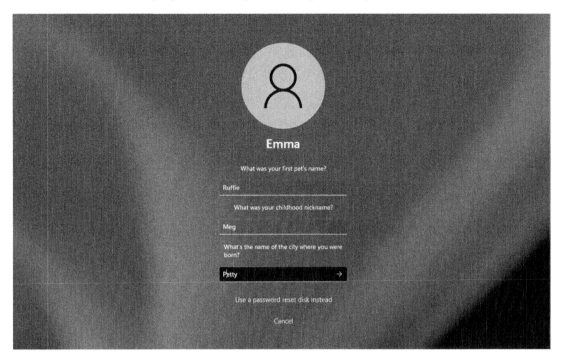

Enter a new password, then click the small arrow to the right.

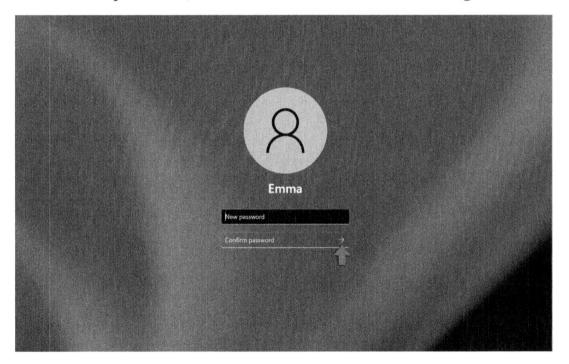

Sign in as usual with the new password.

Changing Passwords

Windows 11 no longer supports passwords for signing into Windows, instead you need to use a PIN, finger print, or facial recognition (if supported). You can change your Microsoft Account password on the web.

Microsoft Account

To change your Microsoft Account password, open your web browser then navigate to the following website

```
account.microsoft.com
```

Sign in with your Microsoft Account Email address and current password if prompted.

At the top of the page, on the right, click 'change password'.

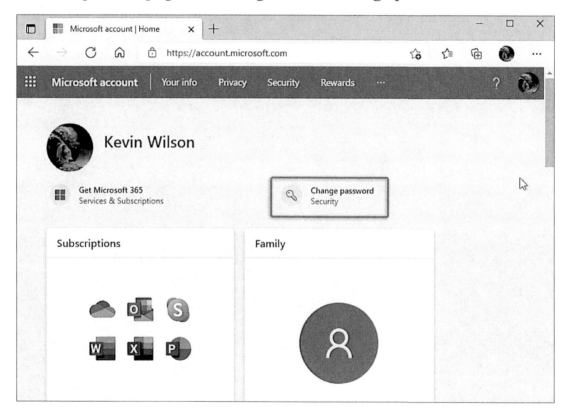

Follow the instructions on screen to change your password.

Windows Update

Windows update usually automatically downloads and installs all updates available for Windows.

Settings

You can find Windows Update in the Settings App on the start menu. Select 'windows update'.

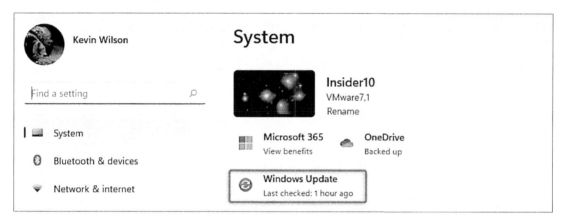

You'll land on the Windows Update page. At the top, you'll see available updates. Click 'check for updates' to check, click 'download now' to download updates.

At the bottom you'll see some options. Here, you can pause updates for a set amount of time - this prevents updates from being installed during this period. You can also see a list of updates in update history

At the bottom, you'll see advanced options.

Let's take a look at the advanced options.

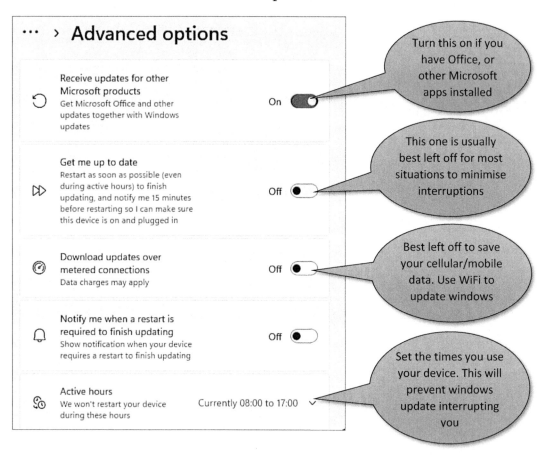

To change active hours, click 'active hours', select 'manual', then choose a start time and an end time.

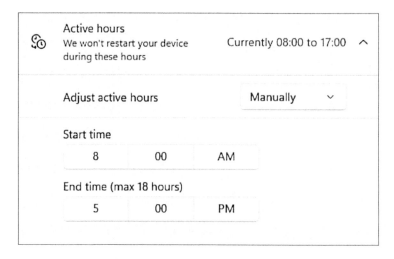

At the bottom of the page, you'll see optional updates. These are usually optional windows features, or device drivers. Click on 'optional updates' to view the options.

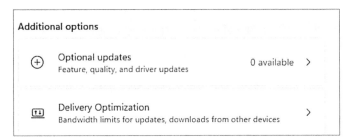

Underneath you'll see delivery optimization. If you have multiple windows 11 devices on your home or office network you can use Delivery Optimization to reduce internet bandwidth consumption by sharing the downloaded updates among the multiple devices on your network. This means that the update packages are downloaded from the internet to a device on the network, the update packages are then shared from this device and made available to other devices on the network, so they can update without having to download the package again from the internet.

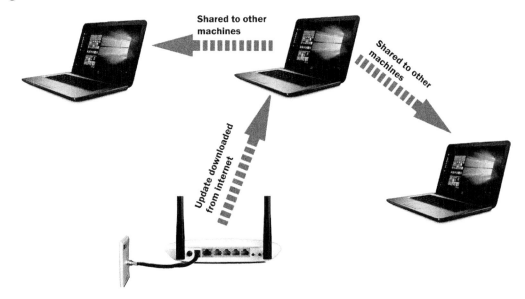

To enable delivery optimisation, click 'delivery optimization'. Click the slider switch to turn it on and select 'PCs on my local network'.

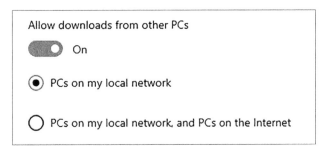

421

Activating Windows

To activate windows, you'll need a license with a product key or a digital license. If your machine came pre-installed with windows 11 or you purchased windows 11 from the Microsoft Store, you most likely have a digital licence meaning Windows 11 will automatically activate.

To activate Windows, open the settings app, select 'system' from the list on the left. Scroll down the list on the right then select 'activation'

Click 'change product key'.

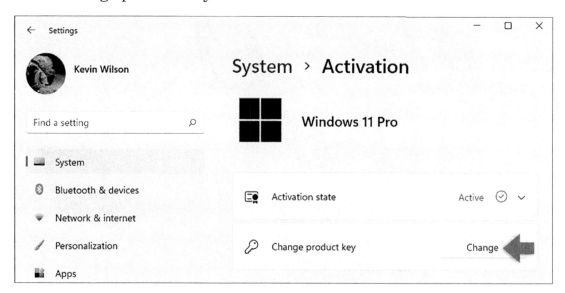

Enter your product key into pop-up box. Click 'next'.

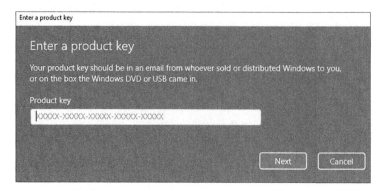

System File Check

System File Check or SFC, is a command line tool that allows you to scan for and restore corrupted windows system files. Useful when troubleshooting certain windows problems.

Open the windows terminal as an administrator - right click on the start button, then select 'windows terminal (admin)' from the popup menu.

Type the following command

```
sfc /scannow
```

SFC will scan your system files and replace any it finds to be corrupt.

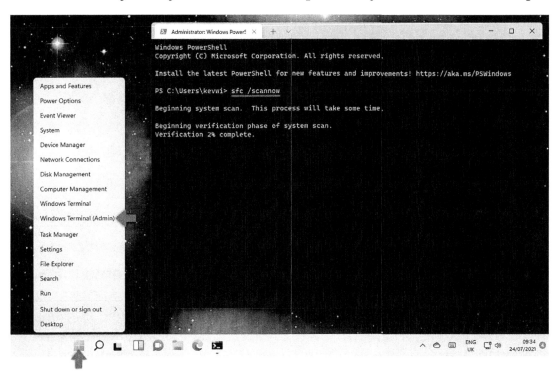

To check the log file, type:

```
notepad $Env:WinDir\Logs\CBS\CBS.log
```

This will open the log file in notepad.

Managing Drives

You can defragment and optimize your drives, as well as clean up temporary files.

Disk De-fragmentation

Data is saved in blocks on the surface of the disk called clusters. When a computer saves your file, it writes the data to the next empty cluster on the disk, even if the clusters are not adjacent. This allows faster performance, and usually, the disk is spinning fast enough that this has little effect on the time it takes to open the file.

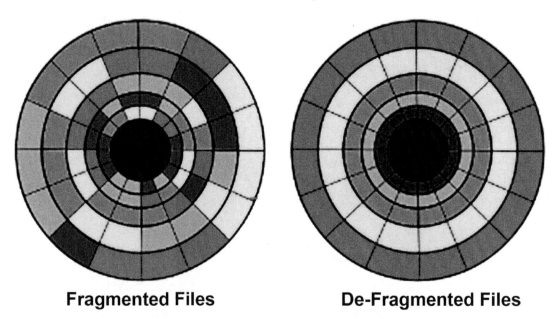

Fragmented Files   **De-Fragmented Files**

However, as more and more files are created, saved, deleted or changed, the data becomes fragmented across the surface of a disk, and it takes longer to access. This can cause problems when launching software (because it will often load many different files as it launches). So bad fragmentation just makes every operation on the computer take longer but eventually fragmentation can cause applications to crash, hang, or even corrupt the data.

It's a good rule of thumb to do this roughly once a month, to keep things running smoothly.

Disk defragmentation only applies to hard drives with mechanical spinning disks (HDD). If you have a solid state drive or SSD, then you don't need to worry about defragmentation. Defragging has no effect on performance with a SSD. Windows 11 will usually detect a SSD and optimise the drive itself using the TRIM command rather than defrag.

To defragment the disk in Windows 11, click the search icon on the taskbar, then type 'defragment'. Click 'Defragment and optimise your drives'.

Select the drive you want to defrag. Click the 'optimize' button.

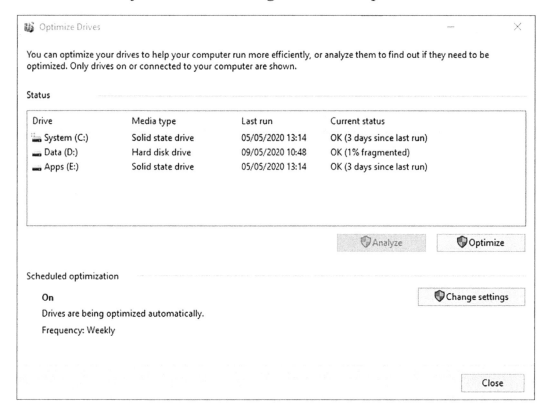

This will start de-fragmenting your disk. This process can take a while.

Disk Clean-Up

Over time, windows gets clogged up with temporary files from browsing the internet, installing and un-installing software and general every day usage. Doing this once a month will help keep things running smoothly.

Click the search icon on the taskbar then type 'disk cleanup'.

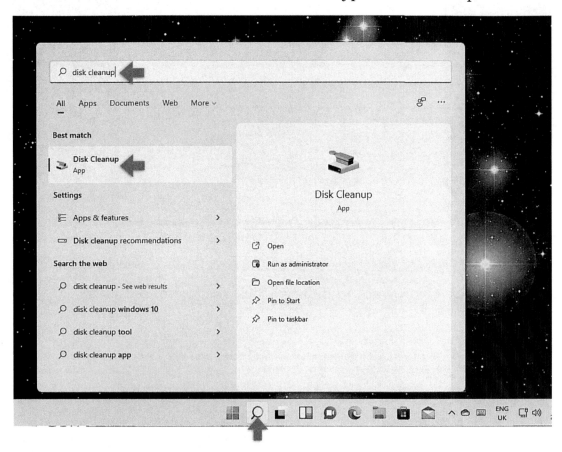

Click 'clear disk space by deleting unnecessary files'

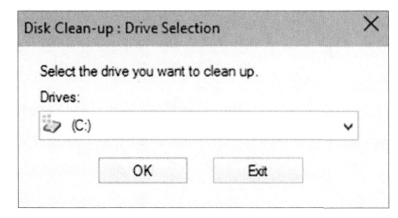

Select drive C, click 'ok'.

In the window that appears you can see a list of all the different files and caches. It is safe to select all these for clearing.

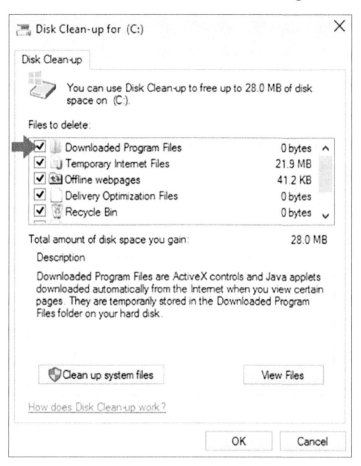

Once you are done click ok and windows will clear out all those old files.

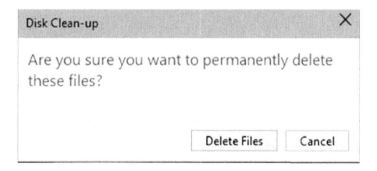

Click 'delete files' on the confirmation dialog box to clear out all the old files

Do the same with the system files. In the window above, click 'clean up system files'.

This helps to keep your system running smoothly. A good rule of thumb is to do this about once a month.

427

Disk Manager

This utility allows you to view and manage disk drives, partitions and volumes. You can also manage external drives such as USB drives (flash drives), and external hard drives. **Use this utility with caution as you can wipe drives, volumes and partitions, which means the data on those drives and partitions will be lost.**

To open disk manager, right click on the start button, select 'disk management' from the menu.

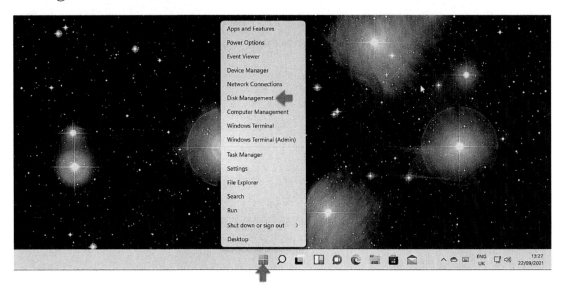

Let's take a look at the main screen.

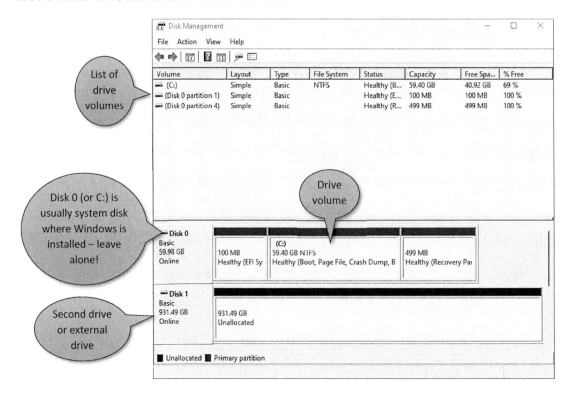

Drive Volumes

Find the drive you want to create a volume on. Disk 1 on this PC is an external hard drive I plugged into a USB port. In this demo, I'm going to create a new volume on this drive.

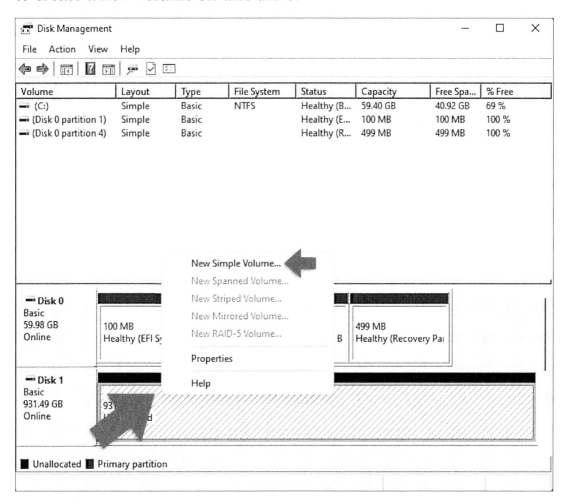

In the lower half of the screen, right click on the unallocated part of the disk, select 'new simple volume' from the popup menu. Click 'next'.

Enter the size of the volume in MB, or leave it as the default if you want to use the whole drive. In this example, I'm creating a volume that is 4GB (4096MB) in size. Click 'next'.

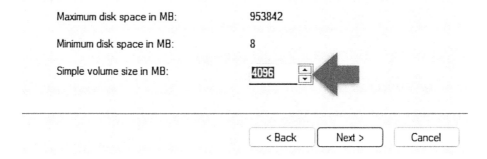

429

Chapter 10: System Maintenance

Assign a drive letter, eg Drive D: Click 'next'.

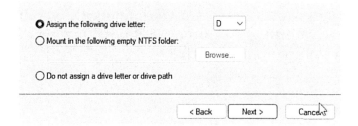

Under 'file system' select a file system. Select NTFS if you use the drive on Windows only. Select exFAT or FAT32 if you use the drive on a Mac, Linux and Windows.

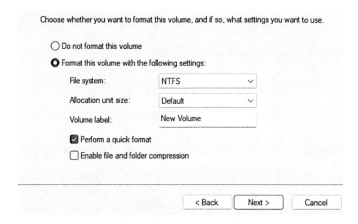

Under 'volume label' give the drive a meaningful name. Click 'next', then 'finish'.

You'll see the partition appear in the bottom half of the screen.

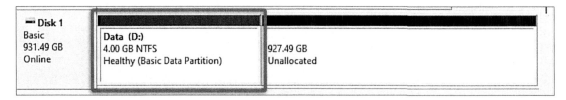

To delete a volume, right click on the volume then select 'delete volume' from the menu. **Use with caution as doing this will wipe the data off the volume.**

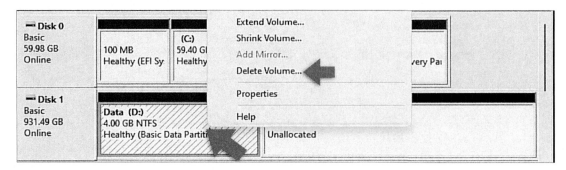

430

Add/Remove Windows Features

You can turn on/off various features in Windows 11. To do this click the search icon on the taskbar, then type 'turn windows features on or off'. Click 'turn windows features on or off' in the search results.

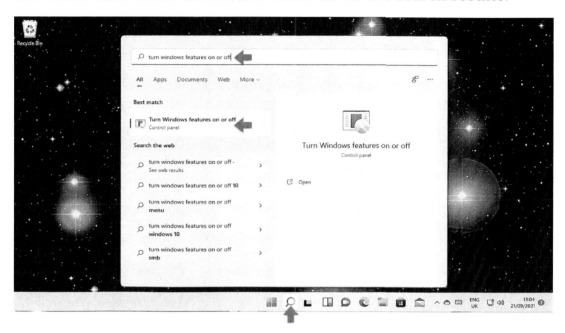

Scroll down the list, select the options you want to install, and deselect the ones you want to remove.

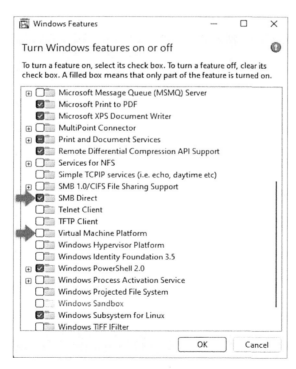

Click 'ok', when you're done. Windows will restart and add/remove your selections.

Maintaining Apps

In Windows 11, you can remove apps you don't use, you can reset apps if they're not working correctly, and you can change which apps run at windows startup.

Removing Apps

To remove apps and programs from your computer, right click on the start button, select 'apps and features' from the menu.

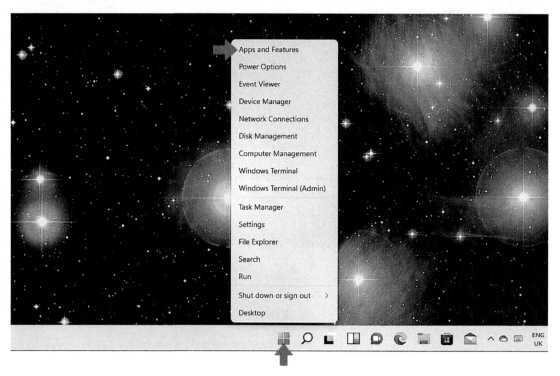

Scroll down to the app you want to remove, then click the three dots icon. Select 'uninstall' from the menu.

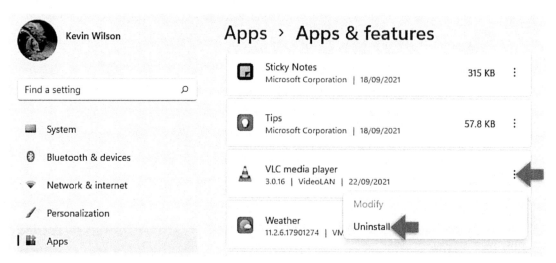

Now, depending on what program you are trying to remove, you might get a screen asking you what you want to do. Click 'next', and run through the wizard.

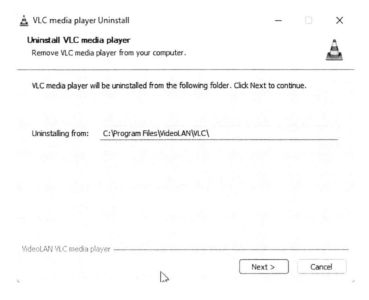

This is the process for removing desktop applications such as Microsoft Office or Adobe Creative Suite.

For apps that you have downloaded from the App Store or ones that come with Windows 11, you can remove them directly from the start menu. To do this, select 'all apps' from the top right of the start menu, then right click on the app you want to remove, select 'uninstall' from the menu.

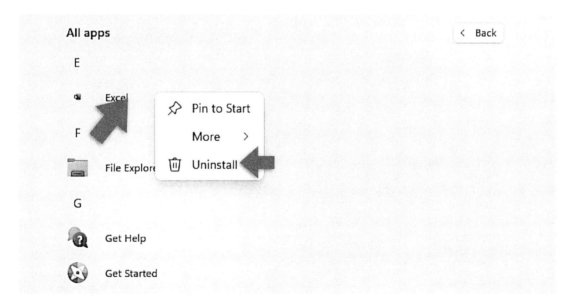

It's good practice to go through the apps and programs installed on your device, and remove the ones you don't use anymore and any old apps. This helps to keep your device running smoothly.

Resetting & Repairing Apps

Sometimes apps can become slow and unresponsive, so in Windows 11, you have the option to reset or repair the app. This will clear all the App's data, history lists, caches, settings and so on. This doesn't clear any of your personal files etc.

To do this, right click on the start menu, select 'apps and features'.

Click the three dots icon next to the app you want to reset, select 'advanced options'.

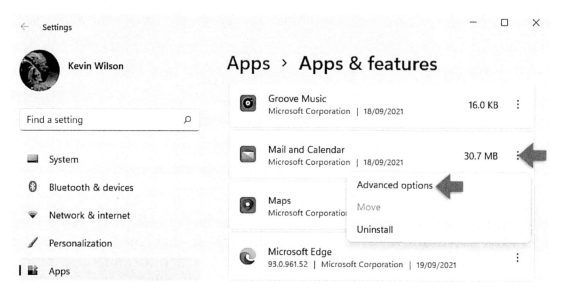

From the advanced options, scroll down the screen, click 'reset' to reset the app, or repair to repair the app.

Terminate

Immediately terminate this app and its related processes.

Terminate

Reset

If this app isn't working right, we can try to repair it. The app's data won't be affected.

Repair

If this app still isn't working right, reset it. The app's data will be deleted.

Reset

Click 'terminate' to close the app down. You can start it up again from the start menu.

Startup Programs

Start up programs automatically start when you start up Windows - this can cause Windows to become very sluggish during start up. These are usually 'helper' apps that are installed with certain pieces of software and most can be disabled without any problem.

To find your startup programs, open your settings app, then select 'apps' from the list on the left hand side. Scroll down, then click 'startup'.

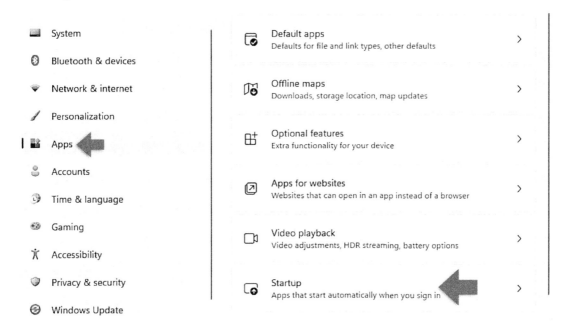

On this screen you'll see a list of apps that are configured to start when Windows starts. Click the sliders next to each app to either enable or disable them - you can turn then on or off.

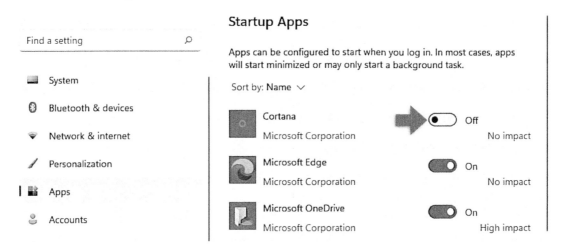

You can turn off most of these, except anti-virus, onedrive, and anything to do with your graphics or sound cards.

System Recovery

If you are having problems, Windows 11 has a section to recover your computer. You can boot to the recovery environment from the settings app. Windows 11 will also startup into the recovery environment after two failed attempts to restart.

To find the recovery options in Windows, open the settings app, select 'system' from the list on the left. Scroll down, click 'recovery'.

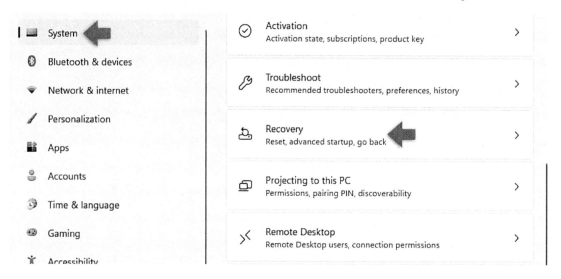

In the first section, under 'recovery options' you can reset your PC - this re-installs Windows 11 leaving all your personal files intact. To do this click 'Reset PC'.

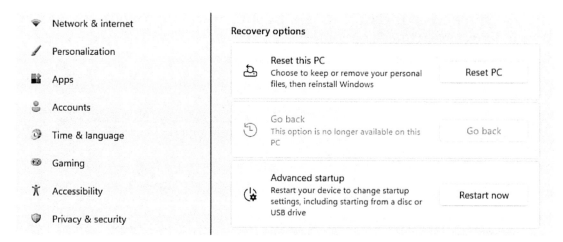

Scroll down to the next section. Here, you can go back to a previous version of Windows 11 - useful if you've installed an update but are having problems. To do this click 'Go back'.

In the section at the bottom, you can boot to the recovery environment under the 'advanced startup' section. To do this click 'restart now'.

Force Windows into the Recovery Environment

If you're having trouble starting Windows, you can force windows 11 to boot into the recovery environment.

To do this, start your machine, then when you see the start up logo screen, hold down the power button until your screen goes blank. *If you don't see the logo you'll need to boot from the installation media - see 'boot from external drive' on page 440 for details.*

Wait a few seconds, then press the power button again to start your machine.

When you see the start up logo screen, hold down the power button again until your screen goes blank.

Wait a few seconds, then press the power button again to start your machine.

This time, allow your device to fully restart. You should see this screen.

Once the WinRE environment starts, you'll see the 'automatic repair screen'.

Click 'advanced options' to begin.

Reset your PC

Boot into the recovery environment as shown in the previous section.

To reinstall Windows 11 for your PC, click 'troubleshoot'.

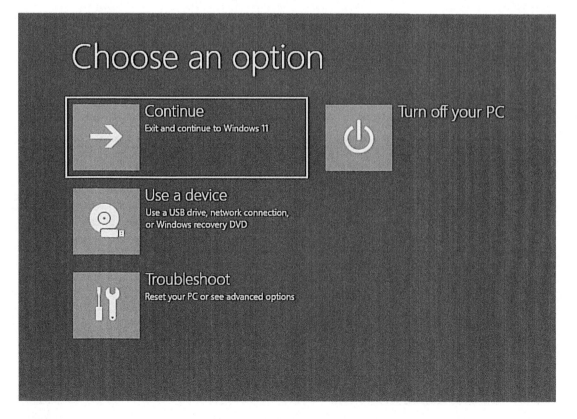

From the 'troubleshoot' screen, click 'reset this PC'.

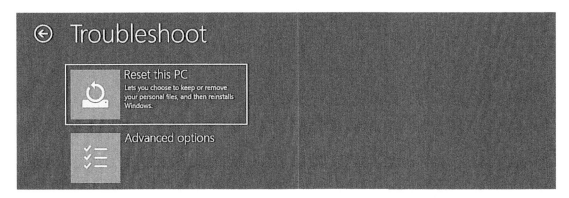

From here you can do a complete re-install by clicking on 'remove everything'. This will remove all your files and applications and reset Windows 11 back to its factory default. Click 'keep my files' to refresh Windows 11. This will delete all your installed applications and settings. Your personal files and data will remain intact.

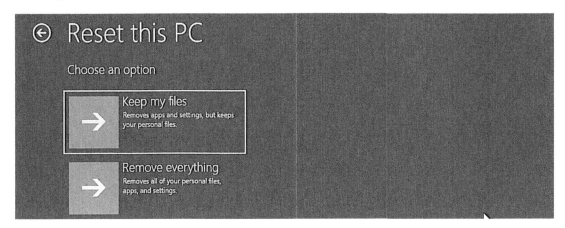

Select where you want to download the installer from. You can download from the cloud meaning the installer will download the installer files from Microsoft's servers to re-install windows. Select this one if you are connected to the internet and have a fast internet connection.

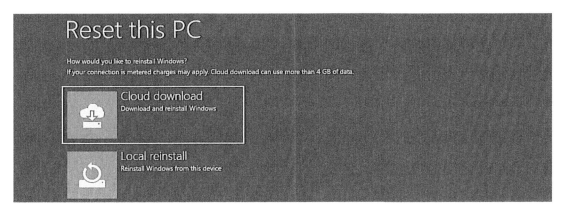

If not, click 'local reinstall' to reinstall Windows 11 from the recovery partition on your hard drive.

439

Boot from External Drive (USB)

First insert the USB drive into a USB port on your PC. Start up your machine.

As the machine boots, have a look at the start up screen for the hot key that displays the boot menu. This key is usually Esc, F8, F10, F11 or F12. You'll have to be quick, as the start up screen is only visible for a split second.

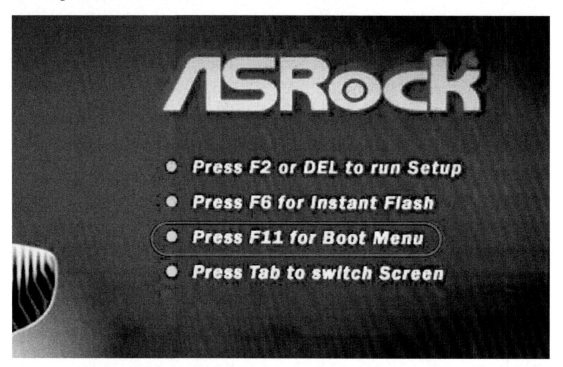

On this particular machine it's F11. *If you're using a surface tablet, press and hold the volume-down button, then press and release the power button.*

Once you find the boot menu select the UEFI USB drive, press 'enter' on your keyboard.

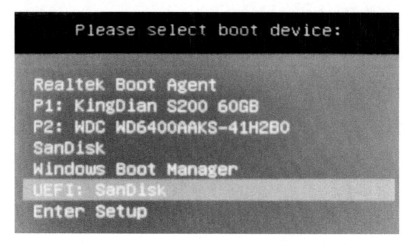

Re-install Windows from USB Drive

Boot your PC from the USB drive. See page 440 for details. Once you boot from the drive, Windows setup will begin.

Select language, time format and your keyboard layout. Click 'next'.

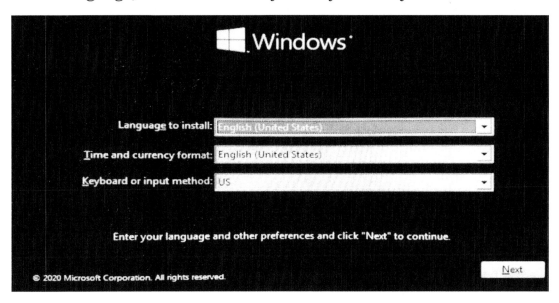

Click 'install now' to re-install windows 11.

On the 'activate windows' screen. Enter your product key - this is usually printed on a label on your PC. If you don't have one, click 'I don't have a product key' on the bottom right, you can activate later.

The product key looks like this: XXXXX-XXXXX-XXXXX-XXXXX-XXXXX

If you're reinstalling Windows, select I don't have a product key. Your copy of Windows will be automatically activated later.

Privacy statement   I don't have a product key   Next

Select the version of Windows 11 you want to install. Eg 'Windows 11 Home', or 'windows 11 pro'. Click 'next'.

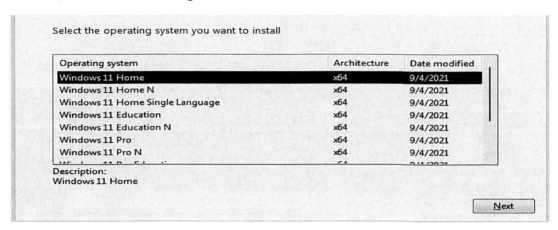

Accept the license agreement on the following screen.

Click 'next'.

Click 'custom: install windows only'.

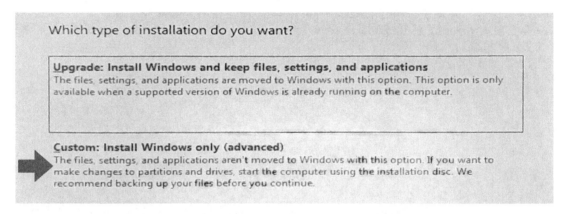

If you see 'partition 1', 'partition 2', and so on, click on each of these then select 'delete'. *Note that this will delete all the information on these partitions - so use with caution. Make sure all this data is backed up if you want to keep it.* This ensures you have a clean drive.

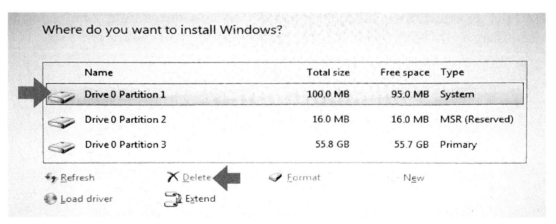

Once all partitions have been deleted, select the drive you want to install windows onto. You should see 'unallocated space' next to the drive.

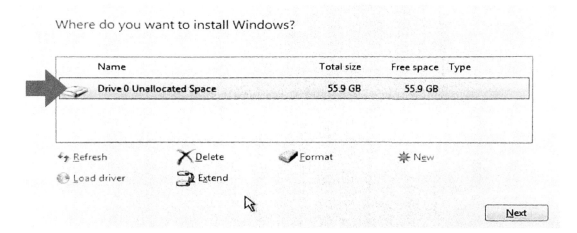

Click 'next' to begin.

Allow Windows to install.

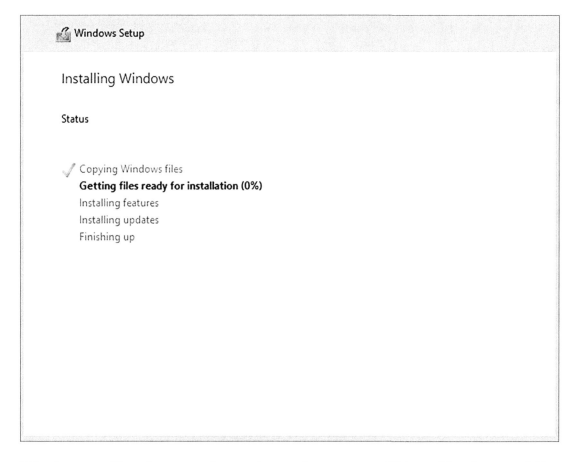

Windows will reboot and continue the setup. This will take a while. When complete, you'll need to run through the initial setup again. See page 31.

Enter UEFI BIOS

Open the settings app, select 'system', then scroll down, select 'recovery'.

Under 'recovery options' click 'restart now'.

From the recovery screen, choose Troubleshoot, then Advanced options.

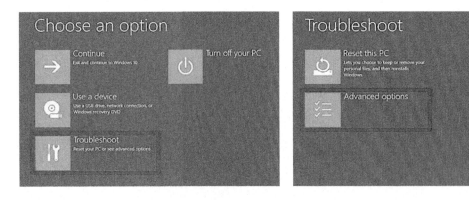

Select UEFI Firmware Settings

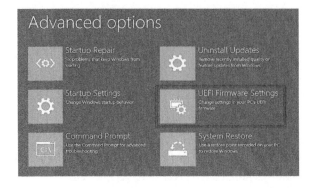

Click 'restart'. Allow your machine will reboot to the UEFI screen.

Media Creation Tool

The Media Creation tool is a utility you can download and run on your computer. This will allow you to create an install DVD or USB flash drive. These can be useful if your machine fails or has problems and will allow you to reinstall Windows 11 on your PC.

First, you'll need to download the utility. To do this, open your web browser and navigate to the following website.

```
www.microsoft.com/en-us/software-download/windows11
```

Scroll down to 'create windows 11 installation media', then click 'download now'.

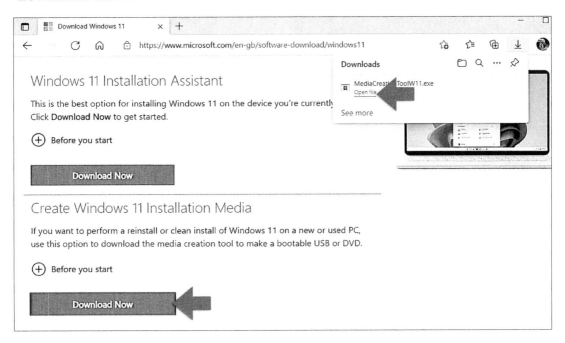

Click on the file in the downloads prompt, or click 'open' if prompted by your browser. If not, you'll find the file in your downloads folder.

Creating a Windows 11 Installation Disk

You can use this tool to create a DVD or a USB flash drive that you can use to re-install Windows 11 on your PC. This media is useful if your PC fails to start or your hard disk fails.

You can start your PC up from the installation media and run the installation process again to restore your computer.

To create the installation media, we are going to use a USB flash drive. Make sure your USB flash drive is at least 8GB.

First, plug your USB flash drive into your PC.

Select your language, edition of Windows 11 (home or pro) and your computer's architecture (usually 64 bit).

Most of the time, the media creation tool will automatically select these settings based on your current version of windows and hardware.

If you need to change then un-tick 'use the recommended options for this PC', then change the language and edition selections.

Click 'next'.

Select your installation media. Select USB flash drive. *If you want an ISO image you can burn to a DVD select ISO file.* Click next.

The media creation tool will scan for your USB flash drive. Select the drive from the 'removable drives' section. Click 'next' to start.

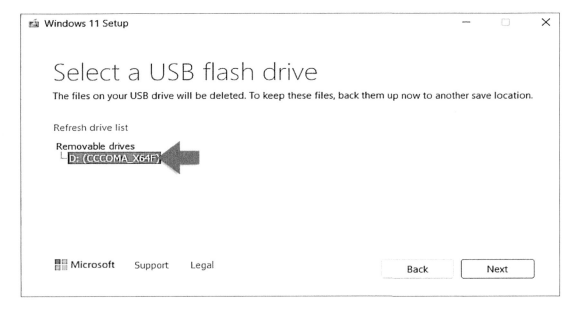

The media tool will start downloading Windows 11. This process can take a while depending on the speed of your PC. Once it has finished, store your USB flash drive in a safe place, as you probably won't need it unless you have problems or want to install a fresh copy of Windows 11.

If you run into problems with your PC, you can always start it up using the flash drive you just created.

Windows Security

Windows Security is the hub for all security features including virus protection, device health, networking, firewalls, internet security, app control and family safety options. Open your start menu, select 'all apps' on the top right. Scroll down the list, then click 'windows security'.

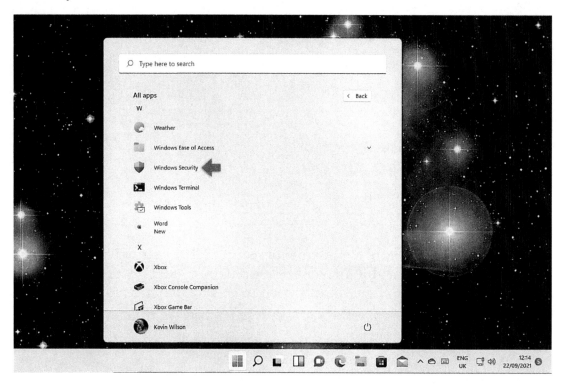

Down the left hand panel and on the 'home' page, you have some options:

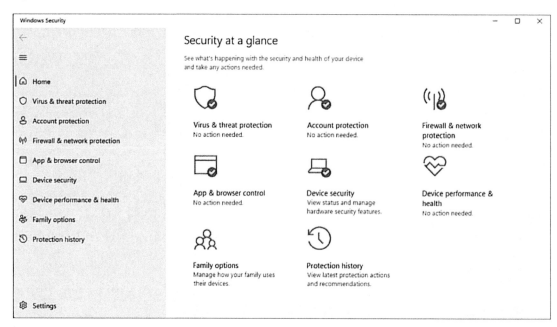

Virus & Threat Protection. From here you can scan for threats with a full system scan which scans system files, apps, as well as your files. You can also perform an 'offline scan', where your system will restart into a 'secure mode' to scan for threats. This scan is useful for removing malware that isn't removed with a full or quick scan. Most detected threats are automatically quarantined.

Account Protection. Security settings for your Microsoft Account, manage sync settings between devices, adjust windows hello sign in options, enable/disable dynamic lock.

Firewall & Network Protection. Here you can troubleshoot network issues with WiFi or internet connectivity and adjust your firewall settings. You can also access firewall settings.

App & Browser Control. Here you can adjust your browser and application security settings such as SmartScreen filter that helps protect you against malicious websites, apps and downloads.

Device Security. Enable/disable core isolation and memory integrity preventing and attack injecting malicious code into processes.

Device Performance & Health. Here you can see any issues arising with drivers, updates, battery life and disk storage space. You also have the option to refresh Windows 11, meaning you can re-install Windows if it is not running smoothly while keeping your personal files safe.

Family Options. This section links you to your family options using your web browser and allows you to monitor your kids' online activity.

Protection History. This shows actions taken on various potential threats, as well as any recommended actions.

Running a Virus Scan

You can run a quick scan that checks your folders, or a full scan that scans every file on your PC. To start, select 'virus & threat protection' from the panel on the left hand side

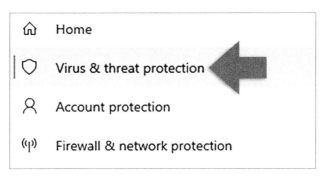

Chapter 10: System Maintenance

From the 'scan screen' click 'scan options'.

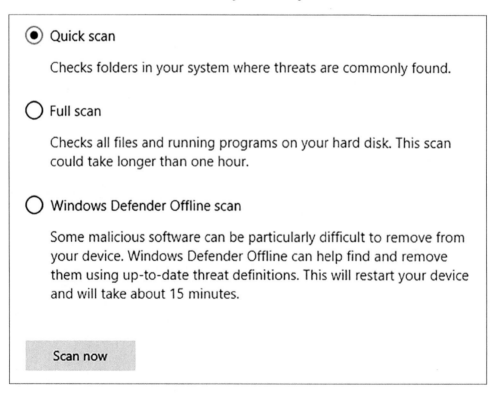

No current threats.
Last scan: 19/02/2019 20:04 (quick scan)
1 threats found.
Scan lasted 2 minutes 42 seconds
39480 files scanned.

Quick scan

Scan options

Allowed threats

Protection history

Select either 'quick scan' to scan system files as well as your personal files. Click 'full scan' to scan every file on your PC.

⦿ Quick scan

Checks folders in your system where threats are commonly found.

◯ Full scan

Checks all files and running programs on your hard disk. This scan could take longer than one hour.

◯ Windows Defender Offline scan

Some malicious software can be particularly difficult to remove from your device. Windows Defender Offline can help find and remove them using up-to-date threat definitions. This will restart your device and will take about 15 minutes.

Scan now

If you are trying to remove malware or a virus and the quick or full scan doesn't remove it, use 'windows defender offline scan' to restart your PC in a secure environment.

Click 'scan now'.

If you selected the 'windows defender offline scan', windows will reboot into a secure environment and scan your system

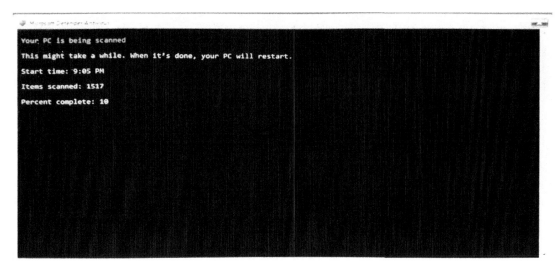

Any malware or viruses that are found will be removed or quarantined. You'll find the results in 'virus & threat protection' under 'protection history'.

Scan a Specified File or Folder

To scan a particular file or folder, open up File Explorer and navigate to the file or folder you want to scan.

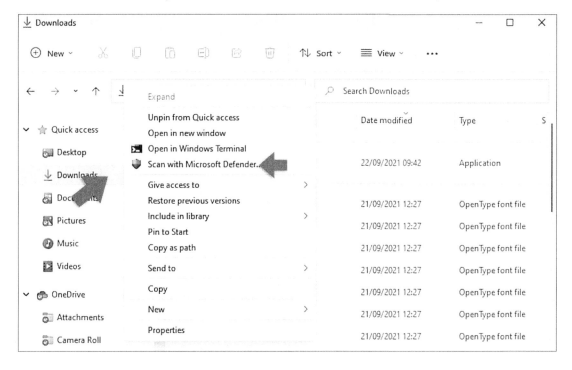

Right click on the folder, select 'show more options', then click 'scan with Microsoft Defender'.

Dealing with Threats

If any of the virus scans detect a threat, they'll appear on the 'scan options' screen. Click on the threat to view details. Select an action, eg 'remove'.

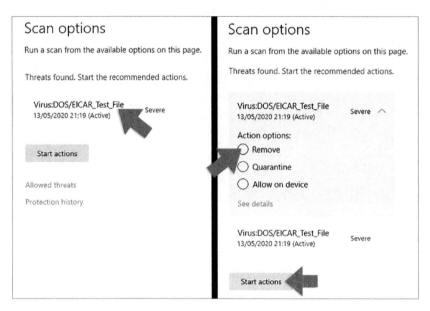

Click 'start actions' to clean.

Threat Protection Settings

Open windows security app, then select 'Virus & Threat Protection'. Scroll down to 'virus & threat protection settings', then click 'manage settings'.

Here, you can enable/disable 'real time protection', 'cloud delivered protection', 'automatic sample submission', 'tamper protection', 'file exclusions', and 'notifications'.

Controlling Folder Access

This feature allows you to protect files & folders from modification by unapproved applications and malware. If any of these applications try to modify files, you'll get a notification allowing you to block the action.

To enable this feature, open Windows Security, Click 'virus & threat protection', scroll down the page, then select 'Manage Ransomware Protection'. Set the 'controlled folder access' switch to 'On'.

Windows Security will normally allow most known applications to access and change data in the folders on your machine. If Windows Security detects an app it doesn't recognise, you'll receive a notification that it has been blocked. Some of the time this will be a legitimate application, so you might need to add the application to the safe list.

To add other applications to the 'safe list', click 'allow an app trough controlled folder access'. Then click 'add an allowed app'.

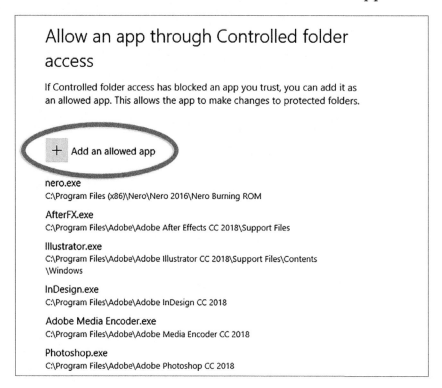

Now in the dialog box that appears, navigate to the folder where the application is installed. This will usually be "C:\Program Files". In this example, I'm going to add 'Adobe After Effects'. So navigate to the folder in 'program files'. Make sure you select the file with the EXE extension, as shown below.

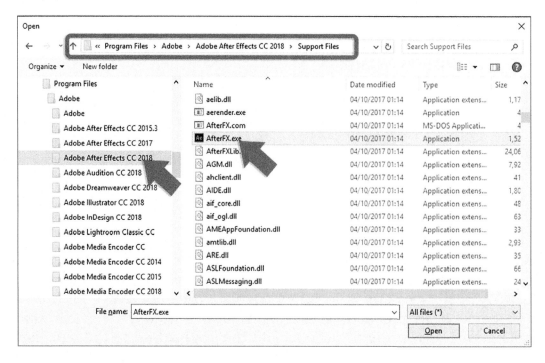

Windows Security will automatically add your system folders and most of your personal folders. You can add any others if you need to. To do this, click 'protected folders' on the 'virus & threat protection' screen.

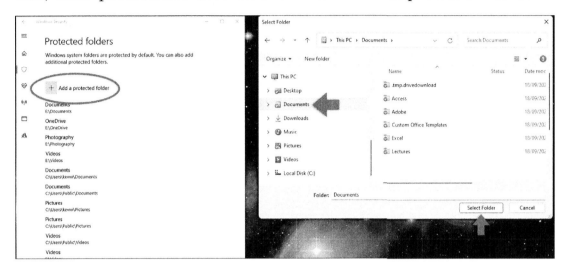

Click 'add a protected folder', then from the dialog box that appears, navigate to the folder you want to protect, click on it, then click 'select folder'.

Exploit Protection

This feature is designed to protect your PC from various types of exploits out of the box and shouldn't need any configuration.

To find this feature, open Windows Security, click 'App & browser control' then select 'Exploit protection' at the bottom of the page.

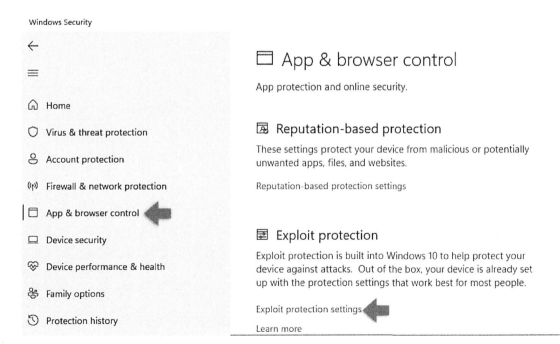

Chapter 10: System Maintenance

The exploit protection settings are divided into two categories: system settings and program settings.

System settings allows you to set the exploit protection globally - for all the programs.

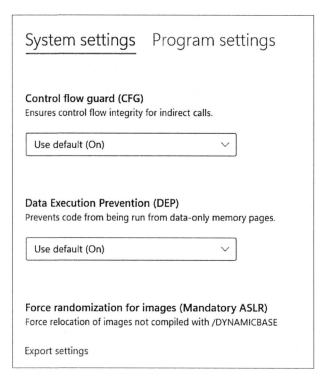

The program settings allows you to override the global system settings for an individual program.

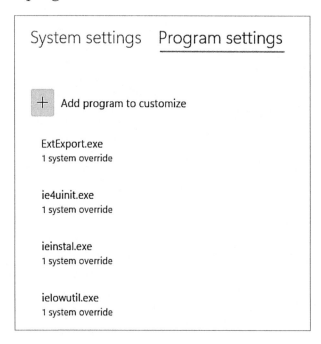

Most of these settings can be left on the default.

Windows Firewall

Windows Firewall is a security feature built into Windows 11. It is designed to filter network traffic to and from your computer and block any malicious attempts to connect to your machine or potentially harmful programs attempting to transmit data.

To open the firewall settings, start windows security - you'll find the icon on your start menu. Select 'firewall & network protection'

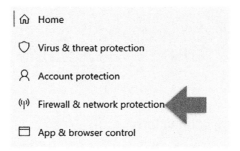

Enable or Disable

Select the network profile. The one your PC is using with have 'active' written next to it. Home networks use the 'private' profile.

Private. Networks where computers at home or office connected to a private, internal network usually a small workgroup.

Domain. Networks where computers are part of an Active Directory domain usually found on large networks in schools, colleges and businesses.

Guest or Public. Networks that are not secure such as wifi hotspots you'd find in a coffee shop, library or any public place.

It's best practice to enable the firewall on all three profiles.

To enable/disable, click on the network profile. Eg 'private network'.

457

Set the slider to 'on' to enable, 'off' to disable.

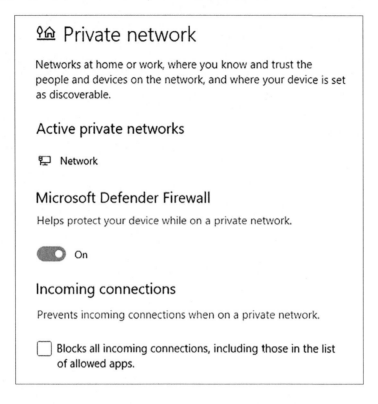

If you're on a public wifi network, enable 'block all incoming connections' on the active network profile.

Allow or Block an App

Select 'firewall & network protection' in Windows Security, then click 'allow an app through firewall'.

Click 'change settings', enter your administrator password if prompted.

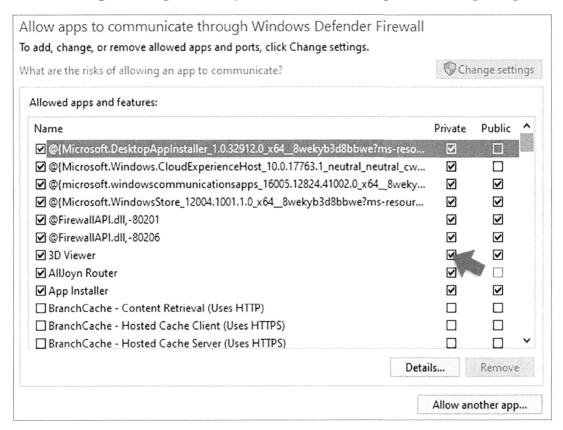

Scroll down the list, click the box next to the app name. Add the tick to allow the app on private and public networks. Remove the tick to block the app.

If you app isn't in the list, click 'allow another app'.

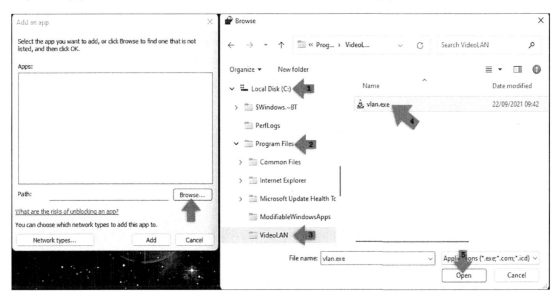

Navigate to the app. This is usually in the 'program files' on the C drive. Click 'open', then back on the 'add an app' screen click 'add'.

Anti Virus Software

Windows security does a reasonable job at keeping you safe, however there are some free third party anti virus utilities worth noting.

Avast

Avast scans and detects vulnerabilities in your home network, checks for program updates, scans files as you open them, emails as they come in and fixes PC performance issues.

You can download it from their website.

```
www.avast.com
```

Scroll down the page until you find 'free download'.

The other two versions here are 30 day trials and will expire after 30 days. You will need to pay a subscription to continue.

When prompted hit 'install'. If the installation doesn't run automatically, go to your downloads folder and run 'avast_free_antivirus_setup.exe', follow the on screen wizard.

AVG

AVG blocks viruses, spyware, & other malware, scans web, twitter, & facebook links and warns you of malicious attachments.

You can download it from their website.

`www.avg.com`

Scroll down and click 'free download'.

The other versions here are 30 day trials and will expire after 30 days. You will need to pay a subscription to continue.

The free version is good enough for home users.

Video Resources

To help you understand the procedures and concepts explored in this book, we have developed some video resources and app demos for you to use, as you work through the book.

As well as the video resources, you'll also find some downloadable files and samples for exercises that appear in the book.

To find the resources, open your web browser and navigate to the following website

elluminetpress.com/win-11/

Do not use a search engine, type the website into the address field at the top of the browser window.

At the beginning of each chapter, you'll find a website that contains the resources for that chapter.

Using the Videos

Type the website url into the address bar at the top of your browser.

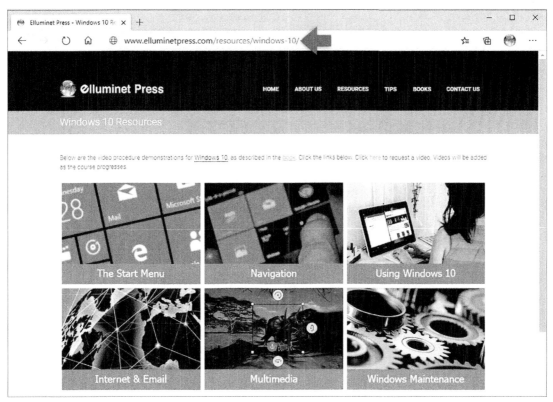

You'll see different categories. Click on these to access the videos.

When you open the link to the video resources, you'll see a thumbnail list at the bottom.

Click on the thumbnail for the particular video you want to watch. Most videos are between 40 and 90 seconds outlining the procedure, others are a bit longer.

Video Resources

When the video is playing, hover your mouse over the video and you'll see some controls...

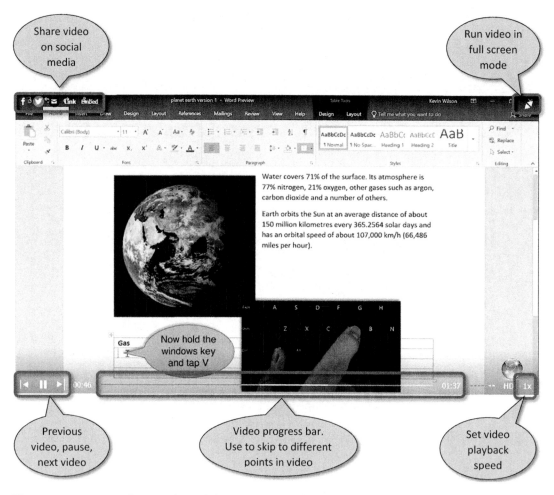

Here, you can share the video on social media, make it full screen. You can also play/pause the video, jump to a particular part of the video using the progress bar and set the playback speed.

You'll also find cheat sheets

Command Prompt   Keyboard Shortcuts   Tips

Here, you'll find short-cuts, updates and tips.

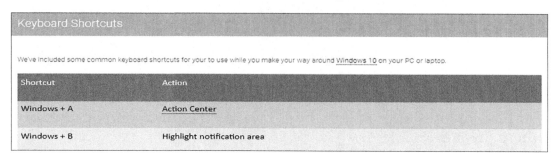

You'll also find a tips section. Here, we'll keep you up to date with the latest tips and tricks to help you get the most out of windows 10.

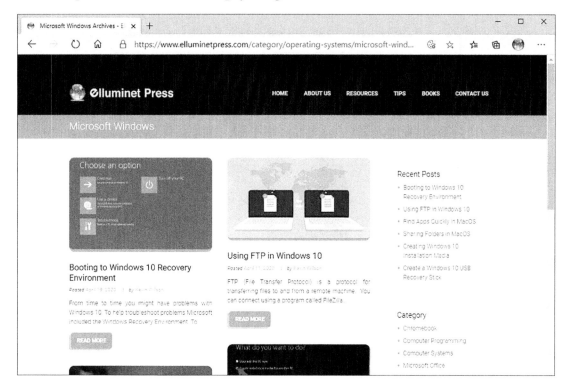

Finally, you'll find a glossary of computing terms.

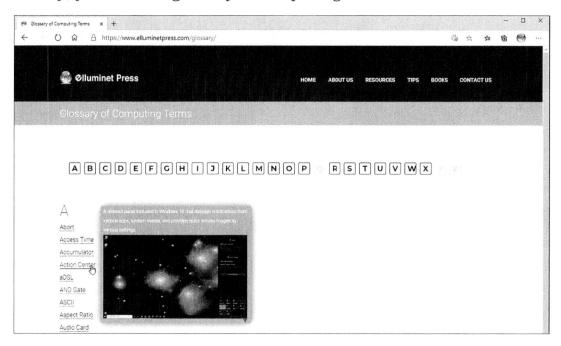

You can find the index here:

www.elluminetpress.com/glossary

This is integrated into the resources section.

Scanning the Codes

At the beginning of each chapter, you'll a QR code you can scan with your phone to access additional resources, files and videos.

iPhone

To scan the code with your iPhone/iPad, open the camera app.

Frame the code in the middle of the screen. Tap on the website popup at the top.

Android

To scan the code with your phone or tablet, open the camera app.

Frame the code in the middle of the screen. Tap on the website popup at the top.

If it doesn't scan, turn on 'Scan QR codes'. To do this, tap the settings icon on the top left. Turn on 'scan QR codes'.

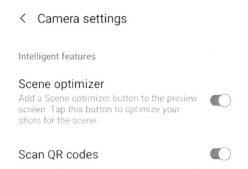

If the setting isn't there, you'll need to download a QR Code scanner. Open the Google Play Store, then search for "QR Code Scanner".

i Index

Index

Index

Index

Index

Index

U

Index

W

SOMETHING NOT COVERED?

We want to create the best possible resources to help you learn and get things done, so if we've missed anything out, then please get in touch using the links below and let us know. Thanks.

 office@elluminetpress.com

 elluminetpress.com/feedback

Printed in Great Britain
by Amazon

14911566R10276